CIPS Study Matters

Level 4

Foundation Diploma in Purchasing and Supply

Effective Negotiation in Purchasing and Supply

Second Edition

Tracy Harwood
De Montfort University

THE
CHARTERED INSTITUTE OF
PURCHASING & SUPPLY®

Published by

The Chartered Institute of Purchasing and Supply
Easton House, Easton on the Hill, Stamford, Lincolnshire PE9 3NZ
Tel: +44 (0) 1780 756 777
Fax: +44 (0) 1780 751 610
Email: info@cips.org
Website: http://www.cips.org

First published June 2006
Second edition published June 2009

Technical reviewer: Eoin Lonergan, Management Development Unit,
London Metropolitan University

Instructional design and publishing project management by Wordhouse Ltd,
Reading, UK

Content management system, instructional editing and pre-press by Echelon
Learning Ltd, London, UK

Index prepared by Indexing Specialists (UK) Ltd, Hove, UK

ISBN 978-1-86124-177-1

Contents

Introduction

This course book has been designed to assist you in studying for the CIPS Effective Negotiation in Purchasing and Supply unit in the Level 4 Foundation Diploma in Purchasing and Supply. The book covers all topics in the official CIPS unit content document, as illustrated in the table beginning on page xi .

Negotiation is an inherently human behaviour, whether it is used to create a solution to a problem or resolve a dispute. It is fundamental to business conduct, whereby purchasers and sellers may enhance their joint and several profitability. Thus, the skill and competence with which the negotiation process is planned, managed and executed remain vital for the purchasing professional.

While approaches to negotiating may vary according to the business context, the substantive issues negotiated have tended to include variables such as price, quantity and sharing of savings. Increasingly, purchasing has become involved in negotiating other factors, such as long-term relationships, trust and risk sharing and supplier integration into the supply and value chain. The recent and rapid emergence of new markets also presents particular challenges.

This course book introduces a wide range of theoretical and practical concepts that underpin sound understanding of negotiation. Development of skill and competence, of course, results from practice – so that bit is down to you!

How to use this book

The course book will take you step by step through the unit content in a series of carefully planned 'study sessions' and provides you with learning activities, self-assessment questions and revision questions to help you master the subject matter. The guide should help you organise and carry out your studies in a methodical, logical and effective way, but if you have your own study preferences you will find it a flexible resource too.

Before you begin using this course book, make sure you are familiar with any advice provided by CIPS on such things as study skills, revision techniques or support and how to handle formal assessments.

If you are on a taught course, it will be up to your tutor to explain how to use the book – when to read the study sessions, when to tackle the activities and questions, and so on.

If you are on a self-study course, or studying independently, you can use the course book in the following way:

- Scan the whole book to get a feel for the nature and content of the subject matter.
- Plan your overall study schedule so that you allow enough time to complete all 20 study sessions well before your examinations – in other words, leaving plenty of time for revision.
- For each session, set aside enough time for reading the text, tackling all the learning activities and self-assessment questions, and the revision question at the end of the session, and for the suggested further reading. Guidance on roughly how long you should set aside for studying each session is given at the beginning of the session.

Now let's take a look at the structure and content of the individual study sessions.

Overview of the study sessions

The course book breaks the content down into 20 sessions, which vary from three to six or seven hours' duration each. However, we are not advising you to study for this sort of time without a break! The sessions are simply a convenient way of breaking the syllabus into manageable chunks. Most people would try to study one or two sessions a week, taking one or two breaks within each session. You will quickly find out what suits you best.

Each session begins with a brief **introduction** which sets out the areas of the syllabus being covered and explains, if necessary, how the session fits in with the topics that come before and after.

After the introduction there is a statement of the **session learning objectives**. The objectives are designed to help you understand exactly what you should be able to do after you've studied the session. You might find it helpful to tick them off as you progress through the session. You will also find them useful during revision. There is one session learning objective for each numbered subsection of the session.

After this, there is a brief section reproducing the learning objectives and indicative content from the official **unit content document**. This will help you to understand exactly which part of the syllabus you are studying in the current session.

Following this, there are **prior knowledge** and **resources** sections if necessary. These will let you know if there are any topics you need to be familiar with before tackling each particular session, or any special resources you might need, such as a calculator or graph paper.

Then the main part of the study session begins, with the first of the numbered main subsections. At regular intervals in each study session, we have provided you with **learning activities**, which are designed to get you actively involved in the learning process. You should always try to complete the activities – usually on a separate sheet of your own paper – before reading on. You will learn much more effectively if you are actively involved in doing something as you study, rather than just passively reading the text in front of you. The feedback or answers to the activities are provided at the end of the session. Do not be tempted to skip the activity.

We also provide a number of **self-assessment questions** in each study session. These are to help you to decide for yourself whether or not you have achieved the learning objectives set out at the beginning of the session. As with the activities, you should always tackle them – usually on a separate sheet of paper. Don't be tempted to skip them. The feedback or answers are again at the end of the session. If you still do not understand a topic having attempted the self-assessment question, always try to re-read the relevant passages in the textbook readings or session, or follow the advice on further reading at the end of the session. If this still doesn't work, you should contact the CIPS Membership and Qualification Advice team.

For most of the learning activities and self-assessment questions you will need to use separate sheets of paper for your answers or responses. Some of the activities or questions require you to complete a table or form, in which case you could write your response in the course book itself, or photocopy the page.

At the end of the session are three final sections.

The first is the **summary**. Use it to remind yourself or check off what you have just studied, or later on during revision.

Then follows the **suggested further reading** section. This section, if it appears, contains recommendations for further reading which you can follow up if you would like to read alternative treatments of the topics. If for any reason you are having difficulty understanding the course book on a particular topic, try one of the alternative treatments recommended. If you are keen to read around and beyond the syllabus, to help you pick up extra points in the examination for example, you may like to try some of the additional readings recommended. If this section does not appear at the end of a session, it usually means that further reading for the session topics is not necessary.

At the end of the session we direct you to a **revision question**, which you will find in a separate section at the end of the course book. Feedback on the questions is also given.

Reading lists

CIPS produces an official reading list, which recommends essential and desirable texts for augmenting your studies. This reading list is available on the CIPS website or from the CIPS Bookshop. This course book is one of the essential texts for this unit. In this section we describe the main characteristics of the other essential text for this unit, which you are strongly urged to buy and use throughout your course.

The other essential text is *Essentials of Negotiation*, 3rd edition, by Roy Lewicki, David Saunders, Bruce Barry and John Minton, published by McGraw Hill in 2003.

This is a concise version of their important text entitled *Negotiation*, 4th edition (2003). As an introduction to the topic, *Essentials of Negotiation* covers the basics, including the nature of negotiation, strategies and tactics for the two main approaches: distributive and integrative negotiation styles, communication, cross-cultural negotiation. The authors are well respected researchers into negotiation and dispute resolution processes, being extensively cited in a wide range of literature.

It is not a practitioner text per se, so may be denser than some texts you will be familiar with. Nonetheless, discussion incorporates our best understanding of the extensive research into negotiating and negotiator behaviour over the last fifty years or so. It is well written, rigorous and engaging. Studies reported on focus on the business (buyer-seller) context, and examine key findings in detail. There are, on the other hand, some studies reviewed which are based on interpersonal, legal and labour – as well as international – relations. Furthermore, the presentation of the material varies from the course book, which will require you to dip in, rather than follow the discourse as it is written.

What is particularly useful, however, compared to many other texts on the subject, is the ability to follow up references to cited work, should your interest and time allow. Negotiation is, after all, a skill that improves with cycles of abstract theorization, reflection and practice – that is, learning! As a scholar of negotiation theory, an avid learner and a keen (if not successful as often as I would like) business person, it is a text I am happy to commend to you.

Second edition amendments

The basic content of this second edition of the course book remains the same as the first edition. There are several small additions to the following areas; SWOT analysis, supply and demand, cost models (in particular standard costs, actual costs and budget costs), conditioning and a new section 20.4 'Improvement, training and development'. These additions help to ensure that the syllabus is covered more fully.

Unit content coverage

In this section we reproduce the whole of the official CIPS unit content document for this unit. The overall unit characteristics and statements of practice for the unit are given first. Then, in the table that follows, the learning objectives and indicative content are given in the left hand column. In the right hand column are the study sessions in which you will find coverage of the various topics.

Unit characteristics

This unit is designed to provide students with the ability to apply a variety of theories relating to negotiation in respect of preparation, planning and participating in the negotiation process.

Students will undertake activities such as cost and market analysis, using information to support the planning of negotiation with suppliers to achieve value for money (VFM). Students also apply their knowledge of various legal implications affecting negotiations.

Negotiating is often a finely balanced activity and involves managing a range of complex relationships, and students should be prepared to effectively manage those relationships, avoiding conflict while maintaining the balance of power.

By the end of this unit, students should be able to plan and prepare how to undertake effective negotiations, and also to understand how they would be able to assess effectiveness.

Statements of practice

On completion of this unit, students will be able to:

- Plan and prepare for negotiations
- Apply a range of negotiation theories in order to achieve set outcomes
- Differentiate between a range of persuasion tools and techniques
- Explain the different approaches required when negotiating in different settings
- Understand how to analyse negotiation performance

Learning objectives and indicative content

1.0 Planning and preparing for negotiations (Weighting 25%)
1.1 Analyse the different phases of negotiation.   Study session 1
- Preparation
- Open
- Test
- Move

Study session 1
Negotiating in different settings

Introduction

Negotiation is often described as both a science and an art: essential to good practice yet a skill that requires honing over time in order to perfect. In business, it is a core competence for effective management.

As a purchaser, you will know that negotiations take place at many different levels:

- Between colleagues within a purchasing department on the division of some task among them.
- Between departments, such as with Production, on agreeing product and service specifications.
- With suppliers, who may have close or distant relationships with the organisation (and the individuals within it) and who may be more or less strategically important to its overall profitability.

The approaches used to reach appropriate outcomes for negotiations will, therefore, vary according to different settings, situations or business contexts.

This session provides you with an introduction and overview to negotiation as it applies to different settings. It firstly considers the definition of negotiation, and its component activities. It then describes two different settings (collaborative and distributive), with a comparison of how each may be used. Finally, the factors that influence the approach taken in purchasing settings are discussed.

'You don't have to blow out the other fellow's light to let your own shine.'
Bernard Baruch, banker and financier, commenting on cooperative business strategies (Nalebuff and Brandenburger, 1996: 4)

Session learning objectives

After completing this session you should be able to:

1.1 Define the term negotiation.
1.2 Describe the different phases of negotiation.
1.3 Identify and describe the collaborative and distributive approaches to negotiating in business.
1.4 Compare and contrast the collaborative and distributive approaches to negotiation.
1.5 Identify the factors that influence the approach taken in negotiations.

Unit content coverage

This study session covers the following topics from the official CIPS unit content document:

1

Statement of practice

Plan and prepare for negotiations.

Learning objectives

1.1 Analyse the different phases of negotiation.
- Preparation
- Open
- Test
- Move
- Agree
- Finalise the deal

Timing

You should set aside about 6 hours to read and complete this session, including learning activities, self-assessment questions, the suggested further reading (if any) and the revision question.

1.1 Defining negotiation

The Oxford Reference Dictionary defines 'to negotiate' as: '1. to try to reach agreement by discussion; to arrange (an affair) or bring about (a result) thus. 2. to get or give the money value for (a cheque or bonds, etc.). 3. to get over or through (an obstacle or difficulty).'

Definitions of negotiation, however, vary according to the context in which they apply. For example, Tracy (1995) defines negotiation as: 'a motivated process of information exchange between or among individuals, groups, organisations, communities, societies and supranational systems with the goal of reaching agreement about certain joint or reciprocal acts.'

Few authors offer a formal definition of negotiation, there being apparently no real consensus on the term! The term is widely applied to different disciplines such as economics, mathematics and social psychology, including international relations, personnel development, management and industrial relations as well as business (purchasing and supply; sales and marketing). A search of the literature reveals, however, five distinct characteristics:

- existence of agreement and conflict between the parties
- bargaining process
- exchange of information
- use of techniques of influence and persuasion
- capability of the parties to reach agreement.

Learning activity 1.1

Make up a definition of negotiation which fits your current business and purchasing circumstances.

Feedback on page 13

2

It is worth noting that definitions have become increasingly complex over time as researchers investigate and understand more detailed aspects of the negotiation process, including how human behaviour, emotions and other intangibles impact on the process and its outcomes. Nonetheless, Lewicki et al (2003a) have simplified a definition as follows:

'[negotiation is a] formal process that occurs when parties are trying to find a mutually acceptable solution to a complex conflict.' (Lewicki et al, 2003: 4a)

As these authors note, the main prerequisite for negotiation to take place is for the parties to be in conflict over issues of common interest about which they wish to come to a mutually satisfactory solution. Conflict, in this instance, does not necessarily imply aggression, as it relates to the division of resources that are required for business continuity – the three Ms of men, money and minutes (where 'men' should be taken to refer to all staff!).

There is general consensus that bargaining is the process by which the solution is reached. Consider this definition:

'[Negotiation is] any form of verbal communication, direct or indirect, whereby parties to a conflict of interest discuss, without resort to arbitration or other judicial processes, the form of any joint action which they might take to manage a dispute between them. Bargaining is the process of negotiating for agreement.'

Morley and Stephenson (1977)

The process of bargaining itself is characterised by exchanges of information on offers, counter-offers and concessions which incorporate the parties' beliefs and expectations. The process incorporates argument and persuasion to influence the other party about the division of available resources.

The term 'resource' is well summarised by Ambrosini (1995) who suggests it consists of both inputs into the production process and capabilities by which resources are used. This author suggests five characteristics of resources:

- Heterogeneity across organisations, that is, different organisations own different resources.
- Scarcity, that is, they must not be possessed by a large number of firms.
- Imperfect mobility, that is, they cannot be traded.
- Imperfect imitability, that is, they cannot be copied.
- They must be valuable.

Implicit within the bargaining process is that the parties are able and willing to reach agreement. Clearly, if one is not, there is little point in entering into a negotiation in the first place!

Self-assessment question 1.1

Define negotiation and at least five distinctive characteristics.

Feedback on page 13

1

1.2 Phases of negotiation

The definition discussed in section 1.1 implies that negotiation is a complex process with several component parts. Lewicki et al (2003b) describe a number of common characteristics for all negotiation situations:

- There are two or more parties who may be acting as individuals, as groups or organisations.
- The parties must search for a way resolve the conflict.
- The parties believe that by using influence they will achieve a better deal, rather than by accepting what is offered.
- The parties prefer to reach agreement, rather than continue to disagree.
- The parties expect to give and take, that is, to modify their demands.
- Success requires management of tangibles (for example, terms of agreement) and intangibles (for example, underlying personal beliefs and values).

In practice, this necessitates the identification and consideration of seven constituent parts. To simplify this, it is useful to identify these as the 'phases of negotiation'. See figure 1.1.

Figure 1.1

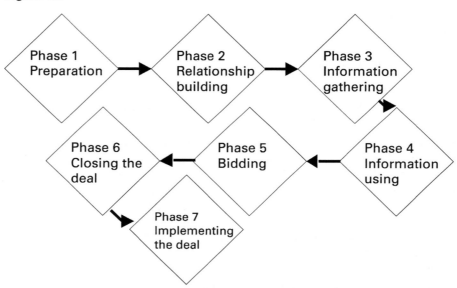

Source: derived from Greenhalgh (2001) in Lewicki et al (2003)

Figure 1.1 illustrates an 'ideal' negotiation process which, in fact, is a rare occurrence (Lewicki et al, 2003). Each phase is briefly described below:

- Preparation: identifying the important issues and goals.
- Relationship building: understanding how you will relate to the other party.
- Information gathering: learning what you need to know about (variables, other party's situation and goals).
- Information using: building the case for the negotiation.
- Bidding: the process of negotiating from initial offer towards the agreement.
- Closing the deal: building commitment from the parties.

- Implementing the deal: a post-negotiation phase. Even after the agreement is reached, there may be loose ends to clarify so there will be follow-ups to the original negotiation.

Depending on normal practice and cultural context, the parties will expend differing energies on each of these phases. Some will spend considerable time building the relationship before entering the subsequent phases, others will spend little time on preparation, depending on their familiarity with the negotiation context and knowledge of the other party.

Learning activity 1.2

What activities would you need to undertake in order to better match your current activities with those suggested in figure 1.1?

Feedback on page 13

It is also important to recognise there are a number of conditions under which it would be unwise to enter into a negotiation at all. Lewicki et al (2003b) identify these as:

- When you could lose everything you have – in which case, choose another option rather than negotiate.
- When you are at maximum (production) capacity.
- When the demands being made on you are unethical.
- When you are not interested in achieving an outcome (that is, you have nothing to gain).
- When you do not have the time to negotiate as you would want to.
- When you cannot trust the other party in the negotiation (and therefore could not trust them to implement the agreed solution).
- When waiting will improve your overall position.
- When you are under-prepared to negotiate.

Now attempt the self-assessment question 1.2 below.

Self-assessment question 1.2

Produce a plan to assist in your preparation for negotiations.

Feedback on page 14

1.3 Collaborative and distributive approaches to negotiating

There is consensus that two distinct negotiating situations occur. Firstly, there are those where agreement is sought through collaboration (integration) and problem solving and those where agreement is reached by distributive (competitive) means:

'A general ideal of negotiation is to achieve outcomes which are integrative in nature. Integrative outcomes are those that provide high joint benefit. By definition, they are represented in decisions where there exists no agreement that all parties would prefer more. This is in contrast to distributive outcomes, where one party benefits at the expense of another, without the concern for dividing all available resources that underlies the integrative outcome concept.'

Aranachalam and Dilla (1995)

Thus negotiations using collaborative or integrative approaches infer that the parties will reach a more mutually agreeable solution than they would otherwise do in a distributive situation. Not surprisingly, there is some disagreement with this contention. For example Hendon and Hendon (1989) say: 'Negotiating is the process you follow to get somebody else to do what you want them to do.'

This is clearly distinct from the collaborative approach and suggests different strategies are used to reach an acceptable outcome, whether or not that favours one of the parties in the negotiation more than the others. Murray (1986) offers stereotypical characterisations of the two types of negotiators, stating:

'the competitive negotiator is a zealous advocate: tough, clever, thorough, articulate, unemotional, demanding, aggressive and unapproachable – a Sylvester Stallone, "Rambo" type who achieves victory by defeating the opponent'

while the problem-solver is:

'also thorough and articulate, but in addition: personable, cooperative, firm, principled, concerned about the other side's interests, and committed to fairness and efficiency – a Jimmy Stewart "Mr Smith Goes to Washington" approach to resolving disputes amicably.'

Authors including Lewicki et al (2003b) have proposed five key methods by which collaborative solutions can be reached:

- Expanding the pie: where resources are scarce, the parties look to increase the available resources.
- Non-specific compensation: in return for compromise, one party is repaid by the other in some unrelated means.
- Logrolling: where several issues are at stake with different priorities, each party concedes on low priorities in exchange for concessions from the other party on issues of higher priority.
- Cost cutting: in return for concessions, one party's costs are reduced or eliminated entirely.
- Bridging: a new option is devised in return for neither party achieving its initial demands.

It is worth remembering, however, that a collaborative negotiation is considered to be less efficient because the search process is lengthier (Bartos, 1995). The five points identified above suggest that extensive exchange of information is required in order for the parties to reach a satisfactory solution. Certainly, the amount of time resource available is a relevant consideration.

Typically, the two approaches (collaborative and distributive) are associated with the outcomes they produce: win-win and win-lose. Originating from game theory, the term 'win-win' describes an outcome of equal (or balanced) value to both parties, based on their respective evaluations of the variables that were traded. In contrast, 'win-lose' describes an outcome where one party is considered to have gained at the expense of the other (sometimes referred to as 'zero-sum'). Ultimately, the 'win-lose' turns into a 'lose-lose' situation for both parties because the losing party refuses to agree further deals with the winner, or else they seek to regain their perceived loss at some future point. Table 1.1 associates the two main approaches of collaboration and distribution with their typical outcomes as discussed. (This is discussed in further detail in study session 10.)

Table 1.1 Win-win and win-lose

	Win-Win	**Win-Lose**
Emphasises	collaboration	distribution
Based on	mutual interest and common goals	opposition and confrontation
Presumes	flexibility	inflexibility
Leads to	joint problem solving	conflicts and disagreement
Results in	both parties reaching an agreement which achieves their objectives	one side 'beating' the other
Appropriate for	long-term contracts and repeat suppliers	one-offs and adversarial suppliers

Learning activity 1.3

Consider which of the two main approaches (collaborative or distributive) is more familiar to your personal work (purchasing) context. Explain the reasons for this.

Feedback on page 14

From this discussion, it is evident that some situations will be more appropriate than others for each of these approaches. For example, it would be potentially destructive to engage in a competitive-style negotiation with a long-term supplier, at least one upon whom you are relying for ongoing supply of some critical component to your production.

Self-assessment question 1.3

What alternative terms are used to describe the 'collaborative' and 'distributive' approaches? Discuss the circumstances that would necessitate the use of each of these approaches.

Feedback on page 14

1

1.4   Comparison of negotiation approaches

First, attempt learning activity 1.4 below.

Learning activity 1.4

Thinking about your own purchasing negotiations, briefly describe different contexts that each approach (collaborative and distributive) may be used in.

Feedback on page 14

Discussion in section 1.3 infers that the two approaches are implemented via differing tactics and behaviours (as will be discussed further in study sessions 9 and 10). It is unrealistic to suppose these approaches occur in isolation of each other since, even when negotiations are essentially collaborative, there is still a need for distributiveness in dividing the resources which are being negotiated over. Table 1.2 compares the two approaches:

Table 1.2 Comparison of collaborative and distributive approaches to negotiation

	Collaborative	**Distributive**
Basic assumptions	• Negotiating world controlled by 'enlightened self-interest'. • Resource distribution system is integrative in nature. • Goal is to achieve mutually agreeable solution.	• Negotiating world controlled by 'egocentric self-interest'. • Resource distribution system distributive in nature. • Goal is to win as much as possible.
Recognised patterns of negotiators	• Maximise returns for organisation. • Focus on common interests. • Understands merits objectively. • Uses non-confrontational debating techniques. • Open to persuasion on substance. • Oriented to qualitative goals.	• Maximise tangible resource gains. • Makes high opening demands. • Uses threats, confrontation and argumentation. • Manipulates people. • Not open to persuasion. • Oriented to quantitative and competitive goals.
Key behavioural elements	• Maximises return within larger time frame. • Considers needs/interests/ attitudes of other side. • Competitive but not antagonistic. • Shares joint gains. • Concentrates on substance. • Considers negotiation as voluntary and superior to non-voluntary processes (for example, adjudication).	• Maximises return from transaction. • Does not consider needs/ interests/ attitudes of other side. • Views disputing processes equally. • Behaves cooperatively only if it helps achieve returns. • Chooses processes similar to military manoeuvres. • Presents strong defence against opposing tactics. • Controls the negotiation for subsequent manipulation.

Source: derived from Murray (1986)

There are, of course, risks associated with rigidly applying each approach (see table 1.3). However, overcoming these risks does not lead to an improvement in the negotiator's skill in that approach. Rather, as suggested by Murray (1986), it leads towards the problem-solving strategy as the negotiator strives to improve his skill to achieve consistently good outcomes. Not only does this infer skilled parties will reach more equitable solutions but, in addition, the individuals involved will derive greater personal satisfaction from the process.

Table 1.3 Risks with collaborative and distributive approaches

	Associated risks
Collaborative	• Has a strong bias toward cooperation, creating internal pressures to compromise and accommodate.
	• Avoids strategies that are confrontational because they risk impasse, which is viewed as failure.
	• Focuses on being sensitive to other's perceived interests; this increases vulnerability to deception and manipulation by a competitive opponent; and increases possibility that settlement may be more favourable to other side than fairness would warrant.
	• Increases difficulty of establishing definite aspiration levels and bottom lines because of reliance on qualitative (value-laden) goals.
	• Requires substantial skill and knowledge of process to do well.
	• Requires strong confidence in own ability to assess interests/needs of other side and other's payoff schedule.
Distributive	• Has a strong bias toward confrontation, encouraging the use of coercion and emotional pressure as persuasive means; it is hard on relationships, breeding mistrust, feelings of isolation, frustration and anger, resulting in more frequent breakdowns in negotiations; and distorts communication, producing misinformation and misjudgement.
	• Guards against responsiveness to opponent and is defensive, thereby restricting access to joint gains.
	• Encourages brinkmanship by creating many opportunities for impasse; increases difficulty in predicting responses of opponent because reliance is on manipulation and confrontation to control process.
	• Contributes to overestimation of return possibly through alternatives (for example, court settlement) because focus is only a few main issues rather than the whole deal.

Source: derived from Murray (1986)

Thus it is important that steps are taken to ensure risks inherent in these approaches are minimised by thorough preparation. This means that there must be explicit awareness of the approach that is going to be taken, and that preparation includes measures for overcoming the things that can go wrong as highlighted in table 1.3.

Self-assessment question 1.4

Imagine you are the consultant asked to comment on one of questions raised in *Supply Management's* 'Your Questions Answered' section:

Day rate dilemma: 'I have a vital consultancy supplier that I think is charging too much per day. It is willing to offer a discount if we commit

(continued on next page)

1

Self-assessment question 1.4 *(continued)*

to buying a bigger block of consultants days than we need at the moment. This is not a supplier that we can easily drop, so how should I approach this negotiation?'

Write a commentary to advise which of two main approaches to negotiation may be appropriate.

Feedback on page 15

1.5 Influences on negotiation approaches

There are a number of reasons for the move from negotiations which focus on short-term contracts to long-term close relationships:

- Moving from multiple **sourcing** to single sourcing.
- Threat of buying the suppliers to **outsourcing** and partnership agreements.
- Moving from tactical purchasing to strategic supply management.
- The relationship between price and quality, which has implications for the competence of the supplier.

Ultimately, the most significant reason is the potential for enhanced profitability.

Donaldson (1996) highlighted in addition the issues of **total quality management** (TQM) and innovations in supply chain management: **just-in-time delivery** (JIT), computer-aided design (CAD) and information technology (IT). From a supply chain perspective, Payne and Frow (1997) discuss the relationship between retention and profitability, originally established in the seminal work of Reichheld and Sasser (1990).

As already stated, the underlying premise for collaboration is that both parties commit to adapting their behaviour to ensure relationship longevity. Gronroos (1997, 2000) summarises well the key differences between transaction (or cost-based) exchanges, and the relationship approach, stating that it is the value created throughout the process and resulting from the process that is important to the parties (see table 1.4). This emphasises the important role that negotiations play in **supplier relationship management**.

Table 1.4 Transaction versus relationship exchanges

	Transaction	**Relationship**
Focus	single purchase	supplier retention
Orientation	product features	product benefits
Time scale	short	long
Service level	little supplier service	high supplier service
Commitment	limited	high
Contact	moderate	high
Quality	concern of production	concern of all

derived from Ballantyne et al (2000)

Learning activity 1.5

Identify which approach (collaborative or distributive) you consider to be more appropriate to the following examples. Justify your decisions:

- Early-stage relationship with a potential long-term supplier of small production components.
- An established long-term contractual relationship with an awkward supplier.

Feedback on page 15

In the broader purchasing context, one of the most widely recognised models of buying behaviour is that of Robinson, Faris and Wind's (1967) 'buyclass framework'. This identifies three typical buying situations: new task, modified rebuy and straight rebuy. These are analysed along three dimensions: the information requirements of the purchaser; the consideration of possible alternatives; and the extent of familiarity with the purchasing situation (new task). This model of buyer behaviour is typically associated with a transactional approach and, as such, is useful in describing the nature of information exchange processes with this approach.

Criticisms of the buyclass framework are levied for its: over-simplicity; lack of consideration of personal or organisational characteristics; failure to recognise the complexity of the buyer-seller relationship; and inability to recognise the strategic importance of the purchase.

In turn, more complex models encompass the interrelationships between economic, social and emotional factors. These highlight the stages of relationship evolution which necessitate the use of varying negotiation approaches, clearly leaning towards the collaborative approach. Authors highlight that the driver for collaboration is the increased complexity of the transactions that form the basis of the relationship. The process of relational development necessarily revolves around trust and cooperation, which includes the negotiation process. This is an aspect that is inherently complex to implement but advantages of genuine partnership are noted to be:

- avoidance of adversarial relationships
- elimination of conflict
- agreement on problem resolution, cost and time savings.

Also noteworthy is the evolution in approaches used by salespeople. Rich (2000) confirms relationship 'selling' (and negotiation) has moved from personal selling for short-term goals to a 'life-long process' in order to reap bigger rewards at a later date. Selling behaviour has evolved from traditional models of objection handling and closing (Strong, 1925) to the investigation of needs and consultative models, such as the 'counsellor selling' model (DeCormier and Jobber, 1998). In such circumstances, purchasing negotiators must adapt their behaviour accordingly.

1

Self-assessment question 1.5

List five factors that may influence the approach taken by a buyer in a negotiation.

Feedback on page 15

Revision question

Now try the revision question for this session on page 265.

Summary

This study session has presented an analysis of the definition of negotiation and synthesised this into a number of key characteristics. Common phases for all negotiation situations have been outlined and negotiation phases identified as follows:

- preparation
- relationship building
- information gathering
- information using
- bidding
- closing the deal
- implementing the deal.

Collaborative and distributive approaches have been compared, contrasted and associated with typical outcomes ('win-win' and 'win-lose'). Risks in rigidly applying each approach have been discussed although it has been noted that in overcoming these, there is the potential to enhance personal skills in problem solving.

Finally, historical influences in the development of collaborative approaches to negotiation have been reviewed. These include:

- Moving from multiple sourcing to single sourcing.
- Threat of buying the suppliers to outsourcing and partnership agreements.
- Tactical purchasing to strategic supply management.
- Price to total cost focus.
- Acceptance that the supply base can add significant value and be a source of competitive advantage.

Suggested further reading

Lewicki et al (2003b) on negotiation settings, the conditions for negotiation and the descriptions of negotiator characteristics.

Steele et al (1989) for the overview of negotiation and its basic approaches.

Feedback on learning activities and self-assessment questions

Feedback on learning activity 1.1

Consider the five characteristics of negotiation listed in 1.1:

- existence of agreement and conflict between the parties
- bargaining process
- exchange of information
- use of techniques of influence and persuasion
- capability of the parties to reach agreement.

How many of these did you incorporate into your own definition and, if you left any out, can you explain why?

Feedback on self-assessment question 1.1

You could have used Lewicki et al's definition:

'[negotiation is a] formal process that occurs when parties are trying to find a mutually acceptable solution to a complex conflict.'

Lewicki et al 2003: 4a

Identified characteristics include:

- existence of agreement and conflict between the parties
- bargaining process
- exchange of information
- use of techniques of influence and persuasion
- capability of the parties to reach agreement
- existence of at least two people
- skilled use of power to achieve the outcome.

Feedback on learning activity 1.2

For example, you may want to consider:

- What you currently do to prepare for a negotiation.
- How you build relationships – whether you arrange a preliminary meeting in order to be on more personal terms with them when you meet for the negotiation.
- How you generate relevant and important information both before and during the meeting.
- How you prioritise the information and present your case during the meeting.
- How you develop your concession strategy on the issues you intend to trade.
- How you close the deal, that is, how you build sufficient common ground between yourself and the supplier for the deal to be implementable.
- The processes you go through when implementing the deal – how you monitor and evaluate it.

- What follow-up procedures you have in place when difficulties are identified at the implementation phase.

Feedback on self-assessment question 1.2

Consider the seven different phases of negotiation and ensure your plan includes steps to address each of them (see figure 1.1). You may also have identified a step at which you review the value of entering into negotiation at all – this is certainly worth considering

Feedback on learning activity 1.3

Circumstances may mean either, and probably both, of these approaches are used across the range of negotiation activities you engage in. Things that will influence the approach taken include:

- Type or extent of relationship you have with your supplier (the other party).
- Your position in the marketplace, that is, your relative power to influence the negotiating situation.
- The personalities involved in the negotiation meeting (Mr Smith or Rambo or somewhere in between).
- The amount of available time for the negotiation (which is, in turn, usually influenced by the needs of the immediate stakeholders, such as Production, Finance, and so forth).
- The range of options available to you, including alternatives to negotiating.
- The parties' separate and joint evaluations of the risks associated with the negotiation and its outcome (or failure to reach an outcome).
- The skill of the negotiators.

You may want to further consider how your approach to negotiation has changed over time, as you have become more adept at negotiating with your suppliers and seen the solutions you have reached implemented, perhaps based on your experience of win-lose (or lose-lose) outcomes.

Feedback on self-assessment question 1.3

Collaborative: integrative, problem-solving. This would be used where the parties want to continue working together after the contract agreed has expired, such as where a long-term relationship exists or is desired. It may only be used where the parties have sufficient time and resource available to engage in relational development.

Distributive: competitive, adversarial. This would be used where no relationship exists or is desired between the parties. It may be used where time and resource is limited, where focus is on a limited number of options, such as a price negotiation.

Feedback on learning activity 1.4

Collaborative approach: long-term and contractual relationships, ongoing supplies (repeats), strategically important suppliers (even if small-scale).

Distributive approach: one-offs, strategically unimportant suppliers.

Feedback on self-assessment question 1.4

It appears that the purchaser in this case is focusing on one main issue (price) as a negotiating variable, and so is attempting a distributive approach. It is highly likely that both parties will have prioritised the same issue and, therefore, are in danger of being in direct conflict when attempting to reach agreement.

The purchaser also identifies, however, that the supplier is important to him over the longer term, which emphasises the need for a more collaborative approach. If this is taken, then the purchaser needs to look for more negotiable variables, such as value and benefit to the organisation. In this way, it may be possible to identify more creative ways to reduce the costs, for example, by looking for efficiencies in the task the supplier is undertaking.

It is evident, however, that the purchaser needs to identify the interests of the supplier, and whether a relationship is sought. This will enable the selection of a strategy that achieves the best value for the organisation. Remember, also, it is rare that situations are so 'black and white' that one negotiation approach can be used – personalities are involved (and some of these people will move to other suppliers who are important to you now). Similarly, skill (if not genuine foresight) is required to predict tomorrow's core suppliers to the business.

Note: This is a genuine question published in the June 2005 issue of *Supply Management*. You may also want to review your answer and these comments against the real consultant's, Christopher Barrat.

Feedback on learning activity 1.5

Early-stage relationship: It depends on the strategic importance of the components to the organisation. If they are considered to be core to production, then a more collaborative approach is best.

Long-term contract: It depends on your view of the potential future sales (up the supply chain from Purchasing). If there is long-term potential, necessitating continuation of the relationship, then a more collaborative approach is required. On the other hand, all relationships end, typically as the business evolves and the product portfolio adapts to market needs.

In both cases, it is also important to consider the availability of alternative supply sources, and your organisation's ability to develop a relationship with one or other of these.

Feedback on self-assessment question 1.5

Answers may include:

- Risk and spend profile with supplier – the more you are reliant on them (and the more you spend with them) as a key supplier, the higher the risks.

- Commoditisation of purchased product risk may be lower if the product is available from other sources.
- Supply chain issues.
- Market demand.
- Technological advancements.
- Need to develop trust with a supplier, to enhance problem resolution, cost and time savings.
- Stage of relationship evolution, from early to close relationships.
- Changes in supplier behaviour, including adapability to your evolving products specifications.
- Desire to reduce or avoid adversarial behaviour and non-productive conflict.

Understanding the supplier organisation

Introduction

The historical figure, Sir Francis Bacon, is attributed with the well-known saying: 'knowledge itself is power'. In the context of purchasing and supply, knowledge is derived from the information available to an organisation, which informs the decision-making processes of individuals. For good decisions to be made in a supply situation, it is important for negotiating purchasers to have as full an understanding of the supplier organisation and its market context as possible.

This study session, therefore, focuses on how to generate the appropriate information that will inform the negotiation process. Firstly, the broad purchasing context and the range of information needed by a negotiator is reviewed, with consideration of how the information underpins negotiations. Finally, two specific frameworks which are used to analyse the market context (Porter's Five Forces and PESTLE) are developed for application to a negotiation situation.

'People make mistakes. More interestingly, people make a variety of systematic and predictable mistakes. The predictability of these mistakes means that once we identify them, we can learn to avoid them.'

Max Bazerman, on dealing with complex business problems (Bazerman, 2002: 11)

Session learning objectives

After completing this session you should be able to:

2.1 Review the purchasing context for negotiations in order to understand the supplier organisation.
2.2 Identify the range of supplier information required to underpin a negotiation.
2.3 Use Porter's Five Forces framework to evaluate the competitive environment of a market.
2.4 Analyse a market using the PESTLE framework in order to support negotiations.

Unit content coverage

This study session covers the following topics from the official CIPS unit content document:

Statement of practice

Plan and prepare for negotiations.

Learning objectives

1.2 Identify and evaluate information required to understand the supplier organisation.
   • Supplier information (supply, demand, timings, costings, budget, readiness, capacity, account management structure)

2

- Competitor information, for example supplier competitors
- Oligopoly/monopoly/duopoly

1.3 Analyse market information to support negotiation.
- PESTLE
- SWOT
- Supply and demand

Timing

You should set aside about 5 hours to read and complete this session, including learning activities, self-assessment questions, the suggested further reading (if any) and the revision question.

2.1 Purchasing context for negotiations

Study session 1 identified some of the factors that have influenced the evolution in approaches to negotiation. These clearly highlight the changes in recent industrial times in market forces. There has been a shift from developing efficient and cost-effective production to differentiating an organisation's offer in the marketplace (typically in a situation where supply exceeded end-user demand) and to focusing on quality and ethicality in production and business processes. In short, the Purchasing department's role within the organisation has changed from merely buying to an agreed specification (with Production, Finance, Marketing and other internal stakeholders) to a broader and more strategic focus on smoothing the supply of **raw materials** into valuable products and services for end-user customers, with the organisation as an intermediary between the two.

This necessitates that purchasing has a pivotal role within an organisation. This can only be achieved, however, if individuals undertaking the role have full understanding of the business and purchasing context. Test your understanding of your own context with learning activity 2.1 below.

Learning activity 2.1

What factors influence your own purchasing context?

Feedback on page 27

Gadde and Hakansson (2001) highlight changes in the purchasing context: most organisations are increasingly reliant on outsourcing; are more focused on cooperating with suppliers to ensure supply, and have reduced the number of vendors they use in order to focus effort.

Challenges for procurement identified by Monczka and Morgan (2000) are:

- Increasing efficiency requirements, that is, adding value to the bottom line.
- Making use of information technology.
- Integration and consolidation, most especially in light of a global purchasing context.
- Insourcing and outsourcing, and the nature of relationships with suppliers.

- Strategic cost management.
- 'Network' management – the strategic role of the relationships between suppliers, the purchaser and the organisation's customers.

Within this context, it is the job of the organisation to communicate and exchange information strategically. Gadde and Hakansson (1993) identify three different types of information important to the supply context: technical, commercial and administrative. This information is key to: coordinating the effort between functions within the organisation; influencing internal stakeholders so that they may accept changes; and increasing understanding of external organisations (via the transfer of knowledge between the purchaser and supplier, and vice versa).

At the point of interface between the purchaser and supplier, the key function of negotiation is to achieve **added value** for the organisation. Lewicki et al (2003b) identify that value is predominantly determined by the differences between negotiators. These differences enable the purchasing and supplying parties to create variables and attribute different values to them so that 'win-win' agreements may be reached. Internally, within the organisation, it is more about determining requirements and organising effort for efficient supply.

In a supply context, value is created (Lewicki et al, 2003b) through differences in:

- Interests: This arises from the view each party has of the variables identified and traded. For example, a supplier of components may be more interested in the total value of the deal rather than price whereas Purchasing may be seeking to reduce unit cost.
- Opinions: Each party will have a view, for example, of the relative strategic importance of the relationship; what is important to the supplier may be less so to Purchasing.
- Risk aversion: Purchasing's need to reduce the total cost of ownership may initially result in less risk being taken as it seeks to stabilise a supplier relationship.
- Time preferences: What is critical to the purchaser's production processes may be a small order for the supplier.

These differences are best understood in relation to the broader market context, which influences the way in which business evolves, is operated and controlled. Table 2.1 gives examples of some of the factors that influence the organisational context and how this may impact upon negotiations.

Table 2.1 Contextual influences on negotiations

	Non-task	**Task (negotiation)**
Environmental influence	economic and political climate	potential changes in price
Organisational influences	criteria used to evaluate tender documents	company policies restricting variables negotiated
Interpersonal influences	informal social interactions	dynamics of exchange during the negotiation
Individual influences	beliefs and values	goal of obtaining the best price

Source: Adapted from Drummond and Ensor (2003), originally based on Webster and Wind (1972)

Sheth (1973) also highlights four main factors that influence the decision-making process within the organisation:

- Expectations of the decision-making unit – especially those individuals within the organisation, for example in Finance or Production departments.
- Factors influencing the buying process – for example: perceptions of risk, type of purchase being made, time pressures, the size of organisation, degree of centralisation in the Purchasing department.
- The decision-making process and how conflicts are resolved, including problem solving, persuasive abilities, bargaining skills, exertion of power.
- Situational factors to do with a supplier and their context – for example, cash flow, industrial relations, and so on.

It is evident that negotiators need to have a broad knowledge of factors that are likely to have both direct and indirect influence on the negotiation process as well as the ongoing relationship with a supplier. The factors highlighted above will be discussed further in relation to risk in study session 3.

Self-assessment question 2.1

Why is it important to understand the purchasing context for a negotiation?

Feedback on page 28

2.2 Underpinning the negotiation

This section identifies the range of supplier information required to underpin a negotiation. Negotiations are typically entered into at a number of different stages with suppliers:

- Pre-contract, in order to develop and build a specification for supply and to clarify the terms of any contractual arrangements including how the relationship will work in practice.
- Main negotiation at which terms and conditions of the contract will be agreed as well as any ongoing relationship between the parties.
- Post-contract and relationship review, where terms and conditions may be revisited in the light of evolving market forces or relationship developments, and to resolve any conflicts that may have arisen upon implementation of the main negotiation agreement. Similarly, performance appraisal against key indicators may be evaluated prior to an extension or continuation of contract.

Information needs for each of the different stages of negotiation will obviously differ:

- Pre-contractually, it will be pertinent to obtain competitive information and broad market data.
- For the main negotiation, information will focus on the specifics of the contract (price, volume/quantity, quality, lead times, service/warranty, replacement stock, and so on).

- Contractual review will require performance data and knowledge of relationship development issues.

Broad market data, or macro-environmental forces, are discussed in more detail in sections 2.3 and 2.4. However, it should be recognised that this broad market data and the wider macro-environment forces need to be considered, not in isolation, but in relation to our own organisation and objectives. SWOT, which is an acronym for strengths, weaknesses, opportunities and threats, is the model, analytical framework or checklist used to assess ourselves, and the other parties, against these broader influences. SWOT is not a model for assessing these external influences, but a model for assessing our relative situation regarding these influences within a specific time and context. For example, SWOT analysis carried out prior to negotiating a new contract with three potential suppliers will, in all probability, result in three very different SWOT analyses. It is a common failing when undertaking a SWOT analysis to concentrate on generating a large number of issues under each heading. This is a mistake, as it will distract our focus from those few key issues where the greatest impact will be derived. Any SWOT needs to be done thoroughly and objectively; however, it must ultimately be focused and reduced to a manageable number of issues, which we will be able to use effectively in the negotiation. The value of this model in a negotiation situation is that, if done sensitively, it will help us see where we might be vulnerable, where we have some advantage and where there might be opportunities for concessions, compromise and agreement. SWOT and information pertaining to an identified supplier (SWOT analysis, the regulatory framework for a negotiation and risk assessment) is treated in study session 3.

Learning activity 2.2

Consider your current supplier account management structure and discuss how resources are allocated for each of the following typical types of negotiation:

- pre-contract
- main contract negotiation
- post-contract and relationship review.

What information is needed to support your negotiations at these stages?

Feedback on page 28

Supplier relationships are seen as strategically important resources for an organisation. Nonetheless, an organisation may have greater flexibility to 'shop around' for better prices and different technologies if it avoids engaging in relationships with suppliers. There are, therefore, a number of considerations for relationships (Gadde and Hakansson, 2001):

- The ongoing economic consequences of relationships, the costs of which may be difficult to measure. It is, therefore, important to continually evaluate the benefits as well as the costs to ensure the relationship remains viable. Direct costs may be seen in pricing and other 'hard' terms related to management of the relationship; benefits relate more to savings, such as contribution towards efficiency and

2

impact on revenue generated. Thus, in a negotiation, it is important to understand and evaluate both these constituents.

- The variety of relationships between the organisation and its suppliers – no two relationships can be managed in the same way! Benefits are likely to arise from the different relational approaches which will need to be brought into the open in negotiations.
- Over- or under-involvement in a relationship, which can result in costly inefficiencies that must be corrected. This also requires both parties to consider the nature of interactions (or interface) between the two organisations in order to allocate appropriate resources.
- The need for mutuality, that is, both parties contributing to the relationship for longevity and benefits. This relates to the 'win-win' scenario identified in study session 1.

Thus a range of information is needed to inform negotiations and underpin the agreements reached.

Self-assessment question 2.2

Briefly describe the focus of three typical types of negotiation that a purchaser will enter into with a supplier.

Feedback on page 28

2.3 Porter's Five Forces framework

Porter's Five Forces framework enables analysis of an organisation's competitive environment by focusing particularly on the competition, competitive activity and bargaining power in the **supply chain** – from suppliers through to customers. Identifying and locating power in a market structure enables an organisation to develop strategies to leverage their negotiations. Figure 2.1 illustrates how market forces exert pressure on the competitive environment. (Different forms of power are discussed in study sessions 7 and 9.)

Figure 2.1: Porter's Five Forces framework

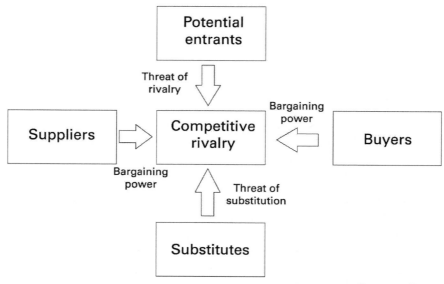

Source: Porter (1985)

2

Suppliers are powerful when:

- There are few other sources of supply for the organisation.
- The suppliers threaten to integrate up the supply chain, in effect becoming a direct competitor to the organisation.
- The costs of switching to other suppliers is great (which will likely be the case if there has been heavy investment in developing a long-term relationship).
- The organisation's business is not key to the supplier.

Buyers, or customers, are powerful when:

- There are few main customers in the marketplace.
- Products are commoditised or standardised, that is, there is little or no differentiation from the customer's perspective.
- The organisation is not a key supplier to the customer.

The threat to the organisation of substitution comes from an indirectly competing product or service. Substitutes may impact on supply and demand. A threat can be identified if:

- The customer is sensitive to pricing and the price of substitute products is low.
- The costs of the customer switching to a competitive product are low.
- The customer has a high propensity to substitute.

The threat of new entrants to the marketplace may be determined by how high the barriers to entry are. These may include:

- The costs of producing for the marketplace.
- The capital expenditure required to establish business.
- Access to appropriate distribution.
- The reaction of existing competitors.

The intensity of rivalry between competitors may depend on:

- The number of competitors in the market. The more there are, the more intense the competitive activity will be.
- The cost structure. High capital investment may result in lower costs because management will want to ensure their machinery operates at optimum capacity, rather than lying idle and waiting for orders.
- The differential advantages between products and services. Products perceived by customers to be differentiated are less likely to attract competitive behaviour.
- The costs involved in customers switching to competing products. If these are high, then customers are less likely to switch, negating the need for such intense rivalry.
- The strategic objectives being pursued by competitors. If a competitor is holding or harvesting their products, then they are not as concerned with highly competitive behaviour.
- The exit barriers. If these are low then more competition will be encouraged into the market, resulting in highly active competitive behaviour as competitors try to gain market share.

2

Basic supply and demand conditions will also impact on the intensity of the rivalry within a market. This will include the supply/demand balance between the market and its suppliers and the supply/demand balance between the market and its customers. Any changes in these basic supply/demand conditions will upset the equilibrium in the market and change the relative influence of these interacting forces in Porter's model. For example, an increase in demand may make a market more attractive to new entrants or stimulate greater competitive rivalry, while a decrease in demand may generate more price focused rivalry and ultimately a loss of competitors from the marketplace. Supply and demand issues are discussed further in study session 6.

Learning activity 2.3

How does competitive rivalry in the supply chain impact on your dealings with customers?

Feedback on page 28

Drummond and Ensor (2003) state that the Five Forces framework enables organisations to ask key questions which need to be understood in the broader market context (see also the PESTLE framework in section 2.4). Questions that need to be considered are:

- How likely are the structures and relationships to change, and are there ways the organisation can benefit from such changes?
- How can the organisation improve its relative position in the market structure? How can competitive rivalry be reduced, and what actions need to be taken with suppliers?
- Why are identified competitors powerful, and can this be reduced? And, if so, how?

In general terms, this model is used to evaluate an overall market structure and an organisation's position within it. This is really the starting point for preparing for a negotiation, as information gleaned from such analysis helps to generate variables that are used in the negotiations.

Self-assessment question 2.3

Draw and label the Five Forces framework diagram correctly.

Feedback on page 29

2.4 The PESTLE framework

This is a framework that enables a wide consideration and evaluation of the macro environment within which the purchasing organisation operates. For example, if the macro-environment indicates customer acceptance of rapid technological change, it may be that a longer-term relationship with a supplier is not desirable. In this case, the development of relationships would be an inappropriate use of resources and a more distributive approach to negotiations is called for.

That said, factors identified within this framework do not typically have direct influence on the negotiation process but usually influence the trading parameters. They are, therefore, important to the negotiation outcome. Specifically, factors will have influence through suppliers, customers, professional standards and regulatory bodies, the government and others.

The PESTLE acronym stands for: Political, Economic, Social, Technological, Legal, Environmental (green). The aim of conducting a PESTLE analysis (variously referred to as PEST, STEP, STEEP, among others) is to identify and understand those critical factors that are likely to lead to change in the organisation's trading environment, and ultimately the implementation of agreements reached.

PESTLE factors include:

Political/legal/regulatory issues

These are government, legal, legislative and regulatory requirements which are modified and introduced from time to time. With an increasingly international focus among businesses, it is particularly important to consider issues from a more global perspective, depending on the organisation's context. Examples of issues that may be considered include:

- The political stability of the region in which the organisation is trading.
- The influence of the government on trade (embargoes and sanctions, restrictive practices).
- The role of pressure groups.
- Taxation influences on pricing.
- Stock and share trading, corporate ownership and periodical financial reporting structures for organisations.

Other aspects that will impact on the organisation include: licensing and trading laws; patent and brand protection; intellectual freedom and transfer of knowledge; data management, including freedom of information and data protection.

Economic factors

These relate to the economic climate in which the organisation and its industry operate, and again, it is worth considering these issues from an international perspective. Economics influence the allocation of resources. Immediate factors may include interest rates, inflation and exchange rates. Remember also the cyclical nature of the economy (boom and bust) and where in the cycle the organisation currently sits, as this will influence how prices will change in the near future.

Social/cultural issues

These are to do with population and demographic trends, lifestyle, cultural habits and habitats, and working practices. An understanding of critical

2

issues and trends in this area will enable better prediction of supply and demand for products and services, and the need for adaptations to these in order to meet evolving market needs. Most governments publish statistics on key changes regularly but, again, it is important to consider global aspects of these issues. For example, while you may be operating in a heavily industrialised economy, others will not and, therefore, product and service demands will differ.

Technological issues

Of all the factors that influence the broader trading environment, it is this area that has had the most significant impact on purchasing and supply in recent years, and will continue to do so. Most new technologies are focused on: collecting and exchanging information, including communications; data and knowledge management processing and systems; technical developments and multi-person interactions. Technologies influence information channel design between organisations. Other technological influences relate to production processes and product designs.

Environmental/green issues

An increasing concern to many, including governments and customers, this is an aspect of the trading environment that cannot be ignored. This is especially so when considering international perspectives because attitudes to such issues often vary according to the wealth of the economy. Included in this category will be issues around the availability and use of natural resources, pollution and waste management.

As well as identifying the critical issues under the PESTLE headings, it is also important to consider the nature of their potential influence, and the likelihood of their occurrence. Indeed, it is recognised that few organisations are able to detect the 'weak signals' that indicate a potentially significant impact on the trading environment (Drummond and Ensor, 2003). A useful additional exercise is, therefore, to rank the issues according to their potential impact on the negotiation outcome and the implementation of the agreement. Extending this further will enable you to plan around issues with suppliers. It will also assist the organisation to plan how it will overcome serious threats to its profitability, cash flow and, ultimately, stability in the marketplace.

Now attempt learning activity 2.4 below. Spend around 45 minutes on this exercise.

Learning activity 2.4

Based on your own experience, undertake a PESTLE analysis of a purchasing situation.

Feedback on page 29

Self-assessment question 2.4

Your organisation is considering the relationship it has with its energy suppliers. Conduct a PESTLE analysis to examine the factors that will impact on business operations and market development.

Feedback on page 29

Revision question

Now try the revision question for this session on page 265.

Summary

This study session has reviewed the range of information that is needed to engage effectively in negotiations. Review of the purchasing context highlighted the importance of understanding the organisation and its operations, including management's view of the strategic importance of supply chain issues.

It was identified that different stages of negotiations have different information needs. In particular the nature of relationships and account structures have the potential to influence the benefits to the organisation, albeit that these may be complex and difficult to evaluate.

Finally, two familiar frameworks, Porters's Five Forces and PESTLE, were used to generate specific information relating to the immediate market structure within which negotiation will take place.

Suggested further reading

Lewicki et al (2003b) for the discussion relating to creating value for negotiation.

Gadde L-E and Hakansson H (2001). Review the changing context of purchasing and supply within organisations; look at the discussion on factors that influence developments in purchasing and supply; also review the discussion on relationship development.

Any strategic marketing and management text, such as Drummond and Ensor (2003), will offer an overview of the PESTLE and Five Forces frameworks, although points will be made more from customer than supplier perspective.

Feedback on learning activities and self-assessment questions

Feedback on learning activity 2.1

A great many factors could be considered here, including:

- The strategic view of purchasing within your organisation.
- The experience of the purchasing team in negotiating both internally within the organisation and externally with suppliers.

- The requirements for supply within the organisation – and the nature of demand for the organisation's products and services.
- The attitude towards ongoing supplier relationships, their development and maintenance as well as dispute resolution processes.
- The types and stages of the contracts the organisation has with its suppliers. For example, is it bound by legal and ethical considerations?
- The organisation's broader market context: its power relative to direct and indirect competitors; its reliance on components suppliers (and their strategic importance to the organisation); its relationship with end-user customers.

Feedback on self-assessment question 2.1

Points to consider in your answer include:

- The evolving nature of the market within which the organisation operates.
- The challenges identified by Monczka and Morgan (2000).
- The differences in value identified by Lewicki et al (2003b).
- Contextual influences on negotiations.
- Organisational decision-making processes.

Feedback on learning activity 2.2

Points to consider in your answer include:

- Pre-contract: supplier structure (decision-making processes, technical abilities, quality and cost issues, capacity, lead times, reputation, other customers); market data relating to supply and demand for organisation's products and services, and potential environmental influences on future supply and demand.
- Main contract negotiation: specification detail, contractual terms and conditions.
- Post-contract: relational performance data, updated market forces data, potential influences on future supply and demand.

Feedback on self-assessment question 2.2

- Pre-contract negotiation, focusing on specification for supply and outline terms. May consider relationship parameters.
- Contract negotiation, focusing on terms and conditions for supply. May include ongoing supply arrangements.
- Post-contract review, focusing on terms and conditions (to resolve conflicts in supply), performance to date (including incentives, such as pay, based on performance review) and market forces.

You may also have discussed that an element of negotiation may also take place while the contract is being implemented, especially if evaluation of performance against agreed terms is proving problematic.

Feedback on learning activity 2.3

This question requires you to examine the supply chain and the competitive forces that exist at each point of exchange (from raw materials suppliers,

2

for example, to component assemblers, to manufacturers, to end user customers). Thus you should identify who competitors are, and why, at each stage – in effect, you are considering who adds value in the supply chain for end customers. You would then examine how competitive the market is and, again, why that is the case.

Factors may include the existence of strong brands which influence demand; relatively few suppliers which, in turn, impacts on the ability of competitors to differentiate themselves; a decreasing customer base, requiring competitors to achieve greater market share to 'stand still' in profit terms, and resulting in the need for reduced supply costs.

Feedback on self-assessment question 2.3

You should not only correctly identify each of the five boxes but also the arrows (in the appropriate direction) and name the forces influencing competitive rivalry (see figure 2.1).

Feedback on learning activity 2.4

Remember to include all of the political/legal/regulatory, economic, social/cultural, technological and environmental/green issues that are likely to impact on the outcome of negotiations and the implementation of agreements reached. Identify, and rank, the issues that are most critical to your negotiations and to the organisation as a whole. Remember also to evaluate how the critical issues are likely to impact on you, and what you may do as a result.

Feedback on self-assessment question 2.4

Examples of factors identified could include, but are not restricted to, the following:

- Political/legal factors: energy suppliers could be restricted to trading in geographic regions; required quality standards impact on costs associated with supply; quotas restrict availability of supply and hold pricing artificially high, or low; the war with Iraq has impacted on fuel supplies and pricing; the demand for energy from a rapidly growing Chinese economy has forced prices high.
- Economic factors: rising oil prices may lead to increased production costs; this will impact on demand for all consumer products, significantly reducing disposable incomes; similarly, changes in interest rates could impact on demand.
- Social/cultural factors: customer demand for more environmentally friendly products could influence choice of suppliers, especially where there is limited cost differentiation perceived by the end-customer.
- Technological factors: availability of alternative energy production technologies, such as renewables (wind and green fuel) may impact on customer demand (although they could be more expensive).
- Environmental factors: local government emphasis on recycling may influence customer demand for renewable energies.

2

Preparing for a negotiation

Introduction

Once you have developed a broad understanding of the market context, the next stage is to prepare the specifics for the negotiation situation. It is worth offering a word of caution here: it is important to evaluate each negotiation situation on its own merits, lest you end up with a suit that is too tight!

This study session focuses firstly on evaluating risk in order to prepare for negotiations. Focus is then turned to preparing for a negotiation by undertaking an analysis of the relative strengths and weaknesses of the organisation and the supplier, as well as the opportunities and threats arising from creating solutions that meet the organisation's needs. The legal framework is considered: the relevance of legal information and its implications for the negotiation. Finally, the session considers the analysis of supplier tenders.

> 'The danger of "fit" is that it is always based on the past. A tailor makes a suit to fit your size at the moment. There is no room for growth.'
>
> **Edward de Bono, management guru and author of *Six Thinking Hats* (2005)**

Session learning objectives

After completing this session you should be able to:

3.1 Undertake risk assessment to prepare for negotiations.
3.2 Produce a SWOT analysis for a negotiation.
3.3 Assess legal information and its implications for negotiations.
3.4 Evaluate and analyse supplier tenders.

Unit content coverage

This study session covers the following topics from the official CIPS unit content document:

Statement of practice

Plan and prepare for negotiations.

Learning objectives

1.4 Assess any legal information and implications for the purchase and supply of goods that might impact upon negotiations.
   • Sale of Goods Act
   • Caveat emptor
   • Negotiating terms and conditions
   • Penalties and damages
   • Unfair Contract Terms Act
1.5 Undertake a risk assessment of conditions that might impact on the negotiation process.
   • Win-lose, win-win and win-perceived-win
   • Generating variables and alternatives
   • Risk assessment matrix

3

Timing

You should set aside about 6 hours to read and complete this session, including learning activities, self-assessment questions, the suggested further reading (if any) and the revision question.

3.1 Risk assessment

An organisation's view of the risks associated with supply will differ according to its view of purchasing. As Gadde and Hakansson (2003) state, if the view is that the organisation is a 'production unit', then emphasis is placed on 'inputs' in terms of raw materials, components and other constituents to the production process. Other views of the organisation are as a 'communicative unit' or a 'capital-earning unit'. These views necessarily emphasise different types of inputs, for example in terms of knowledge and financial efficiency, all with different associations to **risk**. (Refer to study sessions 4, 5 and 6 for more on financial analysis for negotiation.)

The 'production unit' view requires that inputs are classified and categorised. van Weele (2000) uses the following classification system:

- raw materials
- supplementary materials
- semi-manufactured products
- components
- finished products
- investment goods or capital equipment
- MRO items (maintenance, repair, operation supply)
- services.

Each of these types of supply goods presents its own purchasing problems: some require considerable technical competence, some require high administration, and others may be time sensitive in supply and production. These 'problems' may themselves be categorised (see figure 3.1).

Figure 3.1: A categorisation of purchasing situations

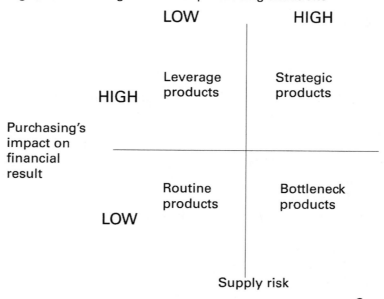

Source: Kraljic (1982)

This model highlights the fact that each category of purchase will have an impact on the bottom line (financial) according to its use, and that risk is associated with supply, depending on the number or range of suppliers in the marketplace. Thus if there are few suppliers and the impact on the organisation's financial situation is high, then the product is seen to be of strategic importance.

Others have categorised risk in different ways, such as by the level and type of organisational member involvement (Drummond and Ensor, 2003):

- Routine order products: these are low risk, with few problems in use or performance.
- Procedural problem products: some training is required in use, with associated risk that users may fail to adopt product successfully.
- Performance problem products: this relates to the ability of the product to meet the user's needs, including its compatibility with existing equipment.
- Political problem products: when there is an impact on another area of the business, politicking may arise from competition within the organisation to 'own' the product.

In relating these models of risk to negotiations, the Kraljic approach emphasises price as a major focus whereas the Drummond and Ensor categorisation enables a broader focus on issues around the integration of the product into the organisation. It can be argued that, since the latter incorporates internal negotiation as well as external negotiation with suppliers, it is more 'win-win' oriented, as it is focused on problem solving and solution building.

Learning activity 3.1

Apply the two models of risk (Kraljic and Drummond and Ensor) to your own organisation in order to categorise supplies. Consider how they compare and contrast.

Feedback on page 40

At this juncture, it is worth noting that individuals and organisations tend to be risk averse. Yet many negotiations fail to conclude with agreement – a failure which in itself can be presumed to be a risk to the parties. Bazerman and Neale (1983) suggest that the reasons for this lie in a number of biases negotiators have in making decisions, including: 'framing' (see below); overconfidence; lack of perspective; escalation; and a fixed pie view. In other words, the parties often favour the 'win-lose' approach. Furthermore, Neale and Bazerman (1991) report on a study where it is suggested that suppliers and purchasers 'frame' the transaction in different terms. Suppliers frame it in terms of gaining resource, are hence averse to taking risks and settle as quickly as possible. On the other hand, purchasers frame the transaction in terms of loss and so seek risk by holding out longer. Whilst this may at first glance favour the purchaser, recall the comment in study session 1: '"win-lose" turns into a "lose-lose" situation for both parties because the losing party refuses to agree further deals with the winner, or else they seek to regain their perceived loss at some future point.'

3

Self-assessment question 3.1

What are the implications of using a supply risk model such as Kraljic's?

Feedback on page 40

3.2 What's SWOT?

A SWOT is an analytical tool that considers internal and external factors that will have an influence on the negotiation. The acronym stands for: Strengths, Weaknesses, Opportunities and Threats. Strengths and Weaknesses are internal to the organisation whilst Opportunities and Threats relate to issues identified, typically, as a result of conducting a PESTLE analysis (see study session 2). An example SWOT analysis is provided in table 3.1.

Table 3.1 Example of factors identified through SWOT analysis

Strengths	Weaknesses	Opportunities	Threats
Our reputation with suppliers.	Cash flow.	New end user customer group identified which will increase demand for product 'x'.	Potential new entrant to the market will influence suppliers of component 'x'.

When applied to a negotiation, the SWOT tool is used to generate and prioritise negotiation variables. The theory behind conducting such an analysis is that the organisation is able to diminish its weaknesses by using its strengths to focus on opportunities. This, in turn, overcomes threats.

This tool can also usefully be applied to the other party. For example, analysis of their known strengths and weaknesses may be extended to analyse other information which is likely to influence their approach, as well as possible alternatives they may be considering (see table 3.2). Clearly, this will involve best guesses but such an exercise enables the purchaser to prepare responses to a range of different scenarios. It is, therefore, a useful tool in putting yourself into the shoes of the other party to consider their situation.

Table 3.2 Analysis of the other party's situation

	Known	Most likely	Alternative possible
Supplier A's strengths	Training and support services.	Ability to commit to long-term contract to train our staff.	Further joint opportunities arising out of partnership.
Supplier A's weaknesses	Production delays impacting on supply.	Future delays to supply arising from installation of new production facilities.	Payment problems with a customer which may mean delays while issues are resolved.

In preparing for the negotiation, both the organisation's (or purchasing's) strengths and weaknesses should be compared with the supplier's. This will help to identify and rank the variables that are to be used in the negotiation process. It is important to recognise that both parties will have strengths they can build upon, and both will want to feel they have utilised their strengths.

Table 3.3 Example of 'theirs' and 'ours' strengths and weaknesses

	Purchaser	Supplier
Strengths	Reputation in the marketplace	Thorough and reliable support services
Weaknesses	Short-term cash flow because of relocation to new site	Production delays because of new machine installation

In the example (table 3.3), both parties have strengths that are complementary to each other – a purchaser's known good reputation will add value to the supplier in the eyes of their other customers. Similarly, the supplier's quality of support services adds value for the purchaser.

Weaknesses may be difficult to identify in a supplier. In this example, the purchaser has identified a cash flow problem but this may be minimised if they are able to accommodate the production delays currently being experienced by the supplier. Thus the purchaser's prioritised negotiating variables generated from this scenario could include:

1 timing of deliveries
2 payment terms
3 support services.

In turn, the supplier may additionally be interested in the use of the purchaser as a reference site.

3.3 The legal framework

Various legal implications arise from the outcome of successful negotiations. Most obvious is that the agreement becomes the basis of a contract between the purchaser and the supplier. Thus the law of contract is an important consideration when preparing for the negotiation, in order that the parties generate an agreement that both are happy to abide by. Jennings (2004) identifies that agreements may include a number of different terms:

- Express terms: those agreed by the parties.
- Implied terms: those not agreed by the parties but which will be assumed by the law, should matters need resort to a court.
- Statutory terms: where the law overrides the explicit terms agreed by the parties.
- Illegal terms: those a court would never enforce even though the parties agreed to them.

Preparation for the negotiation needs to examine these different factors, as they will have a bearing on the way any disputes arising from the agreement will be dealt with. It is worth remembering, however, an old saying that states: when it is necessary to resort to lawyers to resolve disagreements between parties, the only real winner is the lawyer!

Terms and conditions are statements that relate to the extent of the agreement between the buyer and seller. They may be fundamental to the agreement, such that the purchaser may have the immediate right to terminate the arrangement should a breach occur; or they may be incidental, which may have the effect of limiting any claim.

Learning activity 3.3

Examine the range of terms and conditions you use. Explain how these impact on your negotiations.

Feedback on page 41

To be legal, the contract does not have to be written, although it is more often than not a good idea. Indeed, some agreements may require written contracts under the law, such as land purchases or financial credit arrangements. Written contracts also provide the parties with evidence of agreement and detail of the terms and conditions of the agreement.

There are, therefore, a range of legal aspects to consider when entering negotiations, which include:

- contracts
- the law (Acts of Parliament)
- terms and conditions that may impact directly on negotiated agreements
- dispute resolution.

The complexity of the law requires, in many cases, that the advice of a professional is sought in order to draw up an appropriate set of terms and conditions, especially where there are long-term implications for both parties. As Murray (2004) says: 'it is far better to have legal advice before the contract is made than be forced to have legal representation in expensive litigation, where two results are possible and one of them is distressing.' Where the aim of the negotiation is to resolve a dispute that has arisen between the parties, an overview of legal implications is clearly relevant.

Full discussion of legal factors is outside the scope of this study session. However, some (UK) laws which may apply include:

- **Sale of Goods** Act 1979: this relates to the purchase and hire purchase of goods and services (including IT equipment and software).
- Supply of Goods and Services Act 1982: this relates to hire, purchase and part-exchange of goods supplied as part of a service.
- Data Protection Act 1984: this refers to the holding of personal data on automatic equipment (including computers), relevant for personal details on supplier's staff, departmental staff and consultants.
- Fair Trading Act 1973: this concerns the review practices adversely affecting customers through possible monopoly situations; so-called 'collusive tenders' come under the auspices of the Restrictive Trade Practices Act 1976.
- Competition Act 1980: this relates to anti-competitive practices.
- Unfair Contract Terms Act 1977: this considers the role of civil liability for breach of contract or negligence by contract terms identified under the Supply of Goods and Services Act 1982.
- Limitation Act 1980: this sets out guidance for taking action on breach of contract.

Of these, the Sale of Goods Act 1979 defines the title and description of the goods. Similarly, the Sale and Supply of Goods Act 1994, which supplements the 1979 Act, defines:

- Satisfactory Quality: the goods meet standards that a 'reasonable person' would state as satisfactory based on the description of the goods, price and other relevant facts pertaining to the goods;.
- Fitness for Purpose: the goods are fit for the purpose that they are supplied for.

The term 'caveat emptor', meaning 'let the buyer beware', is relevant (although the term pre-dates statutory law on merchantable quality). In effect, this means that the onus is on the purchaser to ensure the product is fit for purpose.

International negotiations are especially challenging in terms of understanding the legal information and the implications for negotiation. Differences in legal systems are the most obvious challenge: the UK legal system is based on precedent and legislation whereas many other countries use a system based on codification of legal principles (such as the US and some countries within the European Union). A further layer of complexity is often added where there are regional guidelines on the application of local laws, such as in the EU. In preparation for the negotiation, it is important to consider, for example, the implications of taxation, labour codes and standards, differences in contract law and its enforcement. Cross-cultural negotiations are considered further in study session 16.

3

Feedback on page 42

3.4 Analysing supplier tenders

Tenders can be open, restricted or selective (Lysons, 2000), where the supplier may be self-selecting or already known to the purchaser. Other forms of tendering enable the purchaser to engage the supplier in a negotiation, which is an exception rather than a rule. The Department of Trade and Industry (DTI) in the UK has a clear and concise set of tendering guidelines which they issue to their potential suppliers, but which make no mention of negotiation:

- Ensure suppliers are treated equally by providing all tenderers with the same information.
- Be clear about the evaluation criteria at the outset, specifying commercial, technical and financial terms.
- Evaluate on the basis of commercial compliance, including any acceptance of terms and conditions specified, delivery, payment arrangements, ownership, et cetera.
- Evaluate on the basis of technical information relating to specification of goods, services and their value, including performance, standards, quality, operation/maintenance, standardisation, support services, consumables, training, sampling, warranties.
- Evaluate on the basis of financial costs and benefits, including **life cycle cost**, quantifiable benefit, fixed and variable pricing, component/spare part costs, current conversions, financial risk analysis.
- Compare tender documents received.

EU directives suggest that negotiation may occur when there are irregularities in the tendering process, when the tender cannot be complied with or when the supplies are for developmental purposes (Lysons, 2000). Since tendering is not always viable, because of cost, time factors and rigorous procedures, post-tender negotiation, or 'PTN', is a way that organisations can build some flexibility into the tender process.

In preparation for negotiation, problems may arise from the tendering process because of the inter-relational distance between the purchaser and the supplier: the lack of contact between the parties immediately restricts a key source of information. Nonetheless, there are circumstances where accountability is a primary concern in the process, arising from different corporate governance systems, such as a public sector organisation seeking private sector suppliers of some product or service. The process of tendering, therefore, overcomes some of the questions that may be asked as a result of public scrutiny in the ultimate selection.

Learning activity 3.4

Reflecting on the tendering processes you are familiar with (or alternatively the DTI guidelines in section 3.4), how can the process be improved to enhance a PTN?

Feedback on page 42

Following the tender process, purchasers may enter into a negotiation with the 'best' supplier and, possibly, those closest to them, so long as other tenderers are not disadvantaged (CIPS). Negotiation at this stage is intended to gain further quantifiable benefits and value for money. Any and all terms identified in the original specification are negotiable but, as the DTI warns: 'the cost of negotiating may be high (several staff days per tenderer), so a careful judgment needs to be made on the likely value of any benefit which might be gained.' Financial analysis for negotiation is considered in study session 4-study session 6.

PTN may be used in circumstances that necessitate further evaluation of the supplier's offer. These include (Lysons, 2000):

- Where orders are valued over £100,000.
- Where there is limited differentiation between the tenderers.
- Where the specification of the supplier's offer is unclear.
- Where supply is for more than 12 months.
- Where collusion among suppliers is suspected.
- Where prices appear to be in conflict with the marketplace.

Self-assessment question 3.4

What considerations and controls are needed to ensure PTNs are successful?

Feedback on page 42

Revision question

Now try the revision question for this session on page 265.

Summary

This study session has considered the role of specific types of information that will be used to inform the negotiation process. Firstly, risk was considered in relation to different perspectives of the role of purchasing: as a production unit, a communicative unit and a capital-earning unit. With the production unit view, risk is associated with the different categorisations of products according to their impact on financial results and the supply context.

A SWOT analysis was identified as a framework to highlight the relative strengths and weaknesses of the supplier in relation to the purchaser. This enables the parties to identify and prioritise negotiating variables so that their strengths can be maximised, and their weaknesses and threats overcome whilst realising the opportunities presented to them.

Discussion of the legal framework for negotiations briefly reviewed the broad range of Acts of Parliament (in the UK) that have the potential to impact upon negotiation outcomes. The further complication of international law was briefly discussed. Finally, the role of tenders and post-tender negotiation was reviewed.

Suggested further reading

Lewicki et al (2003b) on framing the negotiation (pages 30-41).

Gadde, L-E and Hakansson, H (2001) on the role of purchasing in the 'new economy'. This text reviews different perspectives of risk.

Feedback on learning activities and self-assessment questions

Feedback on learning activity 3.1

Application of these models depends very much on the circumstances of your organisation, and its relative position in the marketplace. At the very least, you should be able to identify those products and services which are strategically important and those that are routine (the Kraljic model) and those that are politically sensitive inside the organisation (Drummond and Ensor).

What is interesting in these two approaches is that you may find the same supplier being categorised quite differently. If this is the case, you should consider why.

In comparing and contrasting your application of the models, it is also useful to identify the variables you would use in negotiating with the suppliers, arising from their categorisation. Do they differ? Why? For example, delivery may be a key issue for negotiation on products considered to be 'bottleneck', whereas price may be the main issue for routine purchases, and for strategic products the issue may be post-purchase support (for example, training or warranty).

Feedback on self-assessment question 3.1

You may have included:

- Simplifies the nature of the purchasing negotiation task by clarifying the activities to be undertaken.
- Enables purchasing staff to become specialised in negotiations according to category.

3

- Identifies clear link between purchasing and financial management of the organisation.
- Focuses on a small number of variables over which the parties will negotiate, which may lead to 'win-lose' or distributive approach.
- Considers the way production interfaces with its internal stakeholders.
- Highlights the role of knowledge management in the negotiation process.

Feedback on learning activity 3.2

Remember to include some commentary on the impact of the strength and weakness on the organisation, and the reason for the potential opportunity and threat. Once factors have been identified, these can be prioritised for the negotiation.

Feedback on self-assessment question 3.2

Your answer should identify that it is an analytical tool to examine internal organisational strengths and weaknesses and external opportunities and Threats, based on a PESTLE analysis. It may be used to identify the other party's strengths and weaknesses which, when matched against the organisation's, can be used to generate negotiating variables.

Feedback on learning activity 3.3

You may have identified any of the following common terms and conditions:

- exclusion or limitation clauses, which specify the extent of any liability
- retention of title clauses
- penalty clauses, such as for non-performance.

You may also have considered the following implications:

- the scope of the supplier's provision
- quality and quantity
- the standards to be met by the supplier
- when and how the output will be measured
- equipment and materials to be supplied
- other facilities to be provided for the performance of the work
- frequency of measurement and any inspection
- expected start date for the contract
- schedule for the supply of goods and/or services
- preferred payment mechanisms.

In specifying any outputs, you may have identified the following points:

- Completeness: including any ancillary tasks required as well as the main task.
- Clarity: the supplier's role stated unambiguously.
- Measurability: outputs measured in quantitative terms; specification describing how they will be measured and reported, by whom and who pays.

3

- Objectives: the supplier ought to know the purpose of the service and how it relates to policy and objectives.
- Interfaces: responsibilities between the supplier and the purchaser should be identified.
- Resource inputs: for example, standards for the service or equipment (such as British Standard).

Feedback on self-assessment question 3.3

- Penalty: the purchaser may specify the level of penalty if the supplier fails to meet some deadline, say delivery of product or performance of service. It may not necessarily involve recourse to a court to resolve the dispute but may be worked through by adjusting payments against future supplies, if there are any.
- Retention of title: this is where ownership of goods is explicitly withheld by a supplier, usually pending full payment by the purchaser. Such a clause may have implications for products used in a production process, which may make it difficult to sell on the finished product.
- **Arbitration**: specifies the processes by which a dispute may be resolved, such as third parties to be consulted or laws to be enforced (including the country under whose law the agreement is bound).

Feedback on learning activity 3.4

You may have identified some of the following points:

- Explicit statement at the outset that a PTN may be used.
- Greater clarity in the tender specification in relation to commercial, technical and financial evaluation.
- Preliminary consideration of the differences in corporate structures and the need for accountability within public sector organisations.
- Cost-benefit analysis of the tendering and evaluation process.
- Consideration of the suppliers who are likely to submit tenders.
- Analysis of the subsequent costs associated with negotiating post-tender.

Feedback on self-assessment question 3.4

CIPS identifies the following considerations for PTN:

- Will the potential cost savings of PTN cover the costs of preparing for and conducting additional negotiation over above the tendering process?
- Is there sufficient time to hold PTN, with resulting delay to the contract?
- What is the impact on future supply situations?
- Are there any legal or regulatory guidelines that require all tenderers to be treated in the same way, that is, engage in PTN?
- What are the ethical considerations?

CIPS identifies the following controls for PTN:

- Who authorises PTN and who can award the contract?
- Who will negotiate and what team roles will there be?

- What supporting documentation, including for the audit trail following PTN, is there to be?
- How will the PTN process be reviewed, and by whom?

3

Applying financial tools to a negotiation

Introduction

In study session 3, the ability to evaluate the underpinning financials was highlighted as a skill needed in preparation for negotiation. Specifically, financial analysis enables calculation of the impact of an agreement on the organisation's results by considering the costs and benefits associated with the deal. This study session focuses on the approaches to calculating costs in preparation for a negotiation.

Firstly, the concept of fixed and variables costs is discussed in relation to the price variable for negotiations. This is then extended to breakeven analysis, using marginal costing as a basis. The session offers opportunities to practise analytic skills by providing practical examples and learning activities.

'Capital is money, capital is commodities. By virtue of it being value, it has acquired the occult ability to add value to itself. It brings forth living offspring, or, at the least, lays golden eggs.'
Karl Marx

4

Session learning objectives

After completing this session you should be able to:

4.1 Identify and calculate elements of fixed and variable costs to prepare for a negotiation.
4.2 Examine different perspectives on fixed and variable costs.
4.3 Define and undertake a breakeven analysis using marginal costing.

Unit content coverage

This study session covers the following topics from the official CIPS unit content document:

Statement of practice

Plan and prepare for effective negotiations.

Learning objectives

2.1 Identify and calculate elements of fixed and variable costs associated with supply.
- Fixed costs
- Variable costs
- Suppliers' perspective on fixed/variable costs
- Open book costing
2.4 Undertake a breakeven analysis.
- How to demonstrate breakeven through economic charts
- Modeling using breakeven

- Supplier's perspectives on breakeven
- Buyers' perspectives on breakeven

Resources

Calculator and graph paper.

Timing

You should set aside about 5 hours to read and complete this session, including learning activities, self-assessment questions, the suggested further reading (if any) and the revision question.

4.1 Fixed and variable costs

While price is generally a concern for markets, costs are associated with accounting. This is because it is often considered that setting a price is a function of market demand, while calculating total costs is operational and, therefore, the domain of accountancy. Total costs may include both 'fixed' elements and 'variable' elements, that is, ones where increases in activity lead to increases in costs. Definitions for these terms are, following Masterson and Pickton (2004):

- Total costs are the sum of all costs.
- Fixed costs are those that do not vary with output.
- Variable costs are those that do vary with output.

Think about these questions as you continue through this study session:

- Does the overall cost of materials rise if 10,000 items are made instead of 8,000?
- Does the cost of electricity fall if machinery is used for five hours instead of twelve hours?
- Does the cost of employer's liability insurance change with the rate of production?

Fixed costs are those that do not vary with the amount of activity resulting from production, sales or service levels. Examples could be rent, rates or security. Typically, costs are paid periodically (any changes will usually only be due to inflation). This is illustrated graphically in figure 4.1, where a cost of £80,000 is incurred irrespective of the increase in output units.

Figure 4.1: Fixed costs

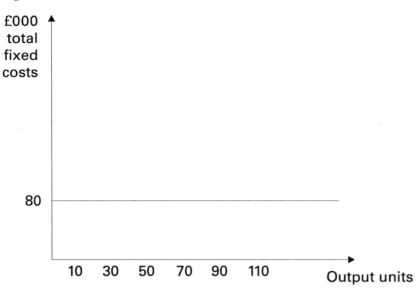

Variable costs vary directly as a result of increases in output. For example, materials used in production will increase with the number of units made (see figure 4.2). These costs are called variable because they vary according to changes in the number of units produced.

Figure 4.2: Variable costs

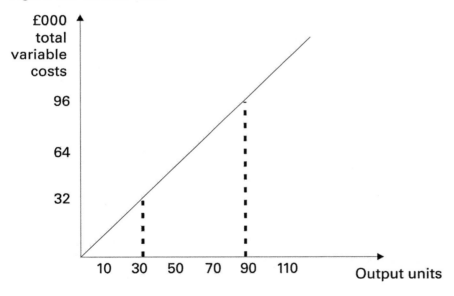

In figure 4.2, a cost per unit of £1,066 is incurred for each unit produced. This is establishing by identifying that £32,000 is incurred with an output of 30 units which increases to £96,000 for 90 units. Thus 110 units would amount to a variable cost of £117,260.

Some costs, however, have both a fixed and a variable component. Supply of telecommunications is an example of this, where there is usually a standing charge made for a telephone connection and additional charges made for calls. These costs are referred to as semi-variable (or also as semi-fixed or mixed costs).

4

Fixed and variable components can be calculated using the following formulae. Firstly, for variable costs (per unit):

- Difference in costs (at two production levels) ÷ Difference in production volume

Then, fixed costs can be calculated as:

- Total costs less total variable costs (at a specified number of units).

Table 4.1 Example of semi-variable cost calculations

Production volume	2,000 units Total costs	8,000 units Total costs
Storage and handling	£20,000	£47,000
Electricity	£15,000	£21,000

Using the example in table 4.1, calculate the variable cost for storage and handling:

- Difference in costs (at two production levels): £47,000 - £20,000 = £27,000
- Difference in production volume (in units): 8,000 - 2,000 = 6,000
- Variable cost (per unit): £27,000 ÷ 6,000 = £4.50.

Now, calculate the fixed costs for storage and handling:

- Total costs at 2,000 units: £20,000
- The total variable costs (at 2,000 units): 2,000 × £4.50 = £9,000
- Fixed cost: £20,000 - £9,000 = £11,000.

At 8,000 units, therefore, the total costs are:

variable cost	(8,000 × £4.50)	£36,000
add fixed costs		£11,000
total costs		£47,000

Work these examples through to see that you have understood the principles and then attempt learning activity 4.1 below.

Learning activity 4.1

Calculate the fixed and variable cost components of electricity in the example in table 4.1.

Feedback on page 55

Calculating fixed and variable costs is an important exercise in preparing for negotiation because it assists in determining the parameters for reaching agreement: it helps to identify costs per unit which can then be used as the basis for comparison with other suppliers. Clearly, the information is important because it reveals the supplier's potential resistance point for the price variable (the lowest they can go and still cover their costs), and enables the organisation to determine its walk away position. It also identifies potential economies of scale where fixed costs may be optimised over a range of different production quantities. Similarly, such analysis will also highlight the minimum number of units that are commercially viable, beyond which there are diseconomies of scale. This aspect of financial analysis is discussed further in study session 6.

Self-assessment question 4.1

Calculate the variable cost for each unit plus the fixed and variable cost components for the following example:

Maintenance costs:

- at 4,630 units = $23,450
- at 11,086 units = $35,200.

Feedback on page 55

4.2 Perspectives on fixed and variable costs

First attempt learning activity 4.2 below.

Learning activity 4.2

Reflecting on a recent negotiation you have participated in, what was the supplier's view of their costs? What evidence did you collect to support your analysis of this view?

Feedback on page 55

The nature of pricing, as previously stated, often reflects factors other than the costs associated with production and supply, such as market forces (competitive parity and customer perceived value) and bargaining power. Obviously, it is important to have a full understanding of how price is determined and, indeed, the PESTLE and Five Forces analyses (see study session 2) should feed into the review of this. In determining price, it is useful to identify the actual costs of the product or service being purchased. This can be obtained in a number of ways:

- Competitive bidding, such as through a tendering process (see study session 3).
- Independent expert analysis, that is, someone who can 'deconstruct' a product or service in order to accurately calculate the cost of each constituent part.
- Review of markets, which is practical for commoditised products and **services** and where information is widely available in various published

forms (internet, trade and industry associations, surveys, catalogues, stock markets).
- Indexed price and cost indicators, such as those found in *Supply Management* (CIPS monthly trade magazine).
- Bespoke or published ad hoc industry reports.

Analysis of data reveals the proportional cost breakdown which enables the purchaser to identify specific variables for a negotiation, for example materials, labour, overheads, profit. Suffice to say, few suppliers without the benefit of a long-term contractual relationship will be keen to reveal their exact cost structures to the purchaser. This is sensitive information about their profitability which has the potential to undermine its position in the marketplace, if the information were to reach, for example, a direct competitor.

Very often, the purchaser's negotiation on price will focus on the profit component of the supplier's offer. This is the most immediate component of the supplier's pricing structure which is negotiable. It is important for the purchaser, at the preparation stage of negotiation, to identify the pricing method that has been used to calculate their offer. Three approaches are:

- mark-up pricing
- full-cost pricing
- contribution pricing.

Mark-up pricing is discussed in study session 5, based on direct and indirect costs. Full-cost pricing uses total costs (fixed and variable costs) as the basis for calculations with a percentage then added on for profit. Profit level is determined by the strategic objectives of the organisation.

Contribution pricing, in contrast, uses the variable costs only; it does not consider fixed costs. It is often used as a short-term marketing strategy, typically with 'loss leaders' and one-off deals. Masterson and Pickton (2004) suggest the approach will be considered by suppliers when:

- Fixed costs are already covered by other customer orders.
- They have capacity to make and supply the order.
- The order will generate goodwill, possibly leading to future orders and, potentially, a long-term relationship.
- The impact of the order on other customers is limited. Suppliers would not want to lose goodwill from their existing customers should they find out a cheaper price has been offered to another organisation, who may be a competitor.

Clearly, the purchaser needs to determine whether the focus on cost is the most appropriate in these circumstances. For a one-off purchase, the answer is probably yes; however, if an ongoing supply situation is sought, then this is unlikely to result in a stable relationship between the parties. Indeed, such a pricing approach may lead to the supplier going out of business!

Overheads should, therefore, be incorporated to reflect the true total costs. These are indirect costs associated with activities such as marketing and manufacturing, and they may fixed or variable. Fixed overheads may include depreciation on capital equipment or some administration costs. Variable overheads may include such things as energy or engineering support. An evaluation of overheads enables the purchaser to understand the relationship between the supplier's cost of production and cost of value adding overheads. Certainly, the purchaser should not pay a disproportionately high price for overheads, which may in fact be used to support supplies to other customers, although this will obviously vary by industry. This is discussed further in study session 5.

When parties engage in an ongoing relationship, it is argued there are cost savings on both sides. On the supplier's side, costs may be reduced because inventory management is streamlined, mark down is minimised and forecasting capacity is simplified (Reichheld, 1996). These savings may be passed on to the purchaser, so that both parties benefit from the enhanced performance.

Where the relationship between the purchaser and the supplier is particularly close, trusting and well protected, such as in a joint-venture or strategic alliance situation, then 'open book' exchanges may occur. Here, the parties endeavour to share intimate information about cost structures related to strategic objectives with one another. Negotiations in this case will tend to focus on creating value for both parties, rather than reducing costs per se (Donaldson and O'Toole, 2002).

Self-assessment question 4.2

What are the advantages and disadvantages associated with open book costing?

Feedback on page 56

4.3 Breakeven analysis

Building on sections 4.1 and 4.2, this section focuses on variable costs, which are also known as marginal costs. These are defined as the cost of one unit of a product or service which would be avoided if the product or service was not supplied.

Consider that fixed costs are 'written off' against sales revenue less variable costs. There is, therefore, a net 'contribution' to profit where revenue is higher than fixed and variable costs. The calculation is written:

- sales revenue - variable costs = contribution
- contribution - fixed costs = profit (or loss)
- breakeven point (units) = fixed cost ÷ contribution (per unit).

An organisation needs to know the point at which its production level becomes profitable, given its costs. Breakeven is the point at which there is no contribution to profit but neither is there a loss to the organisation: that is, total income and total costs are equal. This is known as the breakeven point and is commonly presented as a chart or profit/volume graph (figure 4.3).

Figure 4.3: Breakeven point

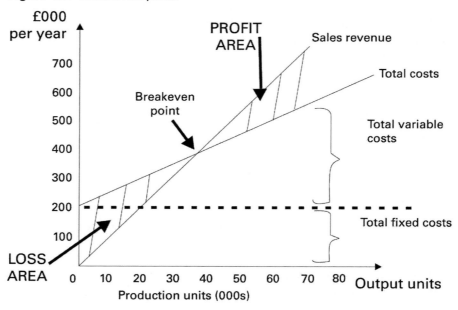

A breakeven analysis is a visual way of representing profitability at different levels of output and is, therefore, a valuable tool in preparing for negotiation. If supplier prices vary, then a new chart will be able to show the impact of the price increase as the breakeven point will be pushed higher.

Learning activity 4.3

How is/might breakeven analysis used/be used within your organisation to model business?

Feedback on page 56

In preparing a breakeven analysis there a number of basic steps to follow. These are worked through with the following example:

- Cantor company produces riding saddles for horses.
- Fixed costs total £150,000.
- Variable costs are £700 per saddle.
- Each saddle sells for £1,800.

1 Decide the scale of the graph, determined by output levels. Draw the vertical (*y*) axis and the horizontal (*x*) axis (see figure 4.4).
2 Plot fixed costs line, remembering to label the line or area.
3 Calculate the variable costs, using the data: for example, 300 units at £700 per saddle = £210,000; 600 units at £700 = £420,000.
4 Draw the total costs line (fixed costs plus variable costs), using the data: for example, at 300 units, fixed costs plus variable costs = £210,000 + £150,000; at 600 units, £420,000 + £150,000.
5 Draw the sales revenue line: for example, sales revenue from 300 units at £1,800 = £540,000; from 600 units at £1,800 = £1,080,000.

6 Mark the breakeven point and the areas below which no profit is made, and above which profit is made.

Figure 4.4: Worked example of breakeven

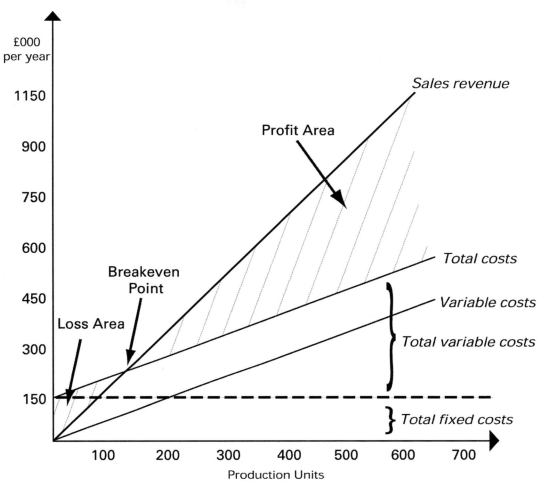

To calculate the breakeven point use the formula: fixed costs ÷ contribution (per unit).

• contribution (per unit) = sales revenue (£1,800) - variable cost (£700)
• £1,800 - £ 700 = £1,100 contribution per unit
• fixed costs = £150,000
• therefore, breakeven is calculated as:£150,000 ÷ £1,100 = 136.3 (137 units).

This figure should accord with the graphic representation!

Self-assessment question 4.3

From the case and data below, model the breakeven point using a graph and calculate the breakeven point:

• Krankit company produces door handles.
• Fixed costs total $200,000.

(continued on next page)

4

Self-assessment question 4.3 *(continued)*
- Variable costs are $2.50 per handle.
- Each handle sells for $5.90.

Feedback on page 56

Revision question

Now try the revision question for this session on page 265.

Summary

This study session has covered a basic introduction to management accounting techniques that are used to prepare for negotiations. It focused particularly on developing an understanding of the terms 'fixed' and 'variable' costs. It was also identified that some costs can be 'semi-variable'. Formulae were presented on how to calculate the total costs, from the sum of fixed and variable costs, and also how to separate fixed and variable costs where this information is presented as a semi-variable cost.

Discussion extended to the supplier's perspective of their costing structure. It was identified that in preparing for a negotiation, the purchaser needs to be examine a range of information in order to determine the supplier's costs. This includes competitive bids, independent expert analysis and review of market data.

It was also identified that suppliers may use a number of different approaches to setting their prices, including mark-up pricing, full-cost pricing and contribution pricing, where contribution was considered to be a short-term strategic offer. Open book pricing was identified as a joint approach to performance enhancement, based on the strength of relationship between the purchaser and the supplier.

Breakeven analysis was presented as a tool to develop understanding of the impact of different prices on profitability: it is a visual way of representing profitability at different levels of output. Six steps were identified in producing a breakeven chart and a formula presented to calculate the exact breakeven point.

Suggested further reading

Lewicki et al (2003b) on knowing your limits and alternatives, and setting targets and openings (pages 47 to 49 of the essential text).

Steele et al (1995) on preparation and planning, which highlights how to seek answers from suppliers on pricing approaches and costing of concessions.

Any introductory management or accounting text on management accounting techniques will include focus on fixed and variable costing and breakeven analysis.

Feedback on learning activities and self-assessment questions

Feedback on learning activity 4.1

At 2,000 units, the total variable cost per unit for electricity is:

- (£21,000-£15,000) ÷ (8,000-2,000) = £1

The fixed cost is:

- £15,000 - £2,000 = £13,000

Therefore, at 8,000 units, total costs are:

variable cost	(8,000 × £1.00)	£8,000
add fixed costs		£13,000
total costs		£21,000

Feedback on self-assessment question 4.1

First, calculate the variable cost:

- Difference in costs (at two production levels) ÷ Difference in production volume
- ($35,200 - $23,450) ÷ (11,086-4,630)
- $11,750 ÷ 6,456 = $1.82

Then, calculate fixed costs:

- Total costs less total variable costs (at a specified number of units).
- At 4,630 units, total costs are: $23,450
- At 4,630 units, total variable cost is: 4,630 × $1.82 = $8,426.60
- Therefore, fixed costs are: $23,450 - $8,426.60 = $15,023.40

At 11,086 units, costs are:

variable cost	(11,086 × $1.82)	$20,176.52
add fixed costs		$15,023.40
total costs		$35,199.92

Feedback on learning activity 4.2

Your answer should cover the following issues:

- Were you able to determine the supplier's pricing approach? Was it based on competitive prices, or some 'cost plus profit' method?
- Did you identify the cost structure used by the supplier, such as the costings for different constituents, including labour?
- What level of **profit** was the supplier making?
- What messages did the concession pattern give you in the negotiation? Did you get an impression of how keen they were to deal with you through their offers on price?

4

- Were they open with you about their price and costings during the negotiation?

Evidence you may have collected to support your analysis:

- competitive bids
- expert advice
- market data
- specific supplier data, such as annual report and accounts or credit scorings.

Feedback on self-assessment question 4.2

Advantages may include:

- Identification of new, shared opportunities which lead to joint gains.
- Reduction in conflict between the parties.
- Influence through expertise.

Disadvantages may include:

- Problems of confidentiality arise if (and when) the relationship dissolves.
- The resultant tie in may, in fact, be due to high switching costs rather than mutuality – this puts added pressure on the relationship to reduce costs and enhance performance values, which may ultimately prove untenable.

Feedback on learning activity 4.3

Your answer could consider the following points:

- Illustrates the point at which the organisation becomes profitable from its production efforts.
- Identifies the range of prices that the organisation will agree to pay for its supplies. It will not want to agree a cost price so high that it cannot achieve a profit from its production capability.
- Evaluates the level of sales that need to be achieved for given levels of supply costs (fixed and variable).
- Highlights the potential contribution to profits from each unit of production.

Feedback on self-assessment question 4.3

Breakeven calculated as follows:

- contribution (per unit) = sales revenue ($5.90) - variable cost ($2.50)
- $5.90 - $2.50 = $3.40 contribution per unit
- fixed costs = $200,000
- therefore, breakeven is calculated as:$200,000 ÷ $3.40 = 58,823.5 (58,824 units).

Figure 4.5: Krankit breakeven

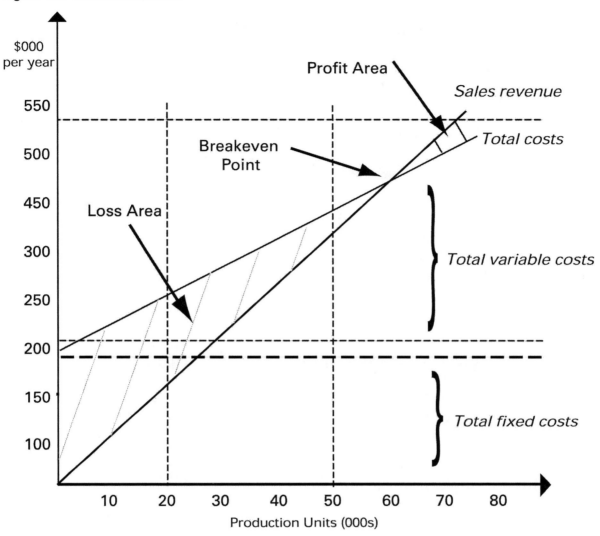

Remember to show all labels for lines and areas you identify on the graph.

4

Analysing financial contribution

Introduction

This study session develops further skills in financial analysis for negotiation, building on study session 4. As Klein argues: 'procurement professionals should be viewed as internal consultants to the budget-holder functions – change agents, with strong commercial acumen, problem-solving skills, analytical ability, and change management skills as well as the professional **procurement** skills of negotiation, tender execution and contract development.'

In preparing for negotiation, this requires the ability to differentiate a range of costs and identify value in different types of goods and services. Goods and services can be for internal consumption, or are for use in producing end-user customer products and/or services. The price paid often reflects the level of need the purchaser has, while the supplier sells on the basis of the value they incorporate into the product or service (Lambin, 2000).

The different types of products and services are, therefore, reviewed in relation to their potential value for and impact upon the organisation. Further types of costs are identified in relation to a range of goods and services and, finally, considerations for cost models are presented.

> 'The ideal is to cut budgets before a sourcing effort, but the finance director must then have confidence in procurement's ability to deliver.'
>
> **Alex Klein, CEO of strategic sourcing and supply chain consultancy, Efficio, commenting on potential returns for an organisation from sound sourcing (2004)**

Session learning objectives

After completing this session you should be able to:

5.1 Identify total costs and its constituents.
5.2 Differentiate between capital goods, consumables and materials, and their value to and impact on the business and its operations.
5.3 Identify and calculate the components of typical costing models.

Unit content coverage

This study session covers the following topics from the official CIPS unit content document:

Statement of practice

Plan and prepare for negotiations.

Learning objectives

2.2 Identify and calculate direct, indirect and standard costs.
   • Difference between direct and indirect costs
   • Standard costs

- Actual costs
- Budget costs

2.3 Identify total costs and margins.
- What total costs are
- What is meant by 'margins'
- Suppliers' margins versus market pricing

Timing

You should set aside about 5 hours to read and complete this session, including learning activities, self-assessment questions, the suggested further reading (if any) and the revision question.

5.1   Pricing and total costs

Total cost was identified in section 3.1 as the sum of fixed and variable costs. Costs may also relate either directly or indirectly to a particular product or service. Thus two additional categories of costs are identified:

- Direct costs are those that are wholly associated with a product or service.
- Indirect costs are those that cannot be traced to a specific product or service.

Direct costs may be broken down further into materials, labour and expenses (see figure 5.1):

Figure 5.1: Costs in a manufacturing organisation

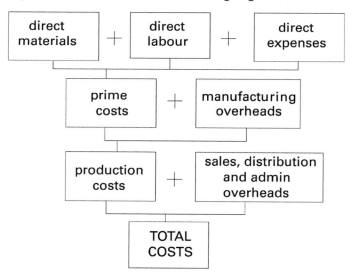

- Materials are those components attributed to a particular product, such as engine parts.
- Labour relates to the wages and salaries of those staff involved in the production process, that is, on the production line.
- Expenses are additional costs associated with the product, such as any special tool hire for the production process.

These three types of direct costs are collectively referred to as 'prime costs'.

Overheads can be similarly classified into production, sales and distribution, and administration. These costs can be apportioned to the product in order to derive total costs. Suffice to say, there are a number of ways that costs can be allocated, using so-called 'absorption' techniques, including:

- Rate of labour per hour, used where labour is the predominant cost.
- Rate of machine hour, used where machinery is the predominant cost.
- Percentage of direct materials cost.
- Percentage of direct labour cost.
- Percentage of prime cost.
- Rate per unit produced.

(Presentation of formulae for each of these is outside the scope of this study session. For further information, refer to a standard management accounting text.)

Services are, not surprisingly, more difficult to cost because of a range of factors, predominantly to do with their perishability. This means that if a service is not provided today, then the opportunity for selling it in that 'space' has passed. Consider a charter aircraft that has only sold half of the seats it has available: does this mean that the service provider will charge twice as much to those passengers it has managed to sell seats to at the point of take-off?

It is argued that the absorption techniques to costing are limited because the tendency is to use only a few different calculations to apportion direct and indirect costs, such as labour and machine hours. Nonetheless, the approach is more commonly used than the marginal costing techniques identified in study session 4, because they are considered to more accurately reflect the total costs of a product.

Learning activity 5.1

Consider how you determine total costs in your own and/or your suppliers' organisations. Can you identify the approach used (marginal costing from study session 4, or absorption costing from this section)? Which works better in preparing for negotiations?

Feedback on page 69

The price a supplier charges may reflect one of three main strategic objectives:

- volume sales
- profitability
- competitive parity.

Clearly, knowledge of the strategy the supplier is pursuing informs the negotiation process. Where focus is on volume, the supplier may be

5

attempting to achieve sales growth; with focus on profit, the emphasis is likely to be on return on investment (ROI); whereas, with competition-oriented pricing, they may be attempting to undermine or merely keep pace with competitors. Given these distinctive approaches, it is evident that total costs will differ using the absorption techniques identified above.

From the purchaser's perspective, there will also be costs and benefits associated with the purchase. Lambin (2000) refers to these as 'transfer' costs, which include:

- The cost associated with incorporating a new supplier's product into the production process.
- The need to adapt or change purchasing habits to accommodate the supplier.
- Any investment in training or support mechanisms.
- Investment in other equipment that is used alongside the supplier's product.

Costs incurred by the purchaser, therefore, go beyond the price agreed with the supplier.

Self-assessment question 5.1

Why is an understanding of cost-based pricing important and how does knowledge of it contribute to a negotiation?

Feedback on page 69

5.2 Impact of supply chain on costing

In section 3.1, different types of goods and services were briefly identified (van Weele, 2000):

- Raw materials: the base products used in the manufacturing process, such as base metals, oil.
- Supplementary materials: materials used in the production process, such as lubricants.
- Semi-manufactured products: pre-processed products for further processing inside the organisation, such as steel plating.
- Components: either specifically designed for the purchaser or predetermined by some standard.
- Finished products: added to the purchaser's product, such as satellite navigation systems to cars.
- Investment goods or capital equipment: for use in the production process over an extended period of time, such as machinery.
- MRO items: maintenance, repair, operation supply.
- Services: from the simple (such as cleaning or gardening) to the highly complex (such as legal advice).

These are used by the organisation in many different ways and, therefore, add value to the organisation differentially. Previous discussion has identified that certain supplies will be identified as more critical to the business than others, depending on strategic objectives. Thus a classification system will be individual to the organisation. There are a number of ways that this can be thought about, beyond the risks associated with supply.

Focusing on projects, such as installing and managing production lines (capital equipment), requires a special order of financial analysis called capital budgeting. This enables the organisation to evaluate the investment over a number of time periods (say, three or four years) that are relevant to the life of the specific project. As a technique for managing costs, it enables calculation of profit for the whole project and, therefore, is a more strategic approach. There are a number of important considerations which will impact on the calculations (Horngren et al, 2005):

- The business environment within which the project will operate – for example, a predicted rise in costs for fuel needed to run the production line.
- The cost of funding the project. If funds are borrowed, then interest rates will apply.
- Predicted taxes on profits.
- Inflation/deflation predictions, which will affect the project over its life.
- The impact of the project on human resources – if the production line is more efficient than workers, then costs go down.

Value chain analysis (Porter, 1985), which is essentially a market-driven tool, can help to identify how purchasing can contribute to the overall business objectives by contributing to all the organisation's functions, including operations, marketing, sales, customer support services.

Value chain analysis focuses on the cost-benefits associated with providing value for end-user customers of the organisation's products and services. Through identification of the value adding components, differential advantage in the marketplace is established. Clearly, without understanding what these value-adding components are, then the role of purchasing will be limited to agreeing specification for supplies with internal value generators (budget holders) where cost is often the major consideration. Implications for negotiation derive from the need to establish an internal mandate for purchasing activities, as well as external negotiation with suppliers. Figure 5.2 illustrates a basic value chain of business functions.

Figure 5.2: Basic value chain of business functions

Source: Based on Horngren et al (2005)

In contrast, the supply chain represents the flow of goods and services from raw materials suppliers to end-user customers. Clearly, purchasing's role

5

within this is to provide economically viable supplies which enable the organisation to meet customer demand.

Learning activity 5.2

Consider how the purchases you negotiate reflect the value chain in your work context.

Feedback on page 69

Emphasis on value and supply chains means that purchaser's focus is on cost, quality, time and innovation, often through a system of continuous improvement. Strategic relationship development with suppliers and customers provides potential for enhancing profitability (Horngren et al, 2005). For example, Donaldson and O'Toole (2002) state that the main advantage of single sourcing, such as through relationship development, is the potential for increased bargaining power. This, in turn, can drive costs down for the purchaser, although indirect costs may rise because more time and effort is invested in managing the relationship.

In this context, the just-in-time approach to production has been a source of financial advantage for purchasing organisations because of:

- lower investment in stocks
- reduced stock handling and holding costs
- reduced risk of stock obsolescence
- reduced storage costs
- reduced total manufacturing costs
- reduced waste because of improved quality.

This does assume, however, that production quality in the organisation is improved.

Self-assessment question 5.2

What performance measures can be used to control just-in-time production? How can knowledge of these contribute to a negotiation?

Feedback on page 70

5.3 Cost models

It needs to be recognised that the costs that organisations use in their calculations are not always the actual costs incurred. There may be reasons why it is not always practical to use the actual costs, for example where costs are subject to short-term fluctuations. In these circumstances organisations will use a model to approximate the cost and reconcile the difference at a later point. Three key definitions need to be highlighted at this point:

1   Actual costs – these are the actual costs incurred during the period which can be allocated directly to a product, service or project. The nature of the product, service or project may be able to accommodate any variations in these costs over a period so the use of alternative models is unnecessary. For example, in a one-off project the actual cost incurred can be allocated direct to that project.

2   Standard costs – are predetermined costs that will be an approximation of what the costs are expected to be over a defined financial period, for example the financial year or a financial quarter. They are used when the costs of inputs can vary, but the outputs need to be costed and priced more consistently for marketing and sales purposes, for example for a shirt manufacturer the actual cost of making a shirt will vary very slightly from shirt to shirt, depending on the amount of waste in the fabric, the sewing thread used and variation in the time to stitch it together. However, the customers who buy these shirts will not want to bother with these very slight variations in the costs and will want a standard, consistent price. Standard costs are usually based on an historical average of the actual costs over time and often adjusted to include an element for performance expectations for the period. This average provides a standard cost that we can use to charge out our product or service at a standard rate for the purposes of simplicity and consistency within our processes and for marketing purposes. Standard costs simplify planning processes and provide a focus for control and performance measurement. However, it must be recognised that this average is unlikely to be entirely accurate and may well lead to an over, or under, recovery of the actual costs incurred. Organisations will measure this difference between the standard cost charged over a period and the actual costs incurred and produce a 'variance report'. This report will highlight the extent of the over or under recovery of actual costs and will be used to adjust the standard cost for the next financial period. The reasons for these variances need to be investigated to ensure that the organisation is not at risk, for example consistent under recovery of actual costs will compromise budgets, forecasts and profit margins, while over recovery might compromise our pricing in the marketplace and our ability to win orders as our prices are too high.

3   Budget costs – are used for longer-term forecasting and pricing purposes and to create budgetary models for broader financial planning. These will also include elements of approximation, averaging and forecasting. For example, broad budget costs used for major project costing may also include elements of standard as well as actual costs to arrive at the overall project cost. Again these budget costs will need to be compared to the actual costs incurred so any variances can be investigated to improve future budgeting.

Exact cost breakdowns differ by industry and by organisation, depending on their unique characteristics. It is, therefore, difficult to present models which are generally applicable. Nonetheless, there are some basic components for costing, which can be identified in the different approaches in calculating costs. Figure 5.3 identifies the elements of a typical model.

Figure 5.3: Elements of a typical cost model

Price to purchaser
(sales price)

Profit

Overhead

Indirect marketing

Indirect manufacturing

Direct marketing cost

Direct labour cost

Direct material cost

Source: based on Lambin (2000)

Cost-based concepts of pricing, for example, identify four aspects which relate to cost and profit requirements:

- The minimum price: based on replacement costs, which implies no profit at all for the supplier. Where the supplier has the opportunity to offset an order against another more profitable one, then this so-called 'floor price' can be used for negotiations.
- The breakeven price: where full costs are covered for a specific volume.
- The target price: representing a price that the supplier is willing to sell at (see also the discussion on negotiation ranges in study session 7). Target price is denoted as:
Target price = direct cost + (fixed cost ÷ expected sales volume) + (expected rate of return on capital invested ÷ expected sales volume)
- The mark-up price: calculated by adding a standard mark-up to the breakeven price, which represents a desired level of profit. Mark-up is calculated as:
Mark-up price = breakeven price ÷ (1 - desired mark-up)

Lambin (2000) points out that although target price and mark-up price are the most commonly used, there is a danger that the relationship between volume and price is overlooked. This is because they merely identify a profit level for a given cost, rather than consider whether or not demand is of an appropriate level to support the volume (and price to the end-customer) identified. For example, an increase in supplies to the market by the organisation may result in customers valuing the product less and therefore paying less. Alternatively, if fewer products are supplied, then demand will be such that customers are prepared to pay more. Either way, this means the price agreed with the supplier needs also to reflect the elasticity of end-customer demand. This is called circular logic (see figure 5.4).

Figure 5.4: Circular logic of pricing

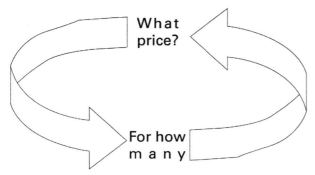

What price?

For how many

Clearly, cost components for services will differ from those for goods, because there will be few raw materials involved in the end product (see figure 5.3). Services costs are likely to be based primarily on expert inputs (people and time), which can be benchmarked against other providers of the service. Consider, for example, the costs that would be involved in marketing consultancy.

Learning activity 5.3

What questions does an understanding of cost-based pricing enable purchasers to ask in preparation for negotiation?

Feedback on page 70

Ultimately, an understanding of costs enables purchasers to set budgets, adding real value to the budget holders, as intimated by Klein's comment at the beginning of this study session. Budgeting is the most common control method used in organisations; it enables setting of activity levels and identifies those activities that are critically important to the business.

In order to set accurate budgets, the key considerations are:

- Cost behaviour: What influences the changes in cost structures?
- Timescales: How do they impact on forecasts?
- Strategic objectives: How does the organisation prioritise the activities it will engage in?

Budgets can be formulated from any of three main bases:

- Historical data: including adjustments for inflation and increases in activity levels.
- Activity: where end-user demand is estimated.
- Zero-based: the analysis of benefits resulting from activities identified as key, usually by senior management, rather than by considering how costs were allocated in previous periods (for example, by using historical data). This approach means that budget holders tend to be less complacent because their objectives are cost/benefit analysed and targeted to meet specific goals (Doyle, 2002).

Self-assessment question 5.3

Draw and label the typical components of a cost model. Use examples to support your answer.

Feedback on page 70

Revision question

Now try the revision question for this session on page 266.

Summary

This study session has identified further definitions of total costs and its constituents:

- Direct costs: wholly associated with a product or service.
- Indirect costs: not associated directly with a product or service.

Direct costs were further broken down into materials, labour and expenses. Different methods of absorption costing techniques were identified, and associated with industries according to their focus on products or services.

Costs and prices were differentiated. Prices were described as being derived from three main strategic objectives of: volume sales, profitability and competitive parity. Capital budgeting, value chain analysis and impact on the supply chain were discussed and negotiating variables identified from consideration of the just-in-time approach to production.

Four aspects of cost-based concepts of pricing were discussed, relating to the organisation's cost and profit requirements:

- The minimum price or 'floor price'.
- The breakeven price.
- The target price.
- The mark-up price.

A key problem was identified with target price and mark-up price in that they assumed a certain volume in order to set price (profit), which may not necessarily reflect what the market will bear.

Typical components of a cost model were identified, based on costing methods. And finally there was a discussion of the considerations for setting budgets.

Suggested further reading

Any management text on costing and budgeting. Focus on the models presented in this study session.

Any text of supply chain management related to cost savings.

Feedback on learning activities and self-assessment questions

Feedback on learning activity 5.1

Points to consider:

- Marginal costing ensures all fixed costs in an accounting period are allocated and it is, therefore, quite a logical calculation; total contribution, however, varies according to volumes. This is relatively straightforward to calculate.
- Absorption costing is more refined and enables apportionment of a range of costs to a product or service, reflecting more accurately the total cost. From a negotiation perspective, it is more difficult to calculate a supplier's cost apportionments, unless you are able to identify the complete range of business activities they engage in and, indeed, their strategic objectives for pricing.

Feedback on self-assessment question 5.1

Your answer should consider the following points:

Importance of cost-based pricing:

- Identifies volume of sales or sales revenue required to cover costs.
- Enables comparison of prices to direct competition.
- If prices go up or down, identifies the volumes required to offset the changes.
- Identifies the rate of return from products at different price levels.

Contribution to negotiation:

- Identifies range of variables for negotiation, including components of prime costs and breakdown of labour.
- Leads to evaluation of transfer costs associated with implementing any deal agreed upon with the supplier.
- Sets ranges for price and other variables in a negotiation.
- Enables profit to be used as a variable which may be used either competitively or collaboratively to achieve outcome benefits for the organisation (and the other party).

Feedback on learning activity 5.2

Your answer should focus on the different functions within the organisation and the range of negotiations you are involved in. For example:

- Design of products and services: possible involvement in supplying expertise on process design.
- Production: the range of supplies needed to make the products, including delivery, quality, and so on.

- Marketing: support services, such as advertising agencies, marketing materials.
- Customer service: support activities which enhance the service delivery (for example, contracting out of call centre support).

Feedback on self-assessment question 5.2

- Financial measures (stock turnover).
- Non-financial measures: such as number of units produced in a given time, stock and quality; or number of units requiring rework or considered to be waste.
- Personal observation of the production effort, which may provide timely information which is relatively easy to interpret.
- Generating and prioritising negotiable variables, for example: delivery volumes, dates, times, quality standards, waste management, stock handling procedures. These may be used as the basis for extending a contract with a supplier or as leverage with a new supplier.

Feedback on learning activity 5.3

Key questions may relate to the intentions the purchaser has for a relationship with the supplier. Answers could include:

- At what volume of sales are costs covered?
- How does price compare with other potential suppliers?
- What is our business worth to the supplier, in terms of market share and profitability?
- At what point of market share could we represent breakeven to the supplier?
- Which costs can be shared to achieve better value between the supplier and the organisation?
- What would be the lowest price that the suppliers could offer us?
- What would be the highest price they could expect us to pay?

Feedback on self-assessment question 5.3

Refer to figure 5.3 for a model illustration. Remember to include direct and indirect costs, all labels, and profit!

Understanding the financial context of negotiations

Introduction

Study sessions 4 and 5 focused on the approaches to calculating costs in preparation for a negotiation and determining the value associated with different types of goods and services. This study session extends the discussion by looking at the supply context more broadly.

Firstly, the concept of supply and demand is discussed in relation to the impact this has on pricing and costs. Financial benchmarking is reviewed as an approach to preparing for negotiation, where pricing and costs in relation to alternatives are considered. Finally, this study session reviews the potential for economies of scale and associated factors, such as the learning and experience curve.

> 'Cost control should be a permanent item on the corporate agenda; continuing economic and cyclical volatility will hasten this trend.'
>
> **Doyle (2002: 13) commenting on the need for strong financial competence in managing an organisation**

Session learning objectives

After completing this session you should be able to:

6.1 Apply the concept of supply and demand to costs and pricing in an organisation.
6.2 Identify techniques for financial benchmarking.
6.3 Analyse the potential for economies of scale in a negotiation.

Unit content coverage

This study session consolidates and builds on the material from study sessions 4 and 5. It considers the financial issues involved in the preparation for the negotiation and develops this material in the broader context of the negotiation. It covers the whole of learning objective 2.0 (2.1–2.4) 'Financial tools for negotiations' from the official CIPS unit content document.

Statement of Practice

Prepare and plan for effective negotiations.

Timing

You should set aside about 5 hours to read and complete this session, including learning activities, self-assessment questions, the suggested further reading (if any) and the revision question.

6.1 Derived demand

Study session 5 identified the circular logic that means cost-based pricing techniques using volume of supply do not necessarily reflect the accurate costs of producing a product. This is because it does not take into account economies of scale or the learning curve for production processes, which may mean that higher volume, or production over a longer time frame, is cheaper. Cost reduction due to increased experience may result from:

- increased labour efficiency
- specialisation in production techniques
- improved performance from equipment used in production
- changes to the resource mix, such as raw materials used
- product redesign, aimed at achieving production efficiency.

Similarly, cost-based approaches do not take into account the impact increased supplies may have on end-user customer demand. Recall the idea presented in the discussion of market forces (see study session 2) where buying power was considered to be strong when there was ample supply of a product, meaning the price may need to be lower to achieve the same demand level. Thus, being able to evaluate an appropriate pricing level for a given demand for a product or service is important. It leads to the notion of elasticity, where sensitivity to price enables calculation of the volume demanded at different pricing levels.

Two ideas are fundamental to elasticity of demand:

- Where price does not result in changes in demand, the product or service is said to be price inelastic.
- Where demand is influenced by price, then the product or service is said to be price elastic.

Price elastic means that the quantity demanded is highly responsive to a change in price. In figure 6.1 a change in price from P1 to P2 results in a large response in the quantity demanded from Q1 to Q2. Price inelastic means that the quantity demanded is highly unresponsive to a change in price. In figure 6.2 a change in price from P1 to P2 results in a small response in the quantity demanded from Q1 to Q2.

Figure 6.1: Price elasticity of demand

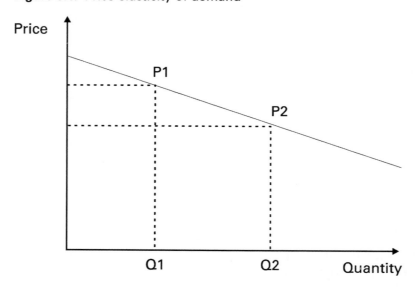

Figure 6.2: Price inelasticity of demand

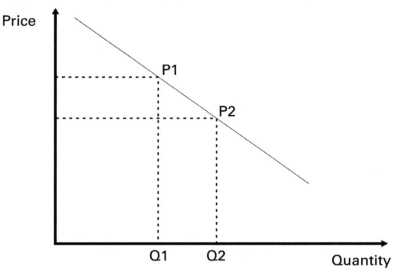

Learning activity 6.1

Describe the impact of **monopoly** and **oligopoly** power on costs and price.

Feedback on page 79

Elasticity of demand can be calculated using one of four main sources of information:

- Expert judgment, where opinions from knowledgeable individuals may enable estimation of demand from changes in pricing.
- Customer surveys, which may predict reactions to pricing fluctuations.
- Experimenting with price, using either simulation or field testing.
- Econometric studies, using extensive market data, such as retail data.

Elasticity of price is calculated as a percentage of the original price – the higher the calculation, the greater the elasticity:

Price elasticity = (% change in quantity demanded) ÷ (% change in price).

For example, if marking up the price of a pack of nails by 10% resulted in a decrease in demand of 25%, then the pack of nails would be described as price elastic. Using the equation above, you would get the following calculation: 25 ÷ 10 = 2.5. If the answer is over 1, the product's demand is described as price elastic.

On the other hand, if marking up the price of a pack of nails by 10% resulted in a decrease in demand of just 5%, then you would produce this equation: 5 ÷ 10 = 0.5. In this case, since the answer is less than 1, the pack of nails would be described as price inelastic.

Lambin (2002) summarises the situations that may mean the purchaser will be less sensitive to price fluctuations:

- Where the supplies represent a small part of the purchaser's costs.

- Where failure of the supplies may carry a high cost for the purchaser.
- Where contributory effectiveness of the supplies leads to high cost savings.
- Where a quality strategy is being pursued by the purchaser.
- Where design or differentiation is a major factor in the purchasing decision.
- Where purchaser profitability is high and supply costs can easily be borne.

The purpose of evaluating price elasticities in preparing for negotiation is as follows:

- Information about the potential direction of prices enables an evaluation of how market demand can be stimulated for increasing profitability.
- Comparing supplier products against one another identifies where market power lies. For example, a more heavily branded product may be less price-sensitive than one that it is not – which, in turn, has implications for profitability for the organisation.
- Comparing supplier prices enables the purchaser to lever a preferred supplier.

Nonetheless, the evaluation of supply and demand using elasticity does have some difficulties in practice. Often, the relationship between price and demand is based on observation of actual demand and is limited to known market situations. It is, therefore, difficult to use as a predictor of supply and demand for a new product, including trial rates and repeat purchases by customers. Moreover, markets are dynamic, responding to a variety of factors, such as may be identified in a SWOT analysis. This means focus on price purely as a predictor of demand is inherently unreliable.

Self-assessment question 6.1

Discuss the impact a 10% increase in price may have on the profitability of a supplier's product range.

Feedback on page 80

6.2 Benchmarking

The purpose of **benchmarking** is to identify the standards of performance. According to Maylor (2003) benchmarking is a 'reference point' and is, therefore, a means by which the purchaser can both evaluate a supplier's offer and measure competing suppliers against one another.

Financial measures of performance (price and cost) may be found in a range of sources, depending on the particular industry in which the purchaser operates (benchmarking 'clubs' and schemes may be used). Information such as that contained in *Supply Management* (Insight section), for example, provides useful initial data on going rates and market prices for a range of widely used raw materials, commodities and services, imports, manufacturers' materials and fuel costs, as well as manufacturers' prices and details of exchange rates and inflation indicators in the UK and Europe.

Another source of benchmarking data is the Centre for Advanced Purchasing Studies ([www.CAPSresearch.org/benchmarking/, CAPS Research]) which provides information on general purchasing activities and performance (including some global trends), such as typical purchasing contracting methods used, or specific industry sector reports (for example oil and gas, and construction).

Other useful data available includes the criteria used for supplier selection, for example:

- price
- quality
- delivery
- reputation
- technical capability
- capacity management.

These may inform the selection and use of negotiating variables. CAPS Annual Supply Management Performance Benchmarking Report may also help to identify performance monitoring variables.

Indeed, performance monitoring of suppliers is a key purchasing activity, and it is in the evaluation of existing contracts that renegotiation plays an important role in achieving cost reductions. For example, research undertaken by CAPS has identified a range of metrics that may be used, relating to finance and compliance, technology, customer satisfaction and supplier diversity. These include:

- Reduction in ownership cost of the product or service.
- Avoidance of higher costs than would have otherwise occurred.
- Improvements in the total value of a purchased product or service.
- Strategic preferred contract supplier relationships.
- Most favourable contract terms and conditions.
- Reduction or elimination of a further cost that would have otherwise occurred.

Many organisations use key performance indicators across a range of industry sectors and which, therefore, enable benchmarking against 'best (KPIs) to monitor performance against specified criteria, which are now developed in class' organisations. For example, the construction industry uses completion rates, budgetary conformance and customer satisfaction to measure the success of its projects.

In order to establish KPIs, however, basic financial measures, such as ratio analysis, may usefully identify:

- The nature of the company, its financial status, its ability to sustain relationships over time, or even its ability to remain in business.

- The types of question the purchaser should be asking in order to avoid future supply problems.
- Comparison with direct competitors which may assist with budget setting.

Types of financial ratio analysis include:

- performance ratios
- financial status ratios
- investor ratios.

In preparing for negotiation, the first two are particularly relevant because they help to answer questions such as financial stability or competitive market position.

Examples of performance and financial ratios are:

- Profit margin (%) = (profit before interest and tax) ÷ sales
- Stock turnover (times) = (cost of goods sold) ÷ (average stock)
- Debtor turnover (times) = credit sales ÷ debtors
- Working capital ratio = current assets ÷ current liabilities.

Learning activity 6.2

Based on your own experience, describe how you would benchmark the financial aspects of the agreements you reach in negotiations.

Feedback on page 80

Using only financial benchmarks to identify the strengths and weaknesses of suppliers is, however, limited. The approach has been expanded to incorporate a variety of indicators which encompass factors including financial, customer, internal business plus innovation and learning perspectives.

Kaplan and Norton (1992) identified this as a 'balanced scorecard' which they describe as: 'a set of measures that gives top managers a fast but comprehensive view of the business. The balanced scorecard includes financial measures that tell the results of actions already taken. And it complements the financial measures with operational measures on customer satisfaction, internal processes, and the organisation's innovation and improvement activities – operation measures that are the drivers of future financial performance.' Using a scorecard approach is valuable in preparing for negotiation because it enables the purchaser to identify the organisation's potential as a longer-term supplier, with the view of matching processes to the organisation's as well as a comparison with other suppliers.

Donaldson and O'Toole (2002) state that there has been limited application of the balanced scorecard approach to supply relationship situations, even though it is a technique widely used in other management fields, such as marketing and project management. They have usefully summarised the types of performance and financial evaluation statements that may be used for supplier relationships (see table 6.1). Such statements can be used in preparing for a negotiation with a potential long-term supplier as well as measuring the outcome.

Table 6.1 Examples of financial and non-financial performance statements

Non-financial performance statements	Financial performance statements
• Lead times for this supplier are shorter than others. • The quality of this supplier's product is higher than others. • Speed of response to problems is quicker than others. • This supplier is involved in the design of our products.	• It would be difficult to switch to an alternative supplier. • Our relationship makes it easy for an abuse of confidence to happen. • Prices we pay in this relationship are lower than in a comparable relationship. • Long-term profitability from this relationship are higher than an alternative.

Source: adapted from Donaldson and O'Toole (2002)

Self-assessment question 6.2

Briefly describe, and comment on, four different financial measures that may be used in preparing for negotiations.

Feedback on page 80

6.3 Economies of Scale

Drummond and Ensor (2003) identify that the single biggest influence on cost leadership of an organisation is its ability to achieve economies of scale. This is because volume drives efficiency and produces purchasing leverage. The potential for achieving economies of scale arises from the view of the supply chain situation. The purchaser needs to determine whether it is better for the organisation to buy in bulk, with the potential to secure quantity discounts but with a trade-off in terms of outlay for managing stock appropriately; or, to utilise a lean supply and strategic relational approach, where the supplier takes a bigger role in managing the supplies so that supply is streamlined and associated wastage is minimised.

Learning activity 6.3

Discuss the advantages and disadvantages of quantity orders on both the supplier and your own organisation.

List the circumstances under which it is appropriate to order: (a) large quantities and (b) small quantities.

Feedback on page 81

Learning and experience, as outlined in section 6.1, can result in efficiency, leading to cost reductions. Experience leads to decreasing costs as a result of increased activity (see figure 6.3).

Figure 6.3: The experience curve

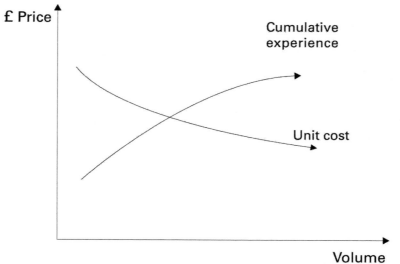

Source: based on Drummond and Ensor (2003)

This is, however, a rather simplistic view since there are other factors to consider, such as quality and service or support levels that a supplier may offer. Indeed, as indicated in figure 6.3, there are diminishing returns from experience (the curves flatten out) because, at some point, an optimal level will be reached beyond which costs will remain static. In practice, this point is likely never to be reached because market dynamics and production processes (for example, through new technologies) may continually evolve,

In a partnership context, a focus on economies of scale and an open-book approach may enable the parties to focus on reducing costs through scale efficiencies in areas such as: information technology, research and development, joint purchasing and overheads management. As Donaldson and O'Toole (2002) identify, negotiation in a relationship may focus more on: bundling of products and services, managing risk, achieving end-customer loyalty, adding value through the relationship and cooperating to compete in the marketplace.

Self-assessment question 6.3

Comment on the methods of analysis that can be used to improve negotiation performance.

Feedback on page 81

Revision question

Now try the revision question for this session on page 266.

Summary

This study session has reviewed how demand is derived from the supply context. Demand was considered to be elastic and inelastic, where the relationship between price and demand is the basic driver of variation.

The impact of market power, resulting from oligopolistic or monopolistic situations, identified that negotiations may achieve higher price reductions where there are more potential suppliers. Four sources of information for calculating elasticity of demand were identified and the purpose of evaluating price elasticities in preparing for negotiation was examined.

Benchmarking was identified as a useful tool in preparing for negotiation because it has the potential to produce basic financial measures, such as ratios that may provide comparisons against industry standards and previous purchasing situations.

Two types of financial ratio analysis were identified as particularly relevant: performance ratios and financial status ratios. These include profit margin (%), stock turnover (times), debtor turnover (times) and working capital ratios.

Cost reduction due to experience effects was also examined and, finally, strategic relationships were identified as producing potential cost reductions through scale efficiencies.

Suggested further reading

Any introductory economics text will review supply and demand concepts, such as price elasticity.

Any introductory financial accounting text will review ratio analyses.

CAPS (http://www.CAPSresearch.org/) is an independent research organisation co-sponsored by the WP Carey School of Business at Arizona State University and the Institute for Supply Management. It has useful research publications by thought leaders in the purchasing and supply context, including development of balanced scorecards for purchasing, and industry-specific purchasing indices.

Steele et al (1989) on costing concessions.

Feedback on learning activities and self-assessment questions

Feedback on learning activity 6.1

A monopoly is where the market is dominated by only one supplier or producer. In such circumstances, costs and price are likely to be high, because:

- There may be high barriers to market entry, protecting the supplier from competitive forces.
- Buyers cannot substitute products or services easily.
- Buyers do not have bargaining power, which would force price down.

- They may be little incentive for the supplier to reduce price.

An oligopoly is where there are a few larger suppliers or producers in the market. Price and costs are likely to be lower because:

- There is free market entry, meaning higher levels of competition, and reduced prices.
- Products may be similar and there may be many more substitutes available to buyers, meaning price will be lower.
- Buyers may be able to play suppliers off against one another.
- Suppliers typically spend a great deal of time observing and reacting to each other's actions.

Feedback on self-assessment question 6.1

Discussion should consider:

- Whether demand for the product is elastic or inelastic.
- Market forces: who has power, and why.
- The nature of any differentiating factors in the product being offered.
- The cost of switching to alternative suppliers: how embedded is the supplier's product in the organisation's processes?
- The type of relationship between the buyer and seller: whether the product is a small or large part of the relationship, and the consequences of failing to agree price.

Feedback on learning activity 6.2

Your answer could consider:

- Comparison with previous similar negotiations.
- Comparison to budget.
- Range of financial options, compared to any industry standards.
- Relationship performance indicators: whether you are achieving your objectives for relational development.

Feedback on self-assessment question 6.2

- Profit margin (%) = (profit before interest and tax) ÷ sales
- Stock turnover (times) = (cost of goods sold) ÷ (average stock)
- Debtor turnover (times) = credit sales ÷ debtors
- Working capital ratio = current assets ÷ current liabilities.

The first three ratios may be used to evaluate supplier performance; the last one to evaluate their financial status.

Using ratios to benchmark performance helps to:

- Identify weaknesses in the supplier's proposition, by comparing it to existing suppliers or 'best in class' suppliers. For example, evaluation may identify profitability, turnover, cash flow and assets which indicate whether the supplier is in a stable trading position and, therefore, an appropriate business partner.

- Establish parameters for the purchaser's negotiation variables: ranges, targets, resistance points. For example, one supplier may be financially weaker than another enabling a tougher negotiation on price, or a lower 'walk away' to reflect higher risk.
- Provides the basis for information exchange about performance and, in so doing, sets the scene for the bargaining phase.
- Communicates to the other party a level of expertise about the underlying cost structures associated with reaching agreement – and the implications of implementation for both parties.

Feedback on learning activity 6.3

Advantages and disadvantages:

- Advantages for the purchaser: stock control managed in-house; critical supply issues minimised.
- Disadvantages for the purchaser: cashflow; potential waste; costs associated with stock control/inventory management.
- Advantages for supplier: supply management, especially where capacity exists; turnover.
- Disadvantages for supplier: poor relationship management with purchaser; potential impact on other customers' supplies.

Appropriate circumstances:

- Large quantities: where stock control is slick and well-managed; where relationship with supplier is poor; where supplies are critical to the business; where the market predicts unfavourable changes to ongoing supply.
- Small quantities: where there is an ongoing relationship with the supplier (contractual terms supporting supply).

Feedback on self-assessment question 6.3

Methods of analysis:

- Accounting methods: performance against budget, or financial outcome (profitability, contribution).
- Ratios or benchmarking: comparison with previous or similar situations.
- Achievement of objectives: comparison against targets.

Comments may include:

- The relationship context and, therefore, the selection of appropriate analytic tools.
- The impact on demand from increasing prices as a result of negotiations.
- The risk associated with non-supply.
- The required level of profitability/contribution to the organisation.
- The costs associated with managing stock in-house.
- The switching costs associated with securing supply from an alternative.

6

6

Study session 7

The negotiation process

Introduction

The case of the two sisters clearly identifies that both have achieved a sub-optimal solution in their negotiation over the orange. What a waste for them – they clearly did not do their homework! Had their preparation identified that they were undertaking tasks that required different parts of the orange, they both would have achieved more from the situation. They did not understand each other's goals or interests in the negotiation.

This study session discusses the importance of developing a negotiating strategy which reflects the parties' goals. An important task is to determine the point at which it is not possible to reach agreement with the other party. This means that targets and negotiation ranges, including the worst case scenario with that party, or an alternative option with another party, should be thought through before the negotiation. These options are reviewed in section 7.2 on identifying alternatives to negotiation and section 7.3 on setting targets and ranges. Finally, section 7.4 reviews how a bargaining position is established and considers the role of negotiator interests and sources of power that influence negotiations.

'Consider a quarrel between two sisters over an orange: a compromise was reached whereby they split the orange in half. Immediately, one sister squeezed the orange portion for juice, and the other used the peel for her cake...'
Fisher and Ury (1981)

7

Session learning objectives

After completing this session you should be able to:

7.1 Develop a negotiation strategy.
7.2 Identify alternatives to negotiation.
7.3 Set targets and compose ranges for negotiation variables.
7.4 Establish the bargaining position.

Unit content coverage

This study session covers the following topics from the official CIPS unit content document:

Statement of practice

Apply a range of negotiation theories in order to achieve set outcomes.

Learning objectives

3.1 Determine the objectives and strategies for negotiation meetings.
  • Integrative versus distributive negotiation
  • Negotiation strategies

83

- Developing ranges and targets
- Best alternative to a negotiated agreement (BATNA)
3.3 Establish the bargaining position of the supplier.
- Parameters for negotiation terms and conditions (purchaser and supplier)
- Who is attending the meeting, why and the level of authority they hold
- Positions and interests
- Power base
- Strength of the purchaser versus the supplier
- Size of the organisation

Timing

You should set aside about 5 hours to read and complete this session, including learning activities, self-assessment questions, the suggested further reading (if any) and the revision question.

7.1 Developing a negotiation strategy

The strategy for the negotiation overarches the phases of negotiation identified in study session 1. Therefore, the first step is to determine the goals for the negotiation: what is to be achieved by entering into a negotiation? This will include an evaluation of priorities. Goals may include tangible and intangible aspects, such as price, contract terms, delivery details and agreement on principles. Lewicki et al (2003b) identify how goals impact on negotiations:

- Goals of both parties are linked together, otherwise there would be no basis for a negotiation!
- There are boundaries for achieving goals, based on the limits set by the parties.
- Goals must be measurable for there to be clarity between the parties on any agreement reached.

Once goals have been determined, the next step is to devise the negotiation strategy, either integrative (collaborative) or distributive (competitive), as described in study session 1. The decision about the overall strategy is usually based on the relative importance of two key factors: the substantive outcome; and the ongoing relationship. Where the relationship and the outcome are both important, then the strategy adopted is collaborative. Where the relationship is less important, then the strategy is more competitive. A third strategy is possible: where the outcome is less important than the relationship, then an accommodative approach may be used (see table 7.1).

Learning activity 7.1

How do internal negotiations impact on the choice of strategy?

Feedback on page 93

Table 7.1 identifies the characteristics of the competitive, collaborative and accommodative strategies for negotiation.

Table 7.1 Characteristics of negotiating strategies

Dimension	Competitive	Collaborative	Accommodative
Goal	Pursued at the expense of others	Joint pursuit	Focus on other party's goals
Motivation	Own outcome	Joint outcome	Other's outcome
Relationship	Short-term	Long-term	May be either
Trust	Low in others	Joint high	One party open and vulnerable
Attitude	I win, you lose	We both win	I lose, you win

Source: derived from Johnston, in Lewicki et al (2003b)

It is important to note, however, that negotiators rarely pursue one strategy in its purest form. Most negotiations reflect the mixed goals and intentions of the parties, and are also constrained by various situational limitations (see figure 7.1).

Figure 7.1: Summary of influences on negotiation strategy

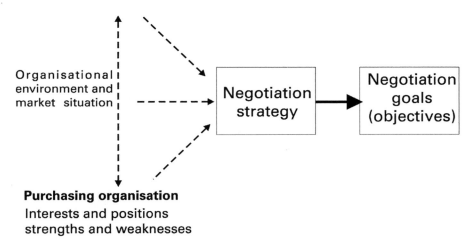

Supplying organisation
Interests and positions
strengths and weaknesses

Organisational
environment and
market situation

Negotiation
strategy

Negotiation
goals
(objectives)

Purchasing organisation
Interests and positions
strengths and weaknesses

Self-assessment question 7.1

Compare and contrast the collaborative, accommodative and competitive negotiation strategies.

Feedback on page 93

7.2 Alternatives to negotiation

Lewicki et al (2003b: 43) state: 'the dominant force for success in negotiation is in the planning that takes place prior to the dialogue.'

Knowing when not to engage at all in negotiation and also when not to continue to engage in negotiation are key considerations in the preparation process. Conditions for not entering a negotiation were outlined in study session 1, including:

- When you could lose everything you have; in that case, choose another option rather than negotiate.
- When you are at maximum (production) capacity.
- When the demands being made on you are unethical.
- When you are not interested in achieving an outcome (because you have nothing to gain).
- When you do not have the time to negotiate as you would want to.
- When you cannot trust the other party in the negotiation (and therefore could not subsequently trust them to implement the agreed solution).
- When waiting will improve your overall position.
- When you are under-prepared to negotiate.

These issues are about knowing the limits of your own and the organisation's capability and willingness to reach an agreement with a specified other party. These issues are discussed further in section 7.3.

An alternative approach to a negotiation will consider how the organisation's objectives could be realised with another (third or fourth) supplier. Clearly, where there are a number of alternative opportunities, then goals for reaching agreement will be higher than if there is only one potential supplier.

Options which limit negotiation may also be considered, for example, mediation or tendering. Mediation uses the services of a third party to negotiate on behalf of the organisation. Tendering limits the opportunity for negotiation because of the specific nature of the supplier selection process.

Learning activity 7.2

Thinking about a typical supply situation, what alternatives do you have to reaching agreement with a particular supplier? How do these alternatives impact on your negotiations?

Feedback on page 94

Fisher and Ury (1991) observed that developing an alternative option to negotiating with a specified party is an important source of power in reaching agreement. They commented that agreement should depend on 'the attractiveness to you of the best available alternative' (Fisher and Ury, 1991: 105). This alternative is commonly referred to as a BATNA, the acronym for 'best alternative to a negotiated agreement'. It is otherwise known as a 'walk-away' position although this specifically relates to the resistance point for a negotiable issue – the point at which the party will not negotiate further. Both parties will have identified BATNAs before entering a negotiation.

As well as being a source of power during the negotiation, a BATNA also performs another important function: protection. For the purchaser, setting a bottom line represents the highest terms (say, price) they are prepared to pay; for the supplier, this will be the lower price they are prepared to sell at. So, identifying the bottom line means there is clarity in any agreement. Identifying a BATNA reinforces the bottom-line and, in effect, curtails 'bad' judgment by providing another solution.

Problems can arise from how the alternatives are viewed but, in reality, few alternatives equate to the original choice. Fisher and Ury (1991) identify these problems with BATNAs:

- Limit the ability to respond to new information gleaned during the negotiation.
- Inhibit creativity, especially through joint exploration of issues, because the bottom line is predetermined by one party.
- Are often set unrealistically high and are difficult to change.

7

Self-assessment question 7.2

Read the case study below. What alternatives does the purchaser have?

Bradcorp, a major construction supplier to Viva Builders, have offered them a 'take it or leave it' price with limited room for negotiation. Viva Builders do not know how the supplier arrives at its prices, its cost structure and reasons for increasing prices. The purchaser for Viva has recently been told that an increase of 55 pence per tonne was the result of higher fuel charges for deliveries. Analysis of this, however, identified that this should be just 5 pence per tonne. When presented with this argument, the supplier's sales reps merely stated that it was what they had been told to do, apparently showing very little understanding of their company's own purchasing strategy. (Based on Blaney, 2005.)

Feedback on page 94

7.3 Targets and ranges for negotiations

A target is defined as the aim for a negotiation at its conclusion, sometimes referred to as an 'aspiration'. Ranges are the best and worst case scenario that the negotiator is prepared to agree. The worst case scenario is often referred to as the bottom line, or a 'resistance point'. (The initial asking point, or starting point, is also important in negotiation – more on this shortly.)

The spread between the best and worst scenarios is the zone of potential agreement. Both parties will, of course, identify a zone of agreement and, for a settlement to be reached in the negotiation, there will obviously be an overlap in these zones (see figure 7.2)!

Figure 7.2: Overlap in zones of agreement

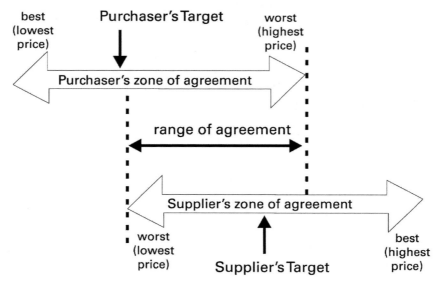

Learning activity 7.3

From the case study below, formulate 'theirs' and 'ours' ranges for the variables you identify.

Xandy is a critical consultancy supplier to Zebra Limited. It appears the day rate being charged by Xandy is too high at £1,320. Xandy have indicated they may be willing to offer a 2% discount if Zebra increase the number of days to ten per month. At the moment, however, Zebra do not feel they need more days than their current six per month.

Feedback on page 94

The different variables to be used in the negotiation will have been identified through the types of analyses described in study sessions 2 to 6. In identifying targets for these variables, however, there are a number of factors to bear in mind:

*   Targets need to be related to stated objectives. Much of the discussion in the previous study sessions has focused on thinking about the other party. It is, however, important that the negotiator does not lose sight of their own position.
*   Target setting requires 'packaging' variables together to create a bargaining mix. Thus preparation needs to evaluate the variables in different mixes.
*   Target setting assumes understanding of 'throwaways' and 'trade-offs' – these are the variables identified as relatively unimportant to the purchaser but which can be used to lever more important variables from the supplier.

From this review, it is evident that the variables for both parties need to be prioritised. Whilst it may be relatively straightforward for the purchaser to undertake this for the organisation, it is true to say it will be more difficult to undertake the task for the supplier. Similarly, identifying a bargaining mix using high and low priority variables should be undertaken for both parties. It is also important to attempt to identify the resistance points of the variables for the other party, that is, the point beyond which they will walk away from the negotiating table.

Self-assessment question 7.3

When both parties prioritise the same negotiation variable highly, there is little opportunity for a collaborative outcome. Discuss this statement.

Feedback on page 95

7

7.4 The bargaining position

Once our objectives have been determined and our targets and the ranges for our negotiations decided it is important to establish our bargaining position. This bargaining position can be enhanced through the use of subtle 'conditioning'. Conditioning, in its broadest sense, is a complex psychological concept which goes far beyond the requirements of everyday negotiations. However, in the context of negotiations it refers to a series of actions or signals that are given, either overtly or covertly, prior to the actual negotiation by one party to another, with the objective of changing or modifying the other party's perceptions and expectations of the forthcoming negotiation. Conditioning helps to establish and manage the expectations of the negotiation and as such it must be remembered that most relationships, and the negotiations that are part of them, are ongoing, so conditioning must be consistent and used sensitively. It is not a face-to-face persuasion technique as the aim is to encourage or develop an appropriate mind-set in the other party, prior to the negotiations, so that our position in the actual negotiation is more readily accepted. The ways in which we can attempt to condition the other might be, for example:

- Sending out invitations to tender (ITT) or requests for quotations (RFQ) – this signals to the marketplace and potential bidders that you are expecting a competitive response to your enquiry.
- Inviting an existing supplier to work with you on a new project without any competitive tendering process signals to the supplier that you are happy with their performance. This may build trust and encourage greater co-operation and support from the supplier, but is also likely to build increased expectations regarding the future of the relationship.
- Using various 'stakeholders' or interest groups to disseminate information to the markets to encourage a particular view or perspective of the business, for example reports regarding customer awards or accreditation, that we have won, may encourage our suppliers to see our business more favourably.

However, it must be recognised that conditioning is a double-edged sword and that our suppliers are also trying to condition us and alter our perceptions and expectations of the forthcoming negotiations, for example:

- They may send out notification that a 10% price increase is imminent, thus conditioning our expectations and our objectives for the negotiations. When we negotiate and reduce this to a mere 5% increase, we feel as though we have won and achieved a saving against our expectations, when an increase of around 5% may well have been their objective all along.
- They may have an ongoing programme of 'hospitality' to build closer working relationships with customers and thus subtly condition the relationship onto a more personal level of trust and friendship. This closer relationship may subconsciously condition our perceptions of the relationship and modify our position and attitude in a negotiation.

It is important to be consistent with the messages and signals that are being sent out as any conflict will undermine the credibility of our message and frustrate our attempts to condition the other party.

Once the issues to be discussed are assembled, the next step is to consider who is going to be involved in the negotiation. Lewicki et al (2003a) identify a range of actors that may influence the negotiation:

- our individual constituents, or negotiators
- their negotiators
- those who influence our negotiators
- those who influence their negotiators
- interested observers of the negotiation.

Thus preparation should examine:

- The range of resources, interest and needs – from a financial analysis, SWOT analysis, and so on.
- Their objectives – information on strategies and targets.
- Their reputation and negotiating style, which can be identified from previous experiences, or from another party who has negotiated with them.
- Their BATNA.
- Their authority: whether the individuals hold their own organisation's mandate to reach agreement.
- The choice of tactics.

From this assimilation of information, it will be possible to determine how best to present a position during the negotiation. Lewicki et al (2003a) suggest considering:

- The range of facts available that support, substantiate or validate the position (or stance) to be taken.
- The availability of data which may be used as back-up or further consultation.
- Whether the issues identified have been negotiated before, or under similar circumstances.

- Patterns of likely response from the other party.
- How to present a convincing argument, and whether to use visual or other aids to support it.

Learning activity 7.4

Reflecting on a recent negotiation, explain how you developed the position you took in the negotiation.

Feedback on page 96

In turn, these actors will be influenced by the context or environment in which the negotiation takes place. As previously identified, these contextual issues may arise from:

Relationship history between the parties and expectations for its future;

- Negotiation success rate of the individuals involved in the current situation.
- Common or accepted practice arising from the legal and ethical context.
- Common or accepted cultural practices.

Furthermore, actors will have their own positions and interests staked in the negotiation, which may not necessarily reflect the organisation's. Lax and Sebenius (1986) identified different types of interest that impact on negotiations in different ways:

- Substantive: economic or financial issues or some other resource.
- Process: personal motivations for entering the negotiation.
- Relational: the reason for sustaining the interaction between the parties.
- Principles: attitudes towards ethics and fairness.

The fact that parties may have more than one type of interest in the negotiation often results in there being differences between them. Interests stem from human values, can change over time, and are difficult to define.

Positions, on the other hand, are best separated from the problem (Lewicki et al, 2003a). By separating the negotiators' underlying positions from the problem, it is possible to build more integrative solutions for the parties by focusing more on their interests. For example, the position of a negotiator may be that they want to achieve a given price, but the underlying motivation, that is, their interest, is that they will receive a bonus for achieving a target at the end of the month for the which the deal is key.

In contrast to interests and positions, an alternative focus may be on the role of power. The balance of power between buyers and sellers has a major influence on negotiation process and outcomes. Power is the direct and indirect pressure brought to bear to achieve a desirable solution (Lewicki et al, 1997). It is intrinsic to all negotiations since there is little point in engaging in negotiation without the ability to commit. In the

7

context of negotiations, power is specific to the parties and their relational dependencies.

Negotiators may influence outcomes by manipulating dependencies to create a relational balance or imbalance between the parties (Lewicki et al, 1997). Typically, an imbalance of power is characteristic of distributive negotiations while a more equal balance is characteristic of integrative negotiations (Phatak and Habib, 1996; Lewicki et al, 1997). Power imbalance creates competitive advantage, enabling the superior party to exert some leverage over the subordinate party, such as that typically seen in retailing (Starkey and Carberry, 1996). The existence of an imbalance does not, however, automatically mean the superior party will exert leverage; indeed, flexibility and fairness in negotiations have an important role to play.

Sources of power are discussed in further detail in study session 9.

7

Self-assessment question 7.4

What influence does the relative size of an organisation have on negotiations?

Feedback on page 96

Revision question

Now try the revision question for this session on page 266.

Summary

This study session has discussed different negotiation strategies that are pursued by the parties and have an overarching impact on the phases of the negotiation. Two key factors were identified of the outcome and the relationship. Characteristics for three different strategies were identified: collaborative, competitive and accommodative.

Alternatives to negotiating were considered. A BATNA was described as a source of influence upon a negotiation outcome, because it gave the parties options other than to agree and is, therefore, protection against bad judgment. A BATNA was identified as the 'best alternative to a negotiated agreement'.

Targets were defined as the aims of a negotiation with ranges being the continuum between the best and worst case scenario that negotiators are prepared to agree. The worst case scenario was described as the bottom line, or 'resistance point'. The spread between the best and worst scenarios was identified as the zone of potential agreement.

The nature of a bargaining position was discussed, including how best to present a position during the negotiation. Interests were identified as emanating from human values and were noted to change over time.

Integrative solutions were highlighted as being more likely if the parties' underlying interests and positions were separated.

Finally, the concept of power was reviewed and noted to derive from a number of sources including: information and expertise, resource control, legitimacy, location in the organisational structure, and the personal and social context.

Suggested further reading

Lewicki et al (2003b) on strategising; positions and interests for both competitive/distributive and collaborative/integrative negotiations; and on power, finding it and using it.

Feedback on learning activities and self-assessment questions

Feedback on learning activity 7.1

In contrast to negotiations with external suppliers, there is often limited scope for the strategic approach to negotiations with internal parties. This is because purchasing individuals invariably have to continue a relationship with members inside the organisation, beyond the current situation. Thus developing and effectively managing the relationship with internal colleagues is more important than the substantive outcome, that is, the terms agreed for a specific negotiation.

You may have also considered the following points:

- Internal negotiations are often about obtaining the mandate to deal with others outside the organisation.
- The focus may be on influencing the internal party to support activities.
- The approach will necessarily be collaborative at best, or otherwise accommodative, depending on how the role of purchasing is seen within the organisation.
- Internal negotiations precede external negotiations with suppliers. Therefore, the strategic approach may depend upon the intentions of others for the future working relationship with the supplier.

Feedback on self-assessment question 7.1

Collaborative strategy:

- It is important to identify goals that are mutually acceptable to both parties.
- Goals may be about developing the relationship through reaching a substantive outcome.
- It will be important to identify solutions together.

Competitive strategy:

- It is necessary to maximise the value of the single deal.
- It is important to influence the supplier's view of the market.

- There is potential to inflate the importance of a deal.
- A fallback is needed if agreement is not reached.

Accommodative strategy:

- An ongoing relationship with the other party is important.
- There is no alternative than to deal with the other party.

Feedback on learning activity 7.2

Your answer should consider the following points:

- The consequences of not reaching agreement with an important supplier.
- Whether there are any realistic alternatives and, if there are, how they impact on the transfer costs to the organisation.
- The specific bases on which alternatives are evaluated, such as costs and benefits to the organisation.
- The way in which negotiation is framed – whether the strategy is competitive, collaborative or accommodative.
- The influence of market forces, including competitive behaviour among potential suppliers, and end-user customer demand for products and services.
- The range of variables used in the negotiation – a limited range if there are a number of acceptable alternatives; a greater range if there are fewer alternatives.
- The limits set on the variables identified – whether high or low.

Feedback on self-assessment question 7.2

There may be few alternatives for Viva if Bradcorp are powerful in the marketplace and there are a small number of other suppliers. The scenario suggests that the negotiation is likely to be competitive, rather than collaborative, being based on few issues – price, delivery terms, volume supply. It is evident that the purchaser's power in leveraging the supplier is limited and consequently the BATNA will be that which achieves short-term goals, such as finding another supplier who is more willing to support the company in achieving its longer term development goals.

Other alternatives could look at increasing negotiating power:

- Collaborate with other purchasers in order to increase spending power.
- Use industry mediators (watchdogs).
- Use tendering, which encourages the supplier to bid against its competitors.
- Use supply chain principles so that value for the supplier and the purchaser in the relationship may be developed.

Feedback on learning activity 7.3

Table 7.2 outlines the possible ranges for variables.

Table 7.2 Possible ranges for variables in Xandy and Zebra negotiation

Possible variables	Zebra (Purchaser) Range	Xandy (Supplier) Range	Comments
Day rate	Best: £800 Target: £1200 Worst: £1320	Best: £1320 Target: £1300 Worst: £1150	• Zone of agreement is between £1150 and £1320.
Discount framework	Best: 10% Target: 5% Worst: zero	Best: 2% Target: 3% Worst: 5%	• Zone of agreement is between 2–5%.
Number of days per month	Best: 8 days Target: 6 days Worst: 5 days (minimum necessary to do job)	Best: 15 days (would generate more income) Target: 10 days Worst: 5 days	• Zone of agreement is 5–8 days. • This may be negotiable if scope of project is reviewed and efficiency savings are achieved.
Project scope (outcome of consultancy project)	Best: quicker outcome Target: as is Worst: reduced outcome	Best: quicker outcome Target: outcome achieved Worst: takes too long	• Zone of agreement is that the outcome is achieved to target date or quicker. • This could be further negotiated if number of days can be altered or efficiency savings achieved which makes the consultants job easier to do.
Efficiency savings	Best: higher saving Target: small saving Worst: as is	Best: higher saving Target: small saving Worst: no saving	• Zone of agreement is that some efficiency saving is achieved.

Feedback on self-assessment question 7.3

This statement is true. There is little opportunity for a collaborative outcome because both parties are diametrically opposed. A highly prioritised price for a purchaser usually means a low price, whereas this will mean a higher price for the supplier. Such a situation may leave limited options for reaching agreement, at least one where both parties achieve a win.

Points for consideration in the discussion include:

- The parties' targets may not overlap.
- Resistance points may be out of each other.
- Zones of agreement may be limited.

- Scope of possible agreement between the parties may be limited to a small number of issues (options/variables).
- Outcome likely to be win-lose (or zero-sum gain) versus win-win outcome.

Feedback on learning activity 7.4

Your position will have been developed from your own personal motivations for entering into the negotiation, albeit influenced by the negotiation task and the relationship your organisation has with the other party. Points to consider include:

- Your needs and interests in reaching agreement with the other party.
- How preparation may have identified a range of possibilities for the negotiation, including the best strategy to use to finalise a deal.
- Your familiarity with and competence in using the tactics that would be most likely to achieve a result.
- The concession patterns that were intended to signal how the negotiation would proceed to the other party.
- The role of any other team members involved in the negotiation, including their needs and interests in achieving an outcome.
- The response of the other party to your approach to the negotiation.

Feedback on self-assessment question 7.4

Imbalance in the relationship between the parties will impact on the negotiating strategy – large organisations do not usually enter long-term relationships with small (SMEs) or medium-sized organisations. Similarly, accountability in the organisational structures will impact on their ability and willingness to engage in relationships. Thus focus will be more collaborative where there is a balance in the relationship, more competitive where there is an imbalance.

Other factors to consider include:

- Use of accommodative strategy.
- Reputation of the parties.
- Social and political influences.
- The influence of the organisation and its members on the position and interests of the individuals involved.
- The organisation's control of resources, especially its information (knowledge management) systems.

Resourcing negotiation stages

'I ask for so little, and boy do I get it.'

Dilbert, management cartoon character, created by Scott Adams (1997) in Lewicki et al (2003a)

Introduction

Dilbert's comment highlights the importance of understanding how to frame and present an argument in a negotiation. This study session discusses the substantive tasks that constitute the different types of negotiation (the distributive and the integrative approach) which determine how issues are presented and discussed. The fundamental differences in the two approaches mean that the process of negotiation is really quite distinctive and, therefore, models are presented and reviewed for each. This is because the costs associated with undertaking the different approaches to negotiation will differ significantly. Similarly, the expectations that the parties have for the benefits they may gain from the negotiation process will differ. For example, in a distributive setting, costs are ideally kept to a minimum and benefits are short term. In an integrative situation, costs are likely to be higher because of investment in the long-term relationship and because the value derived from the benefits will be high.

Progressing to the negotiation meeting, the next consideration are the resources that are allocated to it. These are identified and evaluated in terms of their potential influence on the meeting and its outcome.

Session learning objectives

After completing this session you should be able to:

8.1 Identify and describe typical negotiation tasks.
8.2 Demonstrate an understanding of the key stages of a negotiation.
8.3 Identify resources for the negotiation stages.
8.4 Evaluate the role of resources for managing a negotiation.

Unit content coverage

This study session covers the following topics from the official CIPS unit content document:

Statement of practice

Plan and prepare for negotiations.

Learning objectives

3.2 Identify and explain the key elements of effectively managed, resourced and timed negotiations.
  • Opportunities for conditioning
  • Room layout/surroundings

8

- Psychology surrounding away or at home
- The supplier's position

Timing

You should set aside about 5 hours to read and complete this session, including learning activities, self-assessment questions, the suggested further reading (if any) and the revision question.

8.1   Negotiation tasks

Discussion has so far focused on preparation and planning for negotiation. Activities identified include:

- Defining and assembling the issues and the bargaining mix (market and SWOT analyses; costs and pricing).
- Identifying the positions and interests of both parties.
- Determining limits for the issues identified, including targets (objectives) and opening points.
- Selecting a strategy.
- Planning the issue presentation and defence.

The model presented in section 1.2 outlined the phases of the negotiation, where phases 5 and 6 represent the main negotiation meeting:

- Preparation: identifying the important issues and goals.
- Relationship building: understanding how you will relate to the other party.
- Information gathering: learning what you need to know about (variables, other party's situation and goals).
- Information using: building the case for the negotiation.
- Bidding: the process of negotiating from initial offer towards the agreement.
- Closing the deal: building commitment from the parties.
- Implementing the deal: a post-negotiation phase. Even after the agreement is reached, there may be loose ends to clarify so there will be follow-ups to the original negotiation.

Tactical tasks in negotiations are now discussed in relation to distributive and integrative negotiations.

Tasks for distributive situations include (Lewicki et al, 2003b):

- Obtain information about the other party's resistance point: at what stage will they leave the table? What are their real needs?
- Manage the other party's impressions: the aim is not to reveal your own position while encouraging them to accept your preferred view.
- Modify the other party's perceptions – so that an issue may seem more or less attractive.
- Use the threat of terminating the negotiation (with associated costs of delay) to manipulate other party. Research suggests that most

distributive negotiations are agreed close to the point when one of the parties must leave the table because of a deadline.

Tasks for an integrative situation are fundamentally different to those of a distributive situation (Lewicki et al, 2003b):

- Create a flow of information between the parties, so that solutions can be jointly developed.
- Try to understand the real needs and objectives of the other party; focusing on preferences and interests will achieve this.
- Work on common ground and mutual goals; this helps to minimise the differences between the parties.
- Search for solutions that meet both parties' needs. Remember that the preferred outcome of the negotiation is that both parties achieve a win-win.

Learning activity 8.1

Reflect on a recent negotiation. Did you use breaks in the negotiation meeting by calling a time-out? Why, or why not?

If you did not, could a time-out have improved the outcome? How?

If you did, what is your assessment of how the outcome was improved?

Feedback on page 105

Self-assessment question 8.1

Compare and contrast distributive and integrative negotiation tasks.

Feedback on page 106

8.2   Stages of the negotiation meeting

Comparing typical negotiation meetings for a distributive and an integrative situation reveals different stages. Figure 8.1 illustrates the typical stages of a distributive negotiation; and figure 8.2 the typical stages of an integrative negotiation.

Figure 8.1: Typical stages of a distributive negotiation

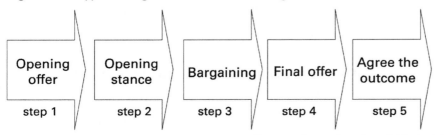

Source: based on Lewicki et al (2003a)

The points to consider at each stage of the distributive negotiation are:

1. Opening offer

Whether too high or too low, the opening offer influences the outcome and research suggests that a high opening offer often results in a higher agreement (Weingart et al, 1990). The message the opening offer sends to the other party may immediately erect a barrier to reaching agreement, or may indicate that you are open to lengthy discussion.

2. Opening stance

The attitude of mind adopted supports the opening offer made. A tough stance generally supports a high opening offer, whereas a friendlier stance supports a more reasonable bargaining position.

3. Bargaining

The pattern of concessions, especially at the beginning of the negotiation, also send messages to the other party about the competitiveness of the situation: small concessions indicate a more competitive position, bigger concessions indicate greater flexibility! Concessions are the central component of the negotiation as they represent the movement between the parties. A competitive negotiation is often considered satisfactory by the parties when they feel they have progressively reached an agreement. Clearly, it is important to have planned how concessions are to be made.

4. Final offer

When there is no more room for concessions, this is as far as the party can go.

5. Agree the outcome

Gain commitment to implement the deal.

Figure 8.2: Typical stages of an integrative negotiation

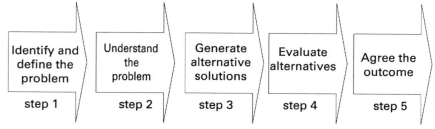

Source: based on Lewicki et al (2003a)

The points to consider at each stage of the integrative negotiation are:

1. Identify and define the problem

This is often the most difficult stage in an integrative situation. The key points for consideration are:

* Define a mutually acceptable problem – one which accurately reflects the situation, rather than inflates it.

- State the problem in practical terms – summarised for greatest clarity.
- Identify obstacles to achieving the goal. A goal may be, for example, 'to cut delivery lead time by five days'; obstacles may be wide-ranging and some may prove impossible to overcome.
- Depersonalise the problem: focus on underlying interests.
- First understand the problem, then work on the solution. If solutions are identified before the problem is fully identified, then there is a risk is of solving the wrong problem!

2. Understand the problem

Focus on interests rather than positions. Dialogue through questioning is the key to this.

3. Generate alternative solutions

It may help to redefine the problem in order to create win-win. It will certainly help if there is a wide range of different variables that can be used as options by the parties.

4. Evaluate alternatives

Select the best alternatives from the range identified at stage 3. Options may be evaluated by:

- Narrowing the range of acceptable options.
- Prioritising options on the basis of quality, acceptability to the parties and any performance standards they meet.
- Agreeing a set of criteria by which to evaluate alternatives.
- Being willing and able to justify preferences for options.
- Being explicit about any influences on selection criteria, such as ethical or legal dilemmas.
- Using colleagues to evaluate options where they are complex.
- Taking time to consider selection.

5. Agree the outcome

Bundle issues together, rather than agree sequentially, and do not agree individual issues until all aspects are considered. Because this can create considerable complexity, it is also worth keeping formality to a minimum until agreement is reached, then recording the final deal.

In both types of situation, managing commitment is a particular challenge. This is discussed further in study session 12.

Learning activity 8.2

When considering the distributive and integrative approaches to negotiation, what are the implications for the types of questions that the parties will ask?

Feedback on page 106

8

Self-assessment question 8.2

Compare and contrast the stages of distributive and integrative negotiations.

Feedback on page 106

8.3 Resources for negotiation

A further consideration for the preparation and planning phase is that of developing and refining the protocol. The process of a negotiation implies the requirement for certain resources to support it. The process is determined by the protocol (Lewicki et al, 2003b) that is to be followed, relating to:

- The agenda for the negotiation: this can be prepared in advance; sometimes, however, especially for complex negotiations, the content of the agenda may well also be part of the negotiation.
- The location of the negotiation: negotiators often perform more effectively when they are 'at home', that is, in an environment they are familiar with. It may, therefore, be appropriate to locate a negotiation on neutral ground, where both parties are on an equal footing.
- The time period: lengthy negotiations will require space and negotiators will require sustenance and comfort breaks. It may also be appropriate to consider the role of time-outs, where the parties have the opportunity to consult with their colleagues.
- The parties' involvement with others: will anyone else be involved in the negotiation, and what role will they play? Will there be anyone on the outside acting as a consultant?
- The consequences of failure: if a deadlock arises, it needs to be determined whether a third party is to be involved, the extent of their involvement and their neutrality.
- Keeping track of the agreement: for complex negotiations, note-taking is an important role, since the notes may form the basis of any written agreement.

Learning activity 8.3

Briefly describe the resources needed for the following example

Aero-engine company, Chunky, wants to achieve long-term supply of high-tech metals for its component manufacturing business from Healtech. It has limited experience of dealing with this company.

Feedback on page 107

Resources were identified in study session 1 as comprising three *M*s: men, money and minutes (where 'men' should be taken to refer to all staff). Thus, in planning resources for a negotiation:

- Team members for the negotiation need to be selected and briefed at preliminary meetings; individual members will need to develop roles for the negotiation meeting.
- Expenses incurred in holding the meeting, and any pre-meeting to discuss agenda items, need to be covered.
- Time will be a factor in preliminaries (team briefings and pre-meetings with the other party) as well as the negotiation itself.

Resources are also about the ability of the parties to satisfy the commitments made as part of the agreement, that is, the substantive content of the negotiation. As Raiffa (2002: 199) reminds us: 'making a deal means matching demand with supply'. In preparing for a negotiation, it is important that the negotiators catalogue the resources they already control and do not need to negotiate over (refer to study session 3 on SWOT analysis).

8

Self-assessment question 8.3

Identify five resource considerations for a negotiation.

Feedback on page 107

8.4 The role of resources

First, attempt learning activity 8.4 below.

Learning activity 8.4

What situational factors influenced the climate of a recent negotiation in your own experience?

Feedback on page 107

The atmosphere, or climate, of a negotiation is often influenced, positively or negatively, by a range of different factors – such as the priorities the parties set on the issues they have identified, and the competitiveness of their pursuit of their goals.

Other factors, some of which have been mentioned previously, include:

- Cultural differences: problems arising from cultural mismatch between the parties, such as when negotiating with an unfamiliar international culture; can also arise when negotiating with an organisation with a more formal structure (this is discussed further in study session 16).

- Timing: the attitudes of the parties to punctuality, both in relation to attending the negotiation and managing deadlines around it.
- The location of the negotiation: whether in familiar surroundings or on neutral ground. If the premises of one or other of the parties are selected, this may negatively influence the other party.
- Room layout: seating patterns, lighting and heat, use of communication aids. Although such factors may seem rather absurd, it is nonetheless difficult to negotiate with an individual who cannot be clearly seen, or who is sitting next to you rather than across a table (in a competitive situation) – although there is limited research to support the psychology behind this.

Lewicki et al (2003a) also identify that the presence of other team members at a negotiation impacts on climate and outcome:

- Integrative agreements are more likely when teams are present. This has been found to be true even if just one side is a team, primarily because there is greater information exchanged between the parties (Thompson et al, 1996).
- Teams can be more competitive. Teams may claim more value in distributing the resource. This is thought to be the case because they are perceived by an individual, or solus, party to be more powerful (Polzer, 1996).
- Pressures to achieve are less in teams than for individuals. Teams seem to split the responsibility between them for reaching agreement, whereas individuals take full responsibility.
- The relationship among team members can affect cohesion. It may seem obvious that teams of friends are more cohesive in negotiations but their focus is more on maintaining the friendship than if the individuals are less familiar with one another.

Individual roles are discussed further in study session 14.

Self-assessment question 8.4

From the discussion in this study session, what resources would you allocate to a distributive negotiation and an integrative negotiation? Justify your answer.

Feedback on page 107

Revision question

Now try the revision question for this session on page 267.

Summary

This study session has identified the specific tasks for the two approaches to negotiation, the distributive and integrative settings. The difference in costs and likely benefits associated with the different approaches to negotiation were highlighted. The processes for the two approaches were presented as being distinct and models were presented of each approach.

The implications for the allocation of resources arising from developing the protocol for each type of negotiation setting were discussed in detail. This included:

- agenda
- location
- time period
- involvement with others
- consequences of failure
- keeping track of the agreement.

Factors that influence the approach taken were reviewed. Finally, team and individual roles were identified.

Suggested further reading

Lewicki et al (2003b) on protocol for negotiation, as part of the planning process; and distributive and integrative negotiation tasks.

Feedback on learning activities and self-assessment questions

Feedback on learning activity 8.1

Time pressure influences negotiations in different ways. Where there is no time pressure, the parties tend to be more integrative; where this is a lot of time pressure, they are more competitive. Nonetheless, time-outs give both parties an opportunity to reflect on progress so far, which can be an important tool for overcoming deadlock, managing conflict and even relationship building. So, depending on the circumstances of the negotiation, and its aims and objectives, time-outs can be used for different reasons.

In integrative situations:

- To give the parties time to reflect on the discussion so far, and to consult with third parties to check specifics and seek additional information.
- To give space to the parties when they are approaching or have approached a deadlock situation.
- To take a breather from the intensity of the negotiation, which may be used for less formal discussion. In turn, this may lead to stronger interpersonal relationships which can be levered for a more collaborative outcome.

In distributive situations:

- To disrupt the flow of the negotiation meeting and, in effect, force the hand of the other party.
- To exert time pressure which may result in the other party making mistakes.

8

Feedback on self-assessment question 8.1

Your answer should consider:

Tasks for the distributive approach:

- Identify and prioritise the variables and likely positions of both your organisation and the other party.
- Produce negotiation ranges.
- Design the most appropriate concession patterns, given the likely stance of the other party.
- Agree within the bargaining range.

Tasks for the integrative approach differ insomuch as the purchaser will need to determine the nature of the relationship, and the intentions of the parties to reach a collaborative outcome. In turn, this will influence: the types of variable and how they are prioritised; concession patterns; and the zone of agreement.

In addition to the points above, you should also consider the available resources, such as time, money, and the skill and preferences of the negotiators.

Feedback on learning activity 8.2

Suffice to say at this stage, there are clear differences in the approach to the other party that will be used by the negotiators. Points to consider include:

- Overall attitude and communication style is important, as it gives messages to the other party about the approach being adopted;
- In an integrative situation, open-ended questions are more about seeking to understand; in a distributive situation they are more about taking up air time.
- The framing of the questions asked is likely to differ between the two approaches. An integrative question may be seeking understanding and clarification, whereas a distributive question may be more probing and intrusive.
- Tough (or hard) questions are more likely to be asked in a distributive situation; whereas in an integrative situation they are likely to be viewed as more manageable.

Question styles are discussed further in study session 12.

Feedback on self-assessment question 8.2

Your answer should consider:

- There is greater emphasis on bargaining in the distributive approach.
- There are greater levels of risk sharing and honesty among the parties in an integrative situation.
- The length of the negotiation will vary – integrative negotiations take longer.

8

- Contributions by the parties may differ. In an integrative situation, both parties are likely to feel they have achieved their aims.
- Bargaining skills, especially when to make an offer and when to concede, are important in a distributive approach.
- Preparation and planning is fundamental to both approaches.

Feedback on learning activity 8.3

The resources should include:

- An agenda should be prepared which includes the key issues that are to be discussed, based on prior research and planning.
- The location could be on neutral ground, to encourage relationship development.
- The time period for negotiation will be high, to give sufficient opportunity to reach agreement.
- The negotiating team will include a range of expertise as well as a note-taker.
- A third party (a mediator or facilitator) may be needed to act as an 'introduction agent'.

Feedback on self-assessment question 8.3

Your answer should include any five from:

- agenda
- location
- time period
- negotiating team, and consultants
- third party (mediator or facilitator)
- note-taker or recorder.

Feedback on learning activity 8.4

Points to consider include:

- cultural differences between the people
- deal size
- expectations of outcome
- balance of power
- timing
- room layout.

Feedback on self-assessment question 8.4

In a distributive situation, a single negotiator may be appropriate. The underlying assumption is that this is a one-off situation, not necessarily focusing on longer-term benefits to the purchaser; therefore, people resources will be kept to a minimum in order to enable maximum return. From an organisational perspective, a solus negotiator may be more effective because of the 'weight' of the responsibility he or she has been given. Time and expenses are also likely to be kept to a minimum.

8

In an integrative situation, the reverse may be true, so a team may be used. Time may be less of an issue and it will certainly be in the interests of the parties to invest in providing a comfortable surrounding for the negotiation.

8

Persuasive techniques

Introduction

Power, influence and leadership are terms that are often used interchangeably in negotiations. In fact, they are ever-present phenomena without which it is impossible to reach agreement!

This study session discusses how power influences negotiations, its sources and how it is used to influence outcomes.

Power can also be used to lift a negotiation out of a deadlock situation (and may well have been exerted to create the deadlock in the first place); therefore, strategies for dealing with so-called entrenchment and intractability in negotiation are discussed. Finally, an overview of game theory is presented.

'[Power is] the capacity to contribute to a pool of resources that is useful to both parties.'

Vitz and Kite, in Pruitt and Carnevale (1993) – a potentially contentious observation, especially when a small buyer tries to deal with a large supplier.

Session learning objectives

After completing this session you should be able to:

9.1 Describe how power influences negotiations, and examine the sources of power in negotiations.
9.2 Describe different techniques for persuading in negotiations.
9.3 Develop strategies for dealing with entrenchment and intractability (turning 'no' into 'yes').
9.4 Describe the basic concepts of game theory.

Unit content coverage

This study session covers the following topics from the official CIPS unit content document:

Statement of practice

Apply a range of negotiation theories in order to achieve set outcomes.

Learning objectives

3.3 Establish the bargaining position of the supplier.
  • Parameters for negotiation terms and conditions (purchaser or supplier)
  • Who is attending the meeting, why and the level of authority they hold
  • Positions and interests
  • Power base
  • Strength of the purchaser versus the supplier
  • Size of the organisation

9

3.4 Evaluate a range of persuasion methods and tactics used in negotiation.
- Threat, emotion, logic, compromise and bargaining
- Tactics
- Creating negotiation leverage
- The psychology of concessions

Timing

You should set aside about 6 hours to read and complete this session, including learning activities, self-assessment questions, the suggested further reading (if any) and the revision question.

9.1 Influence of power

First, attempt learning activity 9.1 below.

9

Learning activity 9.1

Consider a recent negotiation and the impact of using leverage (see below) on outcomes. What leverage did you use and how did it influence the outcome?

Note: **Leverage** in a negotiation is the ability to influence, enforce, exert control or power, or otherwise pressurise the party to behave in a particular manner.

Feedback on page 122

Power is the direct and indirect pressure brought to bear to achieve a desirable solution (Lewicki et al, 1997). Put another way, power is 'the ability to influence or control events' (Donohue and Kolt, 1992). Power occurs when the target accepts the control-claiming move with a concessionary move (Thimm et al, 1995).

Power exists in all negotiations since there may be little point in negotiating without the ability to commit; it is, therefore, specific to the parties and their relational dependencies. Indeed, no party is ever completely powerless and, even where one side has greater power, there exists the possibility of future negotiations, which means there may be little point in exercising any advantage. As Brewster (1989) argues, experienced negotiators always try to 'leave the other fellow with at least his bus-fare home'!

Relational dependencies of parties, in the context of purchasing and supply, arise through the need to transact physical business and, in so doing, create interdependencies (Donohue and Kolt, 1992). Negotiators may influence outcomes by manipulation of the dependencies to create a relational balance or imbalance between the parties (Lewicki et al, 1997). The balance of power between purchasers and suppliers has a major influence on the process and outcomes of negotiation; consider, for example, the relationship between a small purchaser and a large supplier. Indeed, the relative balance of power between the parties is accepted as a predictor of the outcome. Typically an imbalance of power is characteristic of distributive negotiations while a more equal balance is characteristic of integrative negotiations.

Power imbalance creates competitive advantage, enabling the superior party to exert some leverage over the subordinate party. Optimising the power imbalance has received a great deal of attention in recent years, although research suggests that negotiators who place emphasis on power are more likely to achieve only short-term success (Lewicki et al, 1997). The existence of an imbalance does not, however, automatically mean the superior party will exert leverage; superior parties may also wish to act with flexibility or fairness.

The term 'power' is often used interchangeably with leadership, persuasion and influence. For example, Lewicki et al (1997) argue: 'people have power when they have "the ability to bring about outcomes they desire" or "the ability to get things done the way one wants them to be done," suggesting that these individuals are influencing, being persuasive, or being leaders'. This is because sources of power have been identified as being both individual and situational. Harsanyi (1980) argues that power should be defined in terms of: costs, strength, scope, amount and extension of social power. There are, however, very many sources of power used in negotiations. A summary of power sources is shown in table 9.1.

Table 9.1 Sources of power

Source of power	Comments
Information and expert power	• Most common source of power. • Information is accumulated and used to support positions as facts, arguments and viewpoints. • Exchange of information produces a common definition of the situation. • Expert is someone who has gained credibility as a source of specific information. • Relates to the trustworthiness of the provider.
Resource control (reward)	• Power results from the ability to allocate, distribute and create resource scarcity, that is, the ability to reward. • Most important resources are those which have greatest influence on the target, for example: money, supplies, time, equipment, critical services, human resources.
Legitimate power	• Legitimate power is direction from another which must be obeyed. • Usual sources are the social structure, for example: birth, election or entitlement. • Legitimate authority is respect for the holder's position. • Derivatives of power from authority are reputation and performance. • Reputation is image, which is shaped by accomplishments (that is, performance).
Location in the structure	• Power by virtue of the position held within an organisational structure; relates to formal structures.

(continued on next page)

Table 9.1 *(continued)*

Source of power	Comments
	• The more central, critical and relevant an individual is to organisational communication, the more powerful the individual. • The greater discretion, that is, flexibility, the individual has over who receives information, the more powerful. • Power also derives from the support of others as a result of visibility in negotiations.
Personal power	• Converts into influence. • Attractiveness (friendliness and personal charisma) is used to establish a personal relationship, softens the process of negotiation. • Emotion (a component of friendliness), combined with persistence and leading to assertiveness and determination, may be unexpected in a negotiation situation. • Integrity of character, that is, personal values and ethics, assures the other party that any agreement reached will be adhered to. • Persistence and tenacity in creative pursuance of goals.

Source: derived from Lewicki et al (2003b).

Negotiators often try to estimate power balance within negotiations in order to assess the level of control to be exercised over the other party in order to reach a favourable outcome. Donohue and Kolt (1992) suggest two indicators in assessing power:

• the resources available for use by a party
• the willingness of that party to use those resources to influence the situation.

In this sense, power is perceived by the parties. When used, power moves from an amorphous form and becomes an event, although this may result in a loss of power as parties develop 'reference points' and evolve counter moves. Conversely, using power may also have the effect of increasing power by demonstrating a party's willingness to use it.

Power emanates not only from control of physical resources, however, but also from control of the social environment. Negotiation takes place between individuals who manipulate social interaction to reach agreement and draw on their social dependencies to influence and persuade others. Social dependencies, as a source of power, have varying impact on negotiations and are derived, according to Donohue and Kolt (1992), from five key factors (Lewicki et al, 1997):

1   Culture: the values and beliefs an individual holds, translating into customs and norms.
2   Ideology: the individual's beliefs on social order.
3   Institution: the unique social orders, habits and standards of an organisation.
4   Relationship: the relationship specific to a purchaser–supplier dyad, involving control, trust and intimacy.
5   Language: the code of expression of an individual (verbal or non-verbal), used to 'shape' issues.

Power has also been discussed in the context of the bargaining position (refer to study session 7 for further information on this).

Self-assessment question 9.1

Consider the case of a contracted supplier of goods and services who is continually late in delivery. Despite considerable discussion, the supplier is still failing to deliver on time. This supplier is the only supplier in the marketplace; no alternative product can be adapted or used.

Discuss the different types of power that may be used in the negotiation.

Feedback on page 122

9.2 Techniques for persuading

In section 9.1, it was stated that the terms power, influence and persuasion are often used interchangeably in the context of negotiation. Persuasion is really the way in which power is managed by the negotiators. Influence is the resulting effect on the other party when the power move is accepted. Negotiators will try to influence the other party to accept that their view of the situation is best: for example, that the concession offered is not as good as they think it is.

Lewicki et al (2003b) identify that the ability to influence is dependent upon how the communication (message) is sent and received, and whether or not the message is central to the influence. If a message is of central importance, then the receiver of that message will be motivated to process it. Figure 9.1 provides a model of the communication process.

Figure 9.1: The communication process

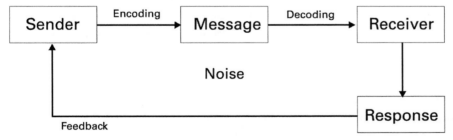

Where the message is central to the influence, the result will be a commitment which is resistant to outside influence and, therefore, long-lasting. Where the message is peripheral, the resulting influence will be merely short-term compliance, open to other influences.

Given the importance of messages in influencing, or leveraging, the other party, it is essential the negotiator selects, organises and presents the ideas appropriately – yet another aspect of the preparation for negotiating. Three issues to consider are:

- the content of the message – what will be conveyed
- the structure of the message – how it will be dealt with
- the style of the message – its presentation.

9

113

Table 9.2 summarises considerations for each of these steps.

Table 9.2 Making messages central to influence

• Content	• Consider how to make the offer attractive to the other party. • Express the message in such a way that they say 'yes'. • Ensure the message is in accordance with the other party's values. • Suggest 'agreement in principle'.
• Structure	• Present the argument from both sides. • Present complex arguments in small components. • Repeat the message. • Conclude the argument.
• Style	• Involve the other party by encouraging participation in the discussion. • Use metaphors to draw attention. • Provoke emotional response. • Say the unexpected!

Source: derived from Lewicki et al (2003b)

Peripheral influence also has a role to play and is more subtle than that outlined in table 9.2. Peripheral influence is exerted by factors such as:

- Credibility of the source of information; for example, the reputation or integrity of the purchaser, or their expertise.
- Personal 'attractiveness', such as the friendliness, likeability or perceived similarity of the purchaser to the supplier negotiators.
- Authority of the purchaser, such as the use of a title (Doctor or Professor) and actual expertise.

It is here that prior conditioning can have a strong influence. As already mentioned in study session 7, conditioning is the process of sending subtle messages prior to the actual negotiation in order to influence the receiver of those messages in such a way that they are more responsive to the more overt messages that are given during the actual negotiation. Conditioning is an activity which makes the communication process flow smoother and the receiver more responsive to our influences. Conditioning helps to set or establish the context in which the receiver will decode our messages. As previously mentioned, the credibility, attractiveness and authority of any source of conditioning information will have an influence on how the message is received and interpreted. Potentially it will make the process of communications during the negotiation easier, provided that the messages and signals are consistent.

The role of the receiver of messages is also important. Consider figure 9.1 where the receiver responds to the message. Aspects of receiving a message include:

- Make eye contact (although there are cultural differences that need to be borne in mind).
- Body position gives signals about attentiveness or respect.
- Facial gestures indicate whether or not messages are being received.

Typical approaches to influencing the other party in negotiation have been identified by a number of authors (see table 9.3). In essence, approaches to influencing can be used to create doubt in the other party about their position or beliefs, or to create movement towards some target outcome.

Table 9.3 Typical approaches to influencing

Approach to influence	Description
Compromise	The search for 'middle ground' by agreeing to 'split the difference', usually on a single variable. Both parties participate.
Bargaining	The use of concessions, based on a bundle of variables to reach agreement. Again, both parties participate.
Coercion	Exertion of power (threat) to force one party to concede.
Emotion	Use of feelings to encourage one party to concede.
Logic	Use of facts to support the argument such that the other party is unable to refuse a concession.

Source: derived from Steele et al (1989)

Learning activity 9.2

Consider the range of approaches to influencing in negotiation (table 9.3). Examine your personal repertoire and explain why you use, or don't use, each.

Feedback on page 122

Self-assessment question 9.2

Identify and briefly describe three techniques for influencing in negotiations.

What approach(es) would you recommend for the scenario outlined in self-assessment question 9.1 above?

Feedback on page 123

9.3 Turning 'no' into 'yes'

Managing conflict is an essential skill and there are a number of important considerations. Conflict is, in essence, a disagreement between the parties on substantive issues, such as incompatibility of goals. Lewicki et al (2003a) identify four levels of conflict:

1 Intrapersonal – within the individual: for example, a disagreement of opinion with a superior may be felt but not expressed.
2 Interpersonal – between people: for example, when the disagreement with another person is expressed.

3 Intragroup – disagreement between members of the same team (for example, the purchasing team).
4 Intergroup – disagreement between the purchasing and supplier teams.

It is commonly held that conflict is competitive, subject to bias and laden with emotion. Parties are often considered to blur the issues, focus on differences and decrease their communication. The outcome is often an escalation of conflict, rather than resolution. Of course, not all conflict is necessarily a bad thing, or indeed, unresolvable over the longer term. Lewicki et al (2003a) highlight some benefits to conflict:

- Discussion leads to greater awareness of problems which may enhance problem solving.
- Conflict challenges current practice, potentially highlighting poor practice.
- Withstanding conflict tests and then builds relationships among colleagues.
- Promotes self-awareness and awareness of others.
- Enhances personal, psychological development, as ways are sought to overcome conflict style and preferences.
- Can be stimulating and fun; adds to the 'spice of life'.

Conflict is more difficult to manage when:

- matters of ethics or principles are involved
- the issues are big, or have considerable consequences
- the outcome is zero-sum – one wins, one loses
- transactions do not lead to a relationship, and have no historical context
- leadership is weak
- there is no competent and neutral third party who can step in to help
- power is unbalanced.

Learning activity 9.3

Thinking about a recent situation where a deadlock occurred, evaluate why it happened and how you overcame it.

Feedback on page 123

Nonetheless, difficult situations arise where a stalemate is reached or breakdown occurs; the parties become frustrated and angry, which may lead to an entrenchment of their positions. These situations can occur because of one or more of the following reasons:

- The way the parties perceive themselves (their personal styles and preferences) are in conflict.
- The substantive issues they are negotiating over are incompatible.
- The process being followed is not acceptable to one or both.
- The context of the negotiation is unfavourable (relating to timing, relationship or cultural aspects).

Conflict resolution is best tackled by first focusing on reducing tension, then managing communication to reflect greater accuracy, and finally focusing on common ground. If the problem remains unresolved, it is at this point that a third party may be used to intervene (Lewicki et al, 2003b).

Conflict resolution, that is, turning 'no' into 'yes', falls under three major categories:

- Challenging perceptions so that the parties adapt their views of issues, that is, *cognitive* resolution.
- Resolving emotional episodes by rebuilding trust and apologising, that is, *emotional* resolution.
- Focusing on the future and implementation, that is, *behavioural* resolution.

Strategies for resolving conflict include:

- Reducing tension: by calling a recess or adjournment and giving the parties time to 'cool off' and then return with renewed focus on resolution; or through active listening, where parties acknowledge the disagreement; or by reciprocal concessions, where making a concession is used as a signal to bring the parties together.
- Improving communication: by putting yourself into the other party's shoes through role reversal or 'imaging', where negotiators think themselves into the other party's position.
- Managing the substantive issues: for example, when conflict escalates, the number of unresolvable issues tends to expand. Techniques for managing the number of issues include: reducing the number of individuals involved in the negotiation, because more people adds greater complexity; bundling the issues together; separating principles away from the issues, or agreeing that there will from time to time be deviations from general principles; avoid precedents which have the potential to restrict agreement; depersonalise issues, by being impartial and acting fairly; and, break big issues down into smaller more manageable ones (the 'salami' tactic).
- Focusing on common ground: such as common 'enemies', expectations, time constraints, and relational benefits.
- Highlighting the attractiveness of options, rather threatening with alternatives.

Clearly, the above are approaches to use in situations where resolution is desired by both parties. There are, of course, situations where one party is deliberately obtuse. These will be discussed further in the next study session.

Self-assessment question 9.3

Describe the influence entrenchment can have on negotiations and why.

Feedback on page 123

9.4   An overview of game theory

Game theory is an approach to analysing situations, such as negotiations, by focusing on the economic efficiency of the outcome through the reduction of events into identifiable stages. The term 'game' is used to describe the interactive process between two or more negotiators (called players) whose interests are interdependent (Zagare, 1984). The seminal work is that of von Neumann (1928) although his later work with economist Morgenstern, entitled *Theory of Games and Economic Behavior* (1944), is seen as the foundation piece of game theory. The theory has, however, been greatly criticised for its limited application to real-world business situations, predominantly because of its highly theoretical nature. This section discusses the basic concepts of game theory, its usefulness and limitations.

Game theory is the abstraction of key features from different situations which have similar patterns of conflict (Zagare, 1984). Of interest in the theory is the outcome, produced when players choose between strategies, broken down by points of decision (referred to as moves) and encompassing both the player's plan and the opponent's beliefs, in the event he does not follow that plan (Rubenstein in Munier and Rulliere, 1993).

Players select strategies to play the game while mathematical functions are used to calculate the consequences of combinations of choices for all players. Players are themselves assumed to evaluate the strategic choices, assigning values (utilities) to each outcome according to their preference. Values may represent, however, purely a rank order of outcomes. Colman (1995) summarises the essential features as follows:

- Two or more decision-makers (players).
- Each player has two or more choices of action (strategies) and the outcome depends on the strategic choice of all players.
- There are distinct numerical payoffs for the strategic outcomes such that all outcomes for all players can be determined.

The skill of players is in choosing the optimum reaction. As Brandenburger and Nalebuff (1995) state: 'you have to look forward far into the game and then reason backward to figure out which of today's actions will lead you to where you want to end up.'

Two generic types of game are played: non-cooperative and cooperative (Brams, 1990). Non-cooperative games, where the outcome depends on the strategic choices of the players, assume that agreement is reached by the players themselves and not enforced by an outside party. These games are also said to be zero-sum in the sense that one player's gain is exactly equal to the other player's loss, that is, the players' positions are diametrically opposed (Zagare, 1984). In such situations, it has been found that the game always results in a minimal, or minimax, solution because players perceive their opponent as malevolent.

An example of the uncooperative type of game is the classic Prisoner's Dilemma in which players have no history of previous games and no second chance to play the game again. It is, therefore, called a 'one shot' game. Briefly, the game comprises two suspects of a major robbery who, on independent questioning, are given a choice to confess. The proposition is such that if suspect A confesses and B does not, A goes free and B is sent down for twenty years in prison; if both confess they each get ten years; if neither confess they each get five years (see table 9.4).

Table 9.4 Prisoner's dilemma payoff matrix

	Prisoner B Stays Silent	**Prisoner B Betrays**
Prisoner A Stays Silent	Each serves 6 months	Prisoner A: 20 years Prisoner B: goes free
Prisoner A Betrays	Prisoner A: goes free Prisoner B: 20 years	Each serves 5 years

The dilemma arises from the lack of trust each suspect has in the other one choosing the strategy which results in a minimum sentence for both, rather than optimising their own position. Thus the game has one steady state, called a Nash equilibrium (confess, confess).

Several possible solutions have been suggested to this type of situation, including Tit-for-Tat (Axelrod and Hamilton, 1981). Here it is suggested, when a series of such games are played, a strategy of retaliation should be adopted after an initial cooperative move: when one player 'defects' the other follows suit immediately. In this way, players learn from each other and gain benefits of cooperation without exploitation. Such a strategy works best, however, under a long-term view of the relationship between players (Nuata and Hoekstra, 1995).

Learning activity 9.4

What assumptions are being made in the Prisoner's Dilemma example?

Feedback on page 124

In contrast, cooperative games presume an agreement is made and, therefore, concentrate on the division of the proceeds resulting from the agreement. Other terms for cooperative games include non-zero-sum, non-strictly competitive games (Zagare, 1984) or pure coordination games (see Neslin and Greenhalgh, 1983). These games have payoffs that are perfectly positively correlated; they may have more than two players and are characterised by high levels of communication. There may also be coalitions between groups of players, adding to the complexity of the game. Zagare (1984) suggests four key differences to zero-sum games:

- Communication: there is none in zero-sum games.
- Information: informing the other party of a player's intention may result in exploitation in zero-sum games.
- Equilibrium: outcomes need not be equal or interchangeable in non-zero-sum games.
- Cooperation: risk is minimised by not defecting in non-zero-sum games.

9

Herbig (1991) suggests nine underlying assumptions of game theory:

1   Complete information: both the rules of the game and the preferred choices of the other players are known.
2   Perfect information: all players have full information of all prior choices when it becomes their turn to move.
3   Rational decision-making: players will choose to maximise their utility.
4   Intelligence: players are able to put themselves in the shoes of their competitors.
5   Competitive behaviour, not cooperative: players tend to act individually.
6   Dynamism: games are dynamic, with changes in each player's position expected over time due, for example, to environmental evolution.
7   Interdependence: decisions by players are interconnected.
8   Time limit: a game's outcome is influenced by its duration.
9   Interaction: the equilibrium among active players.

The usefulness of these assumptions when applied to a business context has been the cause of considerable discussion. The following is a summary, based on Herbig (1991):

• Rationality: individuals do not always act in a rational manner. They may be governed by personal emotive preferences, such as fairness; deliberately try to mislead their opponent; or have different objectives, such as long-term versus short-term perspectives. The irrational behaviour of one party may, however, be completely rational to another particularly if an action is based on different incomplete information.
• Complete information: several studies have alluded to the relevance of complete information in negotiation situations – the more information available to parties, the more successful a particular outcome and the longer a relationship will be. Predictions of the future are, however, probabilistic at best. It is unrealistic to assume any party has complete information in business and, indeed, highly likely one competitor will hold more information than another, particularly about their own position.
• Mixed strategies: in a business context, there is a wide range of choices available to managers, based on a dynamic market context, thus decisions are often not clear-cut (mixed). This is undesirable because of difficulties in determining payoffs, and so on.
• Competitiveness: this is emphasised in zero-sum games, particularly 'one-shot' games, where there is no knowledge of previous interactions and the outcome is always minimum for the parties (minimax), as in the Prisoner's Dilemma. Raiffa (1985) argues that although players may consider themselves strictly opposed, it is rarely true. Rather, disputants are jointly cooperative problem solvers. An example of this is seen in the strategic alliances now common in business, although this may be the result of market economies, rather than a desire for non-competition.
• Reputation: game theory does not formally consider an organisation's reputation or credibility.

General criticism typically alleges that game models are oversimplified and result in unrealistic or unsound choices. Simplicity can often enhance understanding of complex issues and, as suggested by Bennett (1995), there is no guarantee a more realistic model improves performance. Other discussions focus on the fact that game theory has no national or regional identity, being based in mathematics. It thus ignores the cultural overtones (language, religion, values and attitudes, manners and customs, education, social norms) which impact on individual behaviour. Nonetheless, Raiffa (2002) maintains it is useful because it focuses the mind on the other party when preparing for negotiations and can, therefore, provide useful insights into negotiating behaviours.

Self-assessment question 9.4

How does game theory assist in understanding negotiations?

Feedback on page 124

Revision question

Now try the revision question for this session on page 267.

Summary

This study session has reviewed power, persuasion and influence, and how to deal with entrenchment and intractability. It also introduced the concept of game theory.

Power was identified as being the direct and indirect pressure brought to bear to achieve a desirable solution. It exists because parties need to transact business with one another, which creates dependency, although this is rarely balanced between the two. Five sources of power were identified. The term 'power' is often used interchangeably with leadership, persuasion and influence. When evaluating how powerful the other party is, two indicators identified were the resources available for use by a party, and the willingness of that party to use those resources to influence the situation.

The negotiator's ability to persuade the other party was highlighted in the context of communicating messages. Peripheral influence was identified and the role of the receiver was discussed. Techniques for persuading the other party highlighted five different approaches.

Conflict was presented as the disagreement between the parties on substantive issues, such as incompatibility of goals. Four levels of conflict were reviewed. Benefits were also discussed, as were the aspects that make conflict more difficult to manage. Approaches to conflict resolution were reviewed.

Finally, game theory was defined as the abstraction of key features from different situations which have similar patterns of conflict. Two types of game were identified: non-cooperative (zero-sum) and co-operative. Key assumptions were identified and the benefits for negotiation preparation were reviewed.

9

Suggested further reading

Lewicki et al (2003b) on managing conflict (chapter 1); dealing with difficult situations (chapter 9); power: finding it and using it (chapter 6).

Raiffa H (2002). Written by a well respected author, this is a worthwhile read for those interested in game theory and its more modern application to understanding negotiation situations. Start with the introduction to game theory (chapter 4).

Steele et al (1989) on the five approaches to influencing in negotiations.

Feedback on learning activities and self-assessment questions

Feedback on learning activity 9.1

Answers will vary depending on whether you identified a one-off or relational negotiation.

Where a one-off negotiation was identified, it is likely you will have made as much as possible of the different sources of power you had in order to generate a favourable outcome.

In a relational situation, however, power may have been conferred to the other party (by giving away some key information). You may not have used any of your power sources in order to force them into a submissive position because, to do so may have resulted in a short-term gain, but ultimately a longer-term loss for you.

Feedback on self-assessment question 9.1

In such circumstances, it is evident that the supplier has not been performing according to contractual terms and conditions. There would, however, be little point in using a threatening stance to exert pressure on the supplier because both parties need each other. Instead a more accommodative approach is most likely to result in an acceptable solution, albeit it may take some time! Thus, as well as a review of the different sources of power (refer to table 9.1), your answer could have identified:

- Control of physical resources: time, money, staff, products and services; may also relate to reputation, market position, information and knowledge.
- Control of social environment: relating to the skill and competence of the negotiators, influenced by their language, culture, ideology, the relationship and the norms within their organisation.

Feedback on learning activity 9.2

As with previous exercises, your examination of this topic should have taken into consideration the nature of the negotiations you engage in – integrative or distributive.

You may also have discussed aspects relating to the previous section on power. For example, culture, ideology, the organisational context and even language may impact on your preferences. Other considerations may include:

- previous experience
- time available for negotiation
- the extent of your preparation for negotiation
- understanding of the underlying interests, rather than positions
- the substantive content of the negotiation.

Feedback on self-assessment question 9.2

Any three from:

- logic
- compromise
- coercion
- bargaining
- emotion.

See table 9.3 for a brief commentary on each.

The case outlined a scenario where the sole supplier was in a powerful position over the purchaser. The most appropriate forms of persuasion to use would be emotion and logic in order to encourage development of the relationship, rather than coercion to force the supplier into performing. Clearly, it is important to establish why the supplier is not delivering as agreed, and then to find a mutually satisfactory solution whilst remaining firm and assertive. An outcome may include agreement on:

- regular review meetings for feedback
- key performance indicators and benchmarks
- design and implementation of monitoring procedures.

Feedback on learning activity 9.3

Your answer may have considered the following points:

- the nature of competitiveness between the parties
- any specific bias in the individuals involved
- the effect of emotion on how issues were discussed
- the common ground between the parties
- the type of communication and its continuing role within the negotiation.

Feedback on self-assessment question 9.3

Entrenchment can create the following problems:

- Positions become fixed.
- Number of issues to be resolved increases.
- Number of people involved increases, impacting on the complexity of the situation.

9

- Individual sensitivities are heightened, thus increasing tension.
- Negative views of others are reinforced.
- Focus moves to distributive approaches.

These reasons for these problems include:

- Perceptions of personal styles and preferences.
- Nature of the substantive issues being discussed.
- The negotiation process.
- Inappropriate timing for the negotiation.
- Stage, or type, of relationship between the negotiators.
- Lack of cultural awareness of approaches to negotiation, relating to personal and organisational culture.

Feedback on learning activity 9.4

Your answers could consider the following points:

- The parties have not colluded.
- The parties will act in a rational manner, based on evaluation of the possible outcomes.
- The parties act in their own interests only (no honour among thieves, as it were!).
- The prisoners are certainly guilty of some crime but there is insufficient evidence for a conviction, and they both know this.
- The parties assume the worst behaviour of each other.
- The two players act through an intermediary (the questioner) who does not influence their decisions using differential information.
- There is only one opportunity to select a strategy.

Feedback on self-assessment question 9.4

You answer could include the following points:

- The abstraction of complex situations into a few possible outcomes makes it easier to understand the payoffs for each party.
- It enhances preparation by focusing attention on the other party's payoff matrix.
- It provides insights into the other party's behaviour and response patterns.
- It identifies the nature of interaction between the parties – zero-sum or non-zero-sum (win-lose versus win-win scenarios).

Study session 10
Tactics for negotiation

Introduction

Study sessions thus far have identified the nature and underlying assumptions of the two main approaches to negotiation: the distributive and integrative (competitive and collaborative) approaches. This study session identifies the range of tactical tasks that are undertaken using these approaches, including the types of position usually taken by negotiators, and methods for gaining commitment when closing a deal. Finally, the role of ethics and principles is discussed.

'Business executives often hope to "smash the competition". But this can cause them to miss the opportunities that arise from cooperation.'
Bill Trent, principal, McKinsey and Co (Nalebuff and Brandenburger, 1996)

Session learning objectives

After completing this session you should be able to:

10.1 Compare and contrast the tactical tasks undertaken in collaborative and distributive negotiation situations.
10.2 Identify typical positions taken during collaborative and distributive negotiations.
10.3 Assess methods for gaining commitment and closing a deal.
10.4 Evaluate ethical and unethical behaviour in negotiations.

Unit content coverage

This study session covers the following topics from the official CIPS unit content document:

Statement of practice

Differentiate between a range of persuasion tools and techniques.

Learning objectives

3.4 Evaluate a range of persuasion methods and tactics used in negotiation.
  • Threat, emotion, logic, compromise and bargaining
  • Tactics
  • Creating negotiation leverage
  • The psychology of concessions

Timing

You should set aside about 5 hours to read and complete this session, including learning activities, self-assessment questions, the suggested further reading (if any) and the revision question.

10.1 Negotiation tactics

Study session 1 highlighted the two distinctive approaches to negotiation ('Rambo' versus 'Mr Smith Goes to Washington'). Table 10.1 summarises the characteristics of each.

Table 10.1 Characteristics of the collaborative and distributive approaches to negotiation

	Collaborative	Distributive
Appropriate for	• Long-term contracts and repeat suppliers.	• One-offs and adversarial suppliers.
Basic assumptions	• Negotiation world controlled by 'enlightened self-interest'. • Resource distribution system is integrative in nature. • Goal is a mutually agreeable solution.	• Negotiating world controlled by 'egocentric self-interest'. • Resource distribution system is distributive in nature. • Goal is win as much as possible.
Leads to	• Joint problem solving.	• Conflicts and disagreement.
Recognised patterns of negotiators	• Maximises returns for organisation. • Focuses on common interests. • Understands merits objectively. • Uses non-confrontational debating techniques. • Open to persuasion on substance. • Oriented to qualitative goals.	• Maximises tangible resource gains. • Makes high opening demands. • Uses threats, confrontation and argumentation. • Manipulates people. • Not open to persuasion. • Oriented to quantitative and competitive goals.
Results in	• Both parties reaching an agreement which achieves their objectives.	• One side 'beating' the other.
Key behavioural elements	• Maximises return within larger time frame. • Considers needs/interests/ attitudes of other side. • Competitive but not antagonistic. • Shares joint gains. • Concentrates on substance. • Considers negotiation as voluntary and superior to non-voluntary processes (for example, adjudication).	• Maximises return from transaction. • Does not consider needs/ interests/ attitudes of other side. • Views disputing processes equally. • Behaves cooperatively only if it helps achieve returns. • Chooses processes similar to military manoeuvres. • Presents strong defence against opposing tactics. • Controls the negotiation for subsequent manipulation.

Source: derived from Murray (1986)

Tactics associated with distributive approach

Tactical tasks associated with distributive situations, identified by Lewicki et al (2003b), include:

• Assessing the other side's outcome values and their limits for the negotiation, that is, resistance points. This can be achieved by asking direct or indirect questions in order to generate the information needed. Indirect questioning aims to identify how a particular resistance point may have been reached; for example, asking how business is going may elicit the need for certain margins and profitability levels. Direct questioning is, as the name suggests, asking outright what profit the supplier needs to make.

- Managing the other party's impressions so that their view of your position is controlled. Techniques can include masking the information you give out either by giving too much or too little for the other party to be able to evaluate your position, or by being selective in presenting the information, such that the other party is influenced in the way you want. Care must be taken here lest the other party considers that you have deliberately deceived or fabricated information, which may be seen as unethical.
- Changing their perceptions; for example, by making them think that their offer is not so attractive in order to extract a better deal. This equates to concealment, which again, may have ethical connotations, and therefore carries a warning. This approach may involve the cautious release of information which may be seen as good negotiation practice, especially where the negotiators have less experience of dealing with one another.
- Exaggerating the consequences of failing to reach an agreement. This constitutes manipulation; for example, emphasising the cost of failing to reach an outcome by a specified deadline.

As implied by the above commentary, there may be dangers associated with using some of these tactics to the extreme. Indeed, so-called hardball tactics are typical of many texts on negotiation – when used moderately they are gambits which work best when the other party is less well prepared for the meeting. Such tactics are often used to exert pressure on the other party to concede, or act in a manner they would not necessarily wish to do. Lewicki et al (2003b) comment that these tactics 'often do more harm than good in negotiations' and motivate people to retaliate against those that use them.

Nonetheless, commercial reality is that whilst win-win may be sought, the purchaser's role is to achieve the best deal in the circumstances. So, it is important to understand what these tactics are, and how they are used, albeit with great care. Some well-known examples are:

- Good cop/bad cop: where two negotiators will play off against one another to unsettle the other party into an early agreement.
- Lowball/highball: where an opening offer is positioned so low/high that it causes the other party to re-evaluate their position.
- Bogey: where an issue is identified that has little value to one side but is important to the other side; it can then be used in trading during the negotiation.
- The nibble: where a small issue is added in order to close the deal, much like adding a final clause when the deal has almost been struck.
- Chicken: where one party threatens action and the other calls their bluff.
- Intimidation: using anger or guilt to exert pressure.
- Aggression: the hard-nosed bargainer who appears unmovable from their position.

10

- Snow job: where one party overloads the other with information, much of it not useful in reaching an agreement.

There are many more gambits, which include the following (you may want to research these tactics on the internet):

- hard guy/soft guy
- thank and bank
- gimme a kiss (not always ethical)
- outrageous initial demand/'Russian front'
- salami (one thin slice at a time)
- add on
- broken record
- one more thing.

Three strategies for dealing with such hardball tactics are: ignore them, discuss them or reciprocate. How would you deal with them?

Learning activity 10.1

Briefly discuss how you would counter these distributive tactics:

- good cop/bad cop
- lowball/highball
- bogey
- the nibble
- chicken
- intimidation
- aggression
- snow job.

Feedback on page 136

Tactics associated with collaborative approach

Collaborative negotiations have a different approach (see table 10.1). Negotiators aim to (Lewicki et al, 2003b):

- Focus on common ground: this enables the parties to build their relationship and develop understanding.
- Deal with needs and interests, not positions: this leads to greater understanding between the parties. It is helpful when parties reveal their priorities, although not necessarily their positions on those priorities.
- Exchange information and ideas: this creates the conditions for trading. Willingness to share information sends the message that the party trusts the other with that information.
- Create issues for mutual gain: this enhances the possibility of finding a solution.
- Be objective in evaluating performance.

Authors (including Lewicki et al, 2003b) have proposed five key methods by which collaborative solutions can be reached:

1   Expanding the pie: where resources are scarce, the parties look to increase the available resources.

2   Nonspecific compensation: in return for compromise, one party is repaid by the other in some unrelated means;

3   Logrolling: where several issues with different levels of priority are at stake, each party concedes on low priority issues in exchange for concessions on issues of higher priority.

4   Cost cutting: in return for concessions, one party's costs are reduced or eliminated entirely.

5   Bridging: a new option is devised in return for neither party achieving its initial demands.

The key to a collaborative approach is, however, the ability of the two parties to work together to solve problems, rather than competing with each other. This requires faith in one's own ability to problem solve, belief in each other's positions and perspectives, the motivation to work together, trust in each other that neither will abuse the situation, and the ability to communicate effectively.

Exchanging information is the underpinning technique. Czinkota (2000) describes information as 'a crucial strategic resource'. This is because it is easily measured and so can be used to enhance our understanding of relational phenomena. Indeed, the body of literature on game theory (which focuses on developing an understanding of negotiations in a variety of contexts) highlights the importance of information available to decision-making parties, while acknowledging that complete information is a rarity (see study session 9). Baiman et al (2002) state that considerably more information is exchanged between parties in a networked relationship than between parties in an arm's-length relationship, although they also make the important point that information exchanged even in an ongoing and close relationship could be exploited or 'misappropriated'.

Information, which leads to knowledge acquisition, can be categorised into tacit and explicit (or 'operational') forms. It has been suggested (Davenport, 1994) that up to two thirds of information and operational knowledge derives from informal face-to-face interactions (the remaining from documentation), and that tacit knowledge, which is based on personal experience and observation, is seen to be essential for an organisation's success (Dougherty, 1999). Hendon et al (1999) have suggested that a typical US senior manager spends anything up to 50% of a day engaging in information exchange and negotiations.

10

Self-assessment question 10.1

How does a collaborative negotiation differ from a distributive one? Identify a minimum of three factors.

Feedback on page 137

10.2 Positions and interests

Whereas the distributive situation focuses on the positions being taken, the integrative situation works best by identifying and defining the problem to be solved. Fisher and Ury (1991) suggest that interests define the problem whereas positions focus on personal views and, therefore, lead to conflict. By identifying interests, the parties are able to 'look behind' their positions in order to determine where common ground may lie. Fisher and Ury propose a number of stages to consider:

- Ask why the other party takes the position they do; for example, why they need a particular delivery date.
- Ask why not: examine the gaps in their argument, the choices they have made, and why they may have made them. You may want to examine the impact on their interests of the decisions they have made.
- Understand that both parties may have more than one interest in the negotiation.

Consider that the most important interests are those that relate to basic human needs (see Maslow's Hierarchy of Needs model, figure 10.1). It is often helpful, in preparation for the negotiation, to list the interests identified in their potential order of priority for both sides. The model illustrates that where parties are seeking to improve their status (self-actualisation), then these may represent high priority needs.

Figure 10.1: Maslow's Hierarchy of Needs

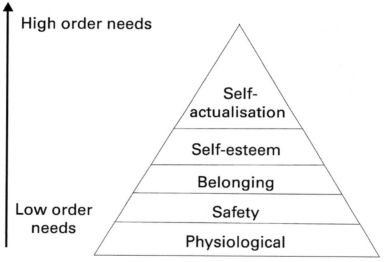

Source: Maslow (1954)

Recommendations for dealing with interests are:

- Make interests alive by providing examples.
- Acknowledge the other party's interests as part of the problem; for example, you could say, 'As I understand it, your interests are…'
- State your justification for a situation before giving the answer. This is more powerful because it keeps the listener involved; the other way around, the other party stops listening in order to plan a response the minute they hear the answer.
- Look forward, rather than backwards. Focusing on where you want to end up is better than rehashing past conflict.
- Be flexible but firm. Know where you are going but be open to creative solutions.
- Be hard on the problem but soft on the people.

Concessions are a key component of the negotiation – without them there would be no negotiation! If one party refuses to move, therefore, there is the distinct possibility of deadlock. Thus concessions are expected by negotiators. It is the way that issues are conceded, or bargained over, that determines the perceptions the parties have of the approach being taken, and it gives the other party's position legitimacy because the movement acts as an acknowledgment. Making concessions, on the other hand, also implies the party is taking a risk, which may lead to reciprocal concessions from the other party, or may signal a weakness to them. To counter this, negotiators often try to 'bundle' the issues and trade them off together, rather than trading issues sequentially, one by one (see figure 10.2).

Figure 10.2: Bundling issues versus sequential agreement

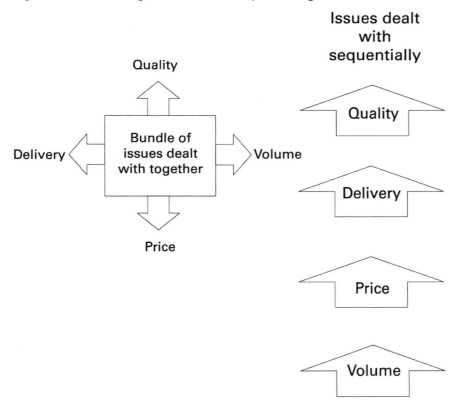

Distributive negotiators typically make an opening offer that is far from their resistance point (their limit or 'walk away' point). It is also often the case that the settlement on an issue occurs on the first or second offer that is better than target (Lewicki et al, 2003b). Thus it is important to identify the other party's bargaining range.

Learning activity 10.2

What do the concession patterns indicated in figure 10.3 suggest to you? Evaluate whether a collaborative or distributive situation is demonstrated.

Triangles and hearts represent the parties. By way of explanation, consider (a): the triangles indicate that each concession made equates to £6, whereas hearts concede at differing £ values.

(continued on next page)

Learning activity 10.2 *(continued)*

Figure 10.3: Example of concession patterns

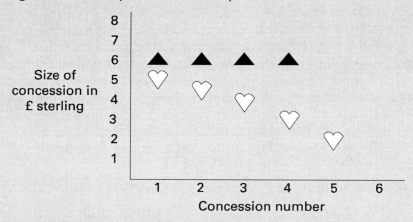

Figure 10.4: Example of concession patterns

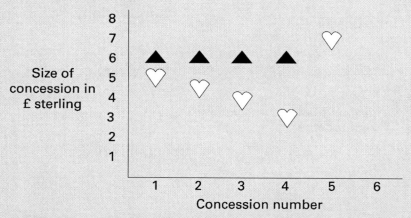

Figure 10.5: Example of concession patterns

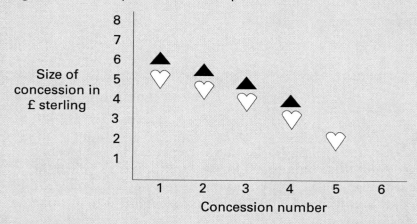

Feedback on page 137

Self-assessment question 10.2

Concession patterns convey messages about positions and interests. Discuss this statement.

Feedback on page 137

10.3 Gaining commitment

Gaining commitment in a distributive negotiation is about getting the other party to agree to a bargaining position on a course of action (Lewicki et al, 2003b). In essence, commitment on an issue guards against ambiguity and reduces the pool of issues left to be negotiated over. As a negotiating tool, commitment can be powerful in that once agreed, most people stick to their position – although therein also lies a difficulty, because the position can also be difficult to retrieve.

Learning activity 10.3

Identify the approaches you have used to gain commitment from a supplier. Explain why you chose them.

Feedback on page 138

Ultimately, once commitment has been gained for all the issues, the parties will want to close the deal. In distributive situations, a number of tactics are identified:

- Make alternative offers that are roughly equal in value to the other party and let them make the choice.
- 'Assume the close': a technique often used by salespeople, where the party does not articulate the deal but merely acts as if a deal has been concluded.
- Splitting the difference typically occurs when the parties have been negotiating for a long period of time. When one party, which started with a high opening position, suggests splitting the difference, then this is a hardball tactic!
- Offers with tight timescales, or 'exploding offers': this type of close pressurises the other party into agreeing and works best in a situation where the aim is to prevent the other party from seeking out a superior offer elsewhere;
- A 'sweetener' is a final, attractive concession that is intended to sway the other party into agreeing.

In more collaborative style situations, by way of contrast, the formal closes identified above are rarely used. This is because the focus of the discussion is on resolving jointly identified problems, gaining momentum and building trust throughout the process through positive communication. The role of trust is evidently important but it is a perceived variable in negotiations. Indeed one study by Hawes et al (1989) found that suppliers often overestimate the level of trust purchasers have in them, with the most important attribute being the supplier's reliability of performance. Other research has postulated the elements of trust in a sales context as being: likeability, competence, customer orientation, honesty and dependability. Trust may be said to exist in the process of the negotiation, in the people involved in the negotiation or in the organisation the negotiator represents.

Conversely, Butler (1996) found the pursuit of self-interests, rather than other's interests, did not effect trust between the parties. This was also

10

suggested by Young and Denize (1994) whose research linked commitment to trust and found that even when relationships between a purchaser and supplier were characterised by low satisfaction levels, the proclivity for the relationship to continue remained.

Self-assessment question 10.3

Identify the pros and cons of the following approaches to gaining commitment:

- splitting the difference
- he sweetener
- exploding offers.

Feedback on page 138

10.4 The role of ethics

Lewicki et al (2003a) define **ethics** in negotiation as being about social standards. These are different from moral standards, which reflect individuals' values and beliefs about wrong doing and appropriateness. Broadly, there are four aspects to ethics that are relevant:

- The expectations for the outcome of the negotiation.
- The legal framework which binds the agreement.
- The cultural values of the organisation that is represented by the negotiator(s).
- The individual's values.

Clearly, what is considered to be ethical, will depend upon practicalities; much like the previous discussion on tactics to be used in a negotiation, the issue is really one of relevance to the situation. Similarly, prudence plays a role – the appropriateness of the tactic to the situation. It is not the intention here to identify right from wrong, but merely to highlight that it is up to individuals to make their decisions based on a justifiable code of conduct.

For example, negotiators often need to resolve the 'dilemma of trust' (Lewicki, 1983) by establishing the true priorities and intentions of their counterparts; however, in so doing they are generally cautious, if not deceitful, about revealing their own priorities and intentions. Lying, which is 'any intentionally deceptive message which is stated' (Bok, in Lewicki, 1983), and deception in negotiation have been identified in a number of tactical guises: misrepresentation of position to opponent, bluffing, falsification, deception, selective disclosures or misrepresentation to constituencies. A primary purpose of lying is to increase the liar's power by providing false information.

Nonetheless, the extent to which the information is accepted as truthful will obviously influence the situation (see study session 9). The issue is

10

really about intentions, motives and the characteristics of the negotiators, their moral development and the social context of the negotiation – the 'nature versus nurture' debate. Consider, again, the so-called hardball tactics identified in section 10.1.

Learning activity 10.4

Reflecting on hardball tactics (see section 10.1), which of these do you consider to be unethical in your organisational (or personal) context and why?

Feedback on page 138

Lewicki et al (2003a) identify a number of ways to deal with deceptive tactics (see table 10.3).

Table 10.3 Uncovering deceptive tactics

Tactic	Techniques for uncovering the deception
Discomfort and relief	Reduce tension by indicating that to confess will be a relief.
Bluff	Indicate that the deception is known about, but not up for discussion.
Minimisation	Assist the other party to find a justification for their deceptive behaviour, but play it down.
Alter information	Overstate a situation with the express intention that the other party corrects you, and in so doing, reveals their true position.
Self-disclose	Reveal information about yourself, including a deception, with the aim that the other party reciprocates.
Direct question	Ask about the deception!
Silence	Create a verbal space such that the other party feels they must disclose information.

Source: adapted from Lewicki et al (2003a)

Finally, CIPS has a personal ethical code on the conduct of business (see CIPS: http://www.cips.org/). The code identifies five key principles relating to:

- integrity
- professionalism
- high standards
- optimal use of resources
- compliance with legal and other obligations.

Self-assessment question 10.4

Review five ethical behaviours identified in the discussion. How do these relate to the CIPS personal ethical code?

Feedback on page 139

10

Revision question

Now try the revision question for this session on page 267.

Summary

This study session has discussed a range of tactical tasks in negotiation. Firstly, comparisons were made between the collaborative and distributive negotiation situations. Tactical tasks associated with both approaches were identified and a range of ploys were reviewed. Information was identified as being the fundamental basis for negotiation.

Discussion then focused on typical positions taken during collaborative and distributive negotiations. It was highlighted that, by identifying interests, it is possible to 'look behind' positions in order to determine the common ground between the parties. Interests were identified as emanating from Maslow's Hierarchy of Needs, ranging from low to high priority, which were considered to be dependent upon the context of the negotiation.

The nature of concessions was discussed and examples presented for comment. It was identified that there are important implicit messages sent when a concession is made which indicate the approach being taken by the negotiator. It was also identified that, in integrative situations, bundles of issues may be conceded, rather than single issues, as is more typical in a distribution situation. Methods for gaining commitment and closing a deal were reviewed. Trust was considered to be a predominating factor in more integrative situations, built by focusing on resolving jointly identified problems and positive communication.

Finally, the role of ethical behaviour in negotiations was discussed. Ethics were considered to be based on four main aspects. A brief review of the personal ethical code was presented.

Suggested further reading

Lewicki et al (2003b) on tactical tasks in negotiations for distributive (chapter 3) and integrative situations (chapter 4), as well as managing difficult negotiations (chapter 9) and ethics in negotiation (chapter 7).

Steele et al (1989) on the phases of negotiation, specifically, the opening to closing stages (chapter 4).

CIPS: http://www.cips.org/. Look up the personal ethical code for business conduct, particularly to help you complete self-assessment question 10.4 above.

Feedback on learning activities and self-assessment questions

Feedback on learning activity 10.1

- Good cop/bad cop: using humour can counter this by deflating the other party.

- Lowball/highball: do not make a counter-offer with this tactic but use thorough preparation to identify an appropriate range; stick to your original ideas and do not move until the other party does; state your understanding of the situation; threaten to leave the negotiation.
- Bogey: sudden changes in position indicate this tactic has been used, so counter by establishing why the party is taking a position that you had not expected from your preparation.
- The nibble: the nibble may be so small it will not be worth losing the deal over, but an appropriate response would be to establish if there are other 'nibbles' that the party wants to include; it might also be useful to have a stock of 'nibbles' to use as counter-trade options.
- Chicken: difficult to defend against this, the tactic should only be used as a last resort; nonetheless a response could be to introduce a counter-chicken threat; thorough preparation and planning, of course, help you to understand the interests and positions behind the tactic.
- Intimidation: discuss the process of the negotiation, and focus on fairness and respectfulness; ignore it – this behaviour only works if the target party lets it!
- Aggression: it may be appropriate to halt the negotiation and discuss the process; a team approach may influence the behaviour; certainly good preparation will enable a better understanding of the other party's interests and position.
- Snow job: ask questions in order to generate information that you understand; try to identify any inconsistencies.

Feedback on self-assessment question 10.1

Any of the characteristics from table 10.1 can be used to compare and contrast the two approaches.

Feedback on learning activity 10.2

The pattern of concessions provides the parties with valuable information about each other's bargaining range and resistance points.

1 Triangles are conceding at the same £ value each move which sends the message that they are able to continue with this strategy, whereas hearts suggest they are getting close to their limits because the £ value of the concessions is getting smaller with each consecutive move.
2 Suddenly, hearts make a dramatic concession (move 5). This may indicate a negotiation tactic is being played, that they are insufficiently prepared, or that they have made a mistake somewhere along the line.
3 Both parties are conceding in a way that indicates they may both be approaching their target or resistance points. There may be high levels of trust in this situation.

Feedback on self-assessment question 10.2

The issues being discussed may be bundled or ordered sequentially and agreed upon by the parties. The latter approach tends to be associated more with distributive while the former, bundling, with integrative situations. Concession patterns may therefore include a number of issues (integrative)

10

compared to only one issue (distributive). They reveal positions and interests: firstly, because of the nature of the issues being discussed (price being the predominant issue in a distributive situation; with more, creative options available in an integrative one); secondly because of the way in which the issues are traded.

Feedback on learning activity 10.3

Approaches:

- use of threats to strengthen a position
- tactical ploys
- ongoing relationship.

Explanations:

- The nature of the relationship you have with the other party (at individual and organisational level).
- The ease with which you are able to extract yourself from the commitment.
- The consequences of not committing during the negotiation.
- The consequences of retracting your commitment at some subsequent point.

Feedback on self-assessment question 10.3

See table 10.2 for pros and cons of gaining commitment.

Table 10.2 Pros and cons of gaining commitment

	Pros	Cons
Splitting the difference	Appears fair to the parties.	Presumes opening position was indeed fair.
The sweetener	May encourage a deal by appearing more attractive.	Associated costs may be high if these are not calculated at the outset as part of the preparation process.
Exploding offers	Potentially ties the other party in.	The party may retaliate because they were pressurised.
	May prevent the other party from considering possible alternatives.	

Feedback on learning activity 10.4

Your answer may have considered the following points:

- The negotiator's experience in using the tactics identified.
- Cultural aspects, such as the organisational, individual and national context.

- The legal framework, including standards or codes of conduct, that overlay the agreements you reach with others, and also the dispute resolution processes to which you may have to resort in the event of contractual breakdown.
- The extent of the other party's familiarity with the tactics – and whether or not the approaches were reciprocated or otherwise responded to.

Feedback on self-assessment question 10.4

Your answer may have considered the following points:

- Being honest, open, truthful – acting with integrity.
- Acting according to a legal framework, code of conduct or other regulatory standard – compliance with legal and other obligations.
- Exhibiting respect for the other party.
- Acting in manner considered to be fair, or principled (professionalism).
- Reciprocating behaviour that is exhibited by the other party.

10

10

Study session 11
Finalising the negotiation

Introduction

This study session reviews the processes of ratifying and evaluating the negotiation outcome. This is the final stage in the negotiation process and is particularly important because successful outcomes to negotiations have a direct role in informing future situations. This is true at the individual, negotiating team and organisational levels for both parties.

Thus the first section reviews the role of ratifying negotiation deals. The next section looks at the negotiation evaluation process. The third at how evaluation informs future negotiations. The final section reviews the legal evaluation and process implications for negotiations.

Session learning objectives

After completing this session you should be able to:

11.1 Explain the importance of ratifying a negotiation.
11.2 Identify and discuss components of a negotiation evaluation.
11.3 Discuss how implementing the agreement influences future negotiations with the same supplier and other suppliers.
11.4 Review the legal implications of negotiation outcomes.

Unit content coverage

This study session covers the following topics from the official CIPS unit content document:

Statements of practice

- Explain the different approaches required when negotiating in different settings.
- Understand how to analyse negotiation performance.

Learning objectives

3.5 Explain how to follow up the negotiation and finalise the deal.
- Informal and formal ratification
- How to evaluate the negotiation process and recommend improvements
- The importance of reviewing the ongoing relationship, including requirements and necessities, to re-negotiate at appropriate intervals

Resources

Any notes from study sessions 1 – 10.

'It comes down to effective communication. You have to be very, very open with one another, with what you expect. What you can do, what you can't do. They can't overestimate their capabilities and promise something they can't deliver. And we can't expect the world.'

Berry Kline, Tom Raglione and Steve Conder, Bristol-Myers Squibb Pharmaceutical Group, commenting on how to avoid problems with partnering (Rackham, Friedman and Ruff, 1996: 224)

11

Timing

You should set aside about 5 hours to read and complete this session, including learning activities, self-assessment questions, the suggested further reading (if any) and the revision question.

11.1 Ratifying negotiations

Ratification is the process of approving, endorsing, confirming or otherwise permitting the agreement reached following a negotiation to proceed to implementation. In fact, it is about the constraints placed upon the negotiators by their constituencies (their own organisations). Ratifying is commonly used in international negotiations, where there are many parties who have vested interests in the outcome. It originated with game theoretic approaches to negotiation (Putnam, 1988).

In business, ratifying negotiation is firstly about ensuring adequate preparation in order that the negotiation takes place with those individuals that have the power to make a decision on the issues. Recall the comment from study session 7, when it was noted that there may be little point in engaging in negotiation without the parties' having the ability to commit. Thus it is worth bearing in mind the seven phases of negotiation previously identified in study session 1:

- Preparation: identifying the important issues and goals.
- Relationship building: understanding how you will relate to the other party.
- Information gathering: learning what you need to know about (variables, other party's situation and goals).
- Information using: building the case for the negotiation.
- Bidding: the process of negotiating from initial offer towards the agreement.
- Closing the deal: building commitment from the parties.
- Implementing the deal: a post-negotiation phase. Even after the agreement is reached, there may be loose ends to clarify so there will be follow-ups to the original negotiation.

Implicit within each of the phases is that both parties, the purchaser and the supplier:

- carry the mandate to enter into negotiation
- are authorised to concede on the issues discussed in the bidding (bargaining) phase
- are formally approved by the respective buying and selling organisations to close a deal and, subsequently, to act upon it.

As Steele et al (1989) imply, if this is not the case, then delays in implementation are certain and failure to implement according to the terms agreed is highly likely. From the negotiator's perspective, this can be detrimental to an ongoing relationship with a supplier and, at worst, can undermine confidence in negotiating competencies. As Lewicki et al (2003a) suggest, however, the requirement for greater accountability within business (the corporate social responsibility agenda) means that ratifying deals is an important aspect to negotiating.

Negotiators need to be sure they have understood the intricacies of the negotiation process and are confident in making complex decisions in agreeing the outcome. Furthermore, the individuals must then be capable of returning to their respective organisations and communicating the agreement back to those with a vested interest, such as those who will implement the deal. An agreement resulting from a negotiation requires that the parties are satisfied with the consequences (Raiffa, 2002). In study session 10 there was discussion of the approaches to gaining commitment from the supplier, but it should be clear from the discussion here that it is important to avoid premature commitment.

Learning activity 11.1

How could you have improved the ratification process of your most recent negotiations?

Feedback on page 152

There are two approaches to ratifying the agreement: formal and informal.

Where formal ratification is sought, the negotiators will take the deal back to their constituency (such as a boss, perhaps a production manager, in the organisation) and present for 'signing off'. The constituency's decision is relatively straightforward: to accept the agreement reached as it is presented. Such a decision will be based on the availability of all salient information related to the deal and its implementation; it is unlikely, for example, that an agreement will be ratified if there is incomplete information.

In contrast, informal ratification is more typically found with internal negotiations. Ratification is often continuous, resulting in pressure to modify terms, which impacts on external negotiations. A usual response to this by a negotiator is to generate indirect support from interest groups (for example, finance) or other vested audiences and so create some form of 'political' pressure to encourage the constituency to ratify.

Clearly, negotiators will most likely be involved with near simultaneous ratification problems – one with their internal constituency to ensure he continues to carry the mandate throughout the negotiation (preparation through to implementation); one on completion of the deal.

For this reason, as Bazerman (2002) comments, it is often worthwhile to include in an agreement a 'post-settlement settlement' (PSS) option. Such an option enables the parties to return to the issues they have agreed at some future point in order to refine the agreement by sharing further information. This then has the potential to conclude with an improved outcome, often referred to as 'pareto-optimal' (Raiffa, 2002).

Self-assessment question 11.1

Compare and contrast approaches to ratifying negotiations.

Feedback on page 152

11.2 Evaluating negotiations

Evaluating negotiation is about measuring its success against specified aims and objectives. Evaluation will relate to all seven of the phases identified (figure 11.1).

Figure 11.1: Phases of negotiation

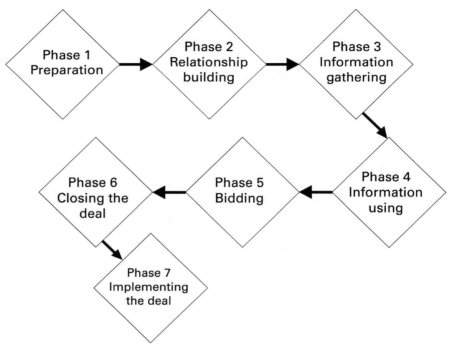

Source: derived from Greenhalgh (2001) in Lewicki et al (2003)

It will be evident from any evaluation that in the event of failure one or more of these phases will not have been attended to adequately. However, negotiation does not take place in a vacuum; the market is dynamic and new information leads to new knowledge on a continuing basis. Thus key considerations may be:

- How has the market changed between the time of the agreement and its implementation, and what impact does that have on the outcome?
- Do the objectives specified remain realistic?
- Can the other party achieve its objectives?

It is often said that, with the benefit of hindsight, the approach to a negotiation would have been different. However, evaluation is not necessarily about self-flagellation, but more about considering how the preparation and planning for the negotiation could be improved for future situations. Lewicki et al (2003b) identify that a negotiator who carefully plans will have:

- Identified the key issues to be resolved.
- Assembled all the key issues – and how they relate to one another.
- Defined and understood the underlying interests on the issues.
- Set limits for issues, including resistance points, the walk-away position, and BATNA.
- Identified targets and objectives, including opening points.

- Appropriately consulted others, including constituents (boss or vested others within the organisation); and understood the level of authority.
- Understood the other party – their goals, issues, interests, strategies, limits, alternatives, targets, openings and authority.
- Identified the strategy which is most likely to achieve agreement.
- Shaped the process of negotiating – which ideas to present first, and how best to present them;
- Decided on the protocol and process to be followed: agenda, who will observe the negotiation, timing and location.

Now build your own evaluation plan (learning activity 11.2 below). This is a substantive exercise – be prepared to spend an hour on it.

Learning activity 11.2

Review study session 1-study session 10 and develop a series of negotiation review questions that may be used to enhance future performance.

Feedback on page 153

Suffice to say, planning the evaluation should also be a key part of the preparation and planning phase. Previous negotiations will have fed into recent negotiations which will inform future negotiations. This is particularly important when dealing with the same party again, as in an ongoing relationship. Relationship history is an important source of power in negotiation, as highlighted in study session 9 (see figure 11.3).

Figure 11.3: Negotiation experience

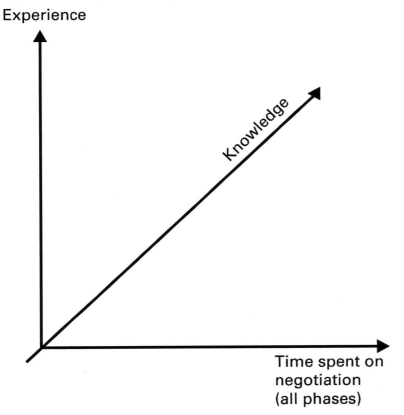

Experience

Knowledge

Time spent on negotiation (all phases)

11

Self-assessment question 11.2

Describe the components of the post-negotiation phase.

Feedback on page 153

11.3 The future

First, attempt learning activity 11.3 below.

Learning activity 11.3

Reflect on the outcome of a recent negotiation and identify why it was successfully implemented.

Feedback on page 154

As illustrated by figure 11.3 in section 11.2, as negotiators develop their knowledge, so their competence grows. This is particularly important when engaging in long-term relationships with suppliers; experience of negotiating with one another builds the body of knowledge and provides the opportunity for shared understanding. This has the potential to lead to 'stickier' solutions, which may be more optimal to the parties.

Previous discussion has highlighted the underlying conditions of relationships between purchasers and suppliers. The mutual benefit of a relationship (for profit or some other gain) requires them to commit to adapting their behaviour to ensure its longevity. Thus negotiators need to develop knowledge of how relationships evolve over time in order that they may facilitate the processes. Drivers for the evolution from transactional to relationship-based exchanges are:

- Retention of suppliers.
- Just-in-time concept, requiring greater openness between buyers and sellers.
- Move from commodity-based transactions to speciality business and higher value-added products, necessitating closer relationships because of a need for more detailed product specifications.
- Trends in outsourcing: partnering agreements that require involved negotiation and conflict resolution processes and, ultimately, lead towards mutually beneficial outcomes.

The negotiation results in an exchange of information which, in turn, can lead to the development of the underlying glue for relationships – trust and commitment. Trust is crucially important in relationships, particularly in the early stages of relational development. Rich (2000) suggests that an understanding of the patterns of behaviour which lead to a 'greater sense of trust' enable the parties to adapt their behaviour in order to improve relationship performance. It is, therefore, important that negotiators accumulate and evaluate their performance in this context to enhance their future negotiations.

Relationships develop from early stages of encounter or 'courtship' to partnership or 'marriage' and, ultimately, dissolution or 'divorce' (Ford, 1980). Dwyer et al's (1987) well-known relational development model, which has subsequently been further researched and adapted (for example, McDonald, Rogers and Woodburn, 2000), highlights that relationships become increasingly collaborative between purchasers and suppliers as the complexity of the transactions increases. Their model shows five stages of relational development in the context of strategically important business relationships, that is, key account or preferred supplier management (KAM), and one further stage of dissolution (uncoupling-KAM). The relational development stages are: Pre-KAM; Early-KAM; Mid-KAM; Partnership-KAM and Synergistic-KAM (see figure 11.4). When this model is successfully implemented, it enhances the opportunity to achieve longer-term competitive advantage through rationalisation of resources.

Figure 11.4: Relationship development model

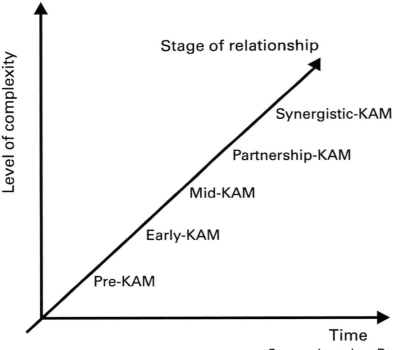

Source: based on Dwyer et al, 1987

Thus negotiation processes and substantive content will differ at different stages of relational evolution. This relates to the discussion in study session 2, which identified that negotiations are typically entered into at the following stages:

- Pre-contract: in order to develop and build a specification for supply and to clarify the terms of any contractual arrangements including how the relationship will work in practice;

- Agreeing the contract: the main negotiation stage, at which terms and conditions will be agreed as well as any ongoing relationship between the parties.
- Contract review: when relationships are reviewed, and where terms and conditions may be revisited in the light of evolving market forces or relationship developments, in order to resolve any conflicts that may have arisen upon implementation of the main negotiation agreement.

Table 11.1 highlights the objectives and strategies for different stages of relational evolution, which also have implications for negotiations with internal constituents.

Table 11.1 KAM objectives and strategies

Development Stage	Objectives and Strategies
Pre-KAM	• Identify key contacts and decision-making unit. • Establish product need. • Display willingness to address other problem areas. • Advocate key account status in-house.
Early-KAM	• Build social network. • Identify process related problems and signal willingness to work together. • Build trust through performance and open communications.
Mid-KAM	• Focus on process related issues. • Manage the implementation of process related solutions. • Build inter-organisational teams. • Establish joint systems. • Begin to perform non-core management tasks.
Partnership-KAM	• Integrate processes. • Extend joint problem solving. • Focus on cost reduction and joint value creating opportunities. • Address key strategic issues of the client. • Address facilitation issues.
Synergistic-KAM	• Focus on joint value creativity. • Create semi-autonomous projects teams. • Develop strategic congruence.

Source: based on Wilson (1999)

The difficulty in preparing for future negotiations within a relationship context is, however, that each relationship often has distinctive characteristics. Thus it is appropriate to have generic evaluation plans which leave room for manoeuvre and flexibility.

Self-assessment question 11.3

Identify three factors that may influence future negotiations.

Feedback on page 154

11.4 Legal implications

Accountability, including social and ethical aspects, has already been highlighted as an important consideration for negotiating. The formal, legal regulatory context is a fundamental aspect of this (see figure 11.5).

Figure 11.5: The negotiator's responsibility

Discretionary responsibility (contribution to community)

Ethical responsibility (do what is right)

Legal responsibility (obey the law)

Economic responsibility (profit)

11

Learning activity 11.4

Explain how the components in figure 11.5 impact on your negotiations.

Feedback on page 154

In study session 3, it was identified that agreements may comprise a number of terms which need to be assessed:

- Express terms: those agreed by the parties.
- Implied terms: those not agreed by the parties but which will be assumed by the law, should matters need resort to a court.
- Statutory terms: where the law overrides the explicit terms agreed by the parties.
- Illegal terms: those a court would not enforce even though the parties agreed to the terms. Nonetheless, such terms may be imposed by the other party through their commercial power: for example, payment of penalties by suppliers following breach (failure to perform).

As was stated, to be legal the contract does not have to be written, although it is recommended. Written contracts provide the parties with evidence of agreement and detail the terms and conditions under which agreement was reached. Common terms and conditions include:

- exclusion or limitation clauses, which specify the extent of any liability
- retention of title clauses
- penalty clauses, such as for non-performance.

These clauses specify:

- scope of the supplier's provision
- quality and quantity
- standards to be met by the supplier
- when and how the output will be measured
- equipment and materials to be supplied
- other facilities to be provided for the performance of the work
- frequency of measurement and any inspection
- expected start date for the contract
- schedule for the supply of goods and/or services
- preferred payment mechanisms.

Model terms and conditions of contract are available from CIPS (see CIPS: http://www.cips.org/) and include core clauses on:

- Insolvency and bankruptcy: outlines the level of security offered in the event that the supplier ceases to trade.
- Force majeure: identifies the conditions under which an agreement is not binding (for example, war, disorder, industrial dispute).
- Confidentiality and data protection: pertains to the flow of sensitive and protected information.
- Termination for breach: relates to the failure by one or other party to perform according to the terms and conditions.
- Terms of payment, including acceptable delay and deductions for defects and non-performance.
- Time of the essence: relates to situations where exact delivery timing is critical.
- Dispute resolution alternatives: outlines the recommended procedures for engaging third parties, especially arbitrators before courts.

It is the negotiator's responsibility to ensure that any deal incorporates the relevant terms and conditions for implementation of the agreement. As indicated, it is also important that the negotiator includes detail of what happens in the event of a breakdown between the purchasing and supplying organisations, including the guidelines that will be used to resolve any disputes that may arise. This requires that negotiators know how and when to resort to third parties (and the law) in the event of dispute. This can become complex when the organisations are engaged in a long-term relationship and when value and benefit are seen beyond the dispute that has arisen. Points to bear in mind are those highlighted originally by Kant (1724-1804) on rule ethics, that is, where the rightness of an action is determined by laws and standards:

- Whose authority acts as guidance on rules?
- When rules conflict, which rules are followed?
- How are the rules adapted to fit the situation?
- What are the consequences of the rules?

11

It is far better to be clear at the outset about the details of terms and conditions that are acceptable, and ensure that agreements reached are win-win.

Self-assessment question 11.4

What steps need to be taken to ensure compliance with legal requirements?

Feedback on page 154

Revision question

Now try the revision question for this session on page 267.

Summary

This study session identified that ratification is the process of approving, endorsing and confirming the agreement reached following a negotiation, and is about the constraints placed upon the negotiators by their own organisations in reaching agreement. It was stated that within negotiation phases both parties, the purchaser and the supplier, should:

- carry the mandate to enter into negotiation.
- be authorised to concede on the issues discussed in the bidding (bargaining) phase.
- be formally approved by the respective buying and selling organisations to close a deal and, subsequently, to act upon it.

Two approaches to ratifying the agreement were identified: formal, where a manager 'signs off' the agreement made by the negotiator; and, informal, where the negotiator needs to gain support from vested parties inside the organisation on a more continual basis. In evaluating negotiation outcomes, it was highlighted that situations are dynamic, which often impedes the evaluation process. Key considerations in evaluating were identified and a ten-step evaluation plan discussed.

Section 11.3 considered the role of developing negotiating experience and recording relational outcomes so that the body of knowledge generated will not be lost. A model of relational development was reviewed and it was highlighted that with each successive stage of relational evolution there may be three negotiation situations. The point was made that each relationship context has distinct characteristics necessitating that generic evaluation plans should leave room for manoeuvre and flexibility.

Legal implications were reviewed in the context of the negotiator's responsibilities. It was noted that whilst the legal and regulatory framework may differ depending on country laws, the negotiator still needs to bear in mind the different types of terms and conditions that impact on agreements.

11

Express terms were reviewed in detail (based on CIPS model terms and conditions of contract). Consideration of the rule bases for negotiations was also briefly reviewed. This included discussion on whose authority would inform any conflict resolution process, particularly when the law is unclear or when the relationship value is greater than the current dispute. Finally, review of compliance with legal requirements highlighted three key stages: preparation, the negotiation itself and post-negotiation.

Suggested further reading

Lewicki et al (2003b) on the planning process and relationship interests.

Steele et al (1989) on the preparation and planning phase.

Shapiro et al (2001) on building relationships.

CIPS: http://www.cips.org/. Ensure you are familiar with the model terms and conditions of contract that form the basis of many contractual agreements and, therefore, highlight some negotiation variables.

Feedback on learning activities and self-assessment questions

Feedback on learning activity 11.1

Your answer could have considered the following points:

- The preparation prior to the negotiation, which may have identified particular issues for the negotiation.
- The market, which may have moved in the direction anticipated.
- The stage of relational evolution, which may have meant you needed to identify additional negotiators on one or both sides.
- The power balance or imbalance between the organisations or negotiators – coercion may have resulted in the weaker party not getting the deal they needed.
- Lack of tracking during the negotiation, leading to poor evaluation of issues traded.
- Under- or over-estimation of the implications of reaching agreement.
- Over-confidence in your or the supplier's ability to 'sell' the deal to organisational colleagues.

Feedback on self-assessment question 11.1

Formal versus informal:

- Formal is used when agreement reached,; informal is used with internal constituencies to ensure the mandate to negotiate continues.
- Formal assumes negotiator has power; informal assumes less power.
- Formal requires that all salient information is exchanged during the negotiation, and that the negotiators have been skilful in using the information they gathered in the preparation phase.
- Informal is a continuous process;

- Informal may require the negotiator to align himself with popular opinion inside the organisation, or even external audiences, in order to exert pressure on the constituency to ratify.
- With both approaches, building a relationship with constituencies is important in order for the negotiator to ratify deals with minimum fuss.

Feedback on learning activity 11.2

You may want to consider your evaluation plan against the diagram (figure 11.2):

Figure 11.2: Planning evaluation

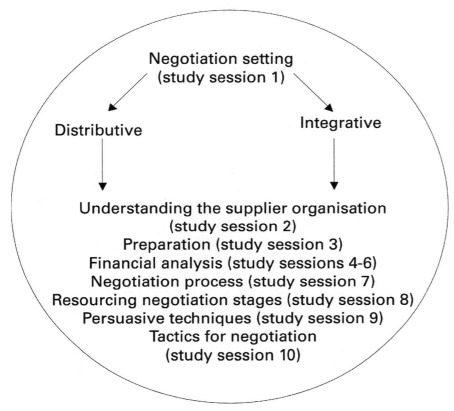

The negotiation setting will clearly influence the way in which your evaluation is conducted, bearing in mind the fundamental differences between integrative negotiations and distributive negotiations. It may be appropriate to consider two evaluation plans!

Feedback on self-assessment question 11.2

Your analysis should have included:

- A plan which evaluates performance against the aims and objectives of the negotiation.
- Analytical review of the agreement reached, or analysis of the outcome.
- Evaluation of your own and your team's performance, highlighting learning points and any areas for development of skills.
- Review of any new information generated from the negotiation meeting which may impact on future situations or agreements.

11

Feedback on learning activity 11.3

Your answer may have considered the following points:

- The thoroughness of the preparation and planning.
- The consequences to one or other party of failure.
- The skill and competence of the individuals involved in the negotiation.
- The similarities between the parties involved.
- The ongoing relationship context: the level of trust and commitment resulting from previous successful outcomes.

Feedback on self-assessment question 11.3

- Experience of the negotiators.
- Relationship development stage.
- Substantive content of the negotiation: whether pre-contract, contract or post-contract review.

Feedback on learning activity 11.4

- All negotiations have specific aims and objectives which include economic benefits to the organisation. If you are working in a commercial context, then this will be defined in terms of profitability, whereas in a public sector context, then cost reductions and value added are more likely to be the focus. It is clearly incumbent upon negotiators to achieve the best they can in the circumstances for their organisation.
- Your comments will obviously depend on the country's law that prevails for your negotiations. The legal framework includes those terms and conditions that you agree to be bound by as purchaser.
- Discretionary and ethical responsibility is likely to depend on your organisation's view of itself within its local and broader environment. You may, for example, be keen to reduce waste from packaging of products supplied as part of your commitment to a green agenda, or you may wish to ensure the deals you agree have more direct benefit, such as a contribution to some local project.
- Ethical responsibility will also include the CIPS personal ethical code of conduct.

Feedback on self-assessment question 11.4

Your answer should have considered the following points:

Before the negotiation

- Ensure preparation and planning have highlighted the relevant terms and conditions of contract with appropriate resistance points ('walk-aways') for each clause.

During the negotiation

- Ensure negotiation includes all relevant aspects of product or service performance, including review of regulatory standards that apply, especially where there is the possibility of any deviations.

11

- Ensure the legal framework that informs the agreement is reviewed in the negotiation process so there is clarity on the terms and conditions between the parties. This should include express, implied and statutory aspects. For example, the negotiation may focus much attention on express terms, but it will also be important to understand the statutory terms that impact on the agreement.
- Ensure that dispute resolution processes have been reviewed adequately, and are understood by both parties, including the identification of any third party facilitator if needed.

After the negotiation

- Ensure the written agreement clearly states the terms and conditions settled on.
- Ensure the terms and conditions are ratified by both party's organisations.
- Monitor and evaluate performance against agreement to ensure standards are maintained within the legal framework.
- Evaluate performance to identify the point at which to begin dispute resolution, including resort to a third party facilitator.

11

11

Effective communication

'The quality of the relationship can be jeopardised through poor and inconsistent communications.'

Chris and Karen Fill (2005: 338) commenting on the weaknesses of personal interaction

Introduction

This study session reviews the role of communication – one of the most demanding aspects of negotiation to prepare for and participate in, because it requires extensive and direct experience in order to perform well.

First, effective communication is reviewed as it relates to negotiations, including techniques for improving communication processes. Then different types of communication are reviewed, relating to verbal and non-verbal forms. Finally, this study session reviews the range of potential difficulties arising from communication.

Session learning objectives

After completing this session you should be able to:

12.1 Appraise what is meant by effective communication in negotiations, including how to improve communication during negotiations.
12.2 Distinguish between different verbal and non-verbal (body language) communication techniques.
12.3 Assess the range of potential communication difficulties experienced in negotiations.

12

Unit content coverage

This study session covers the following topics from the official CIPS unit content document:

Statement of practice

Apply a range of negotiation theories in order to achieve set outcomes.

Learning objectives

4.1 Evaluate the relative importance of verbal and non-verbal communications in negotiation situations.
- Reducing the potential for conflict
- Sales influencing tools
- The other person's perspective
- Body language
- Behavioural technologies

Timing

You should set aside about 5 hours to read and complete this session, including learning activities, self-assessment questions, the suggested further reading (if any) and the revision question.

12.1 Effective communication

Previous discussion has identified that communication is the exchange of information which, in turn, leads to trust and commitment. Communication is the process by which business relationships are formed; value is added through the communication frequency and physical proximity between purchasers and suppliers (Boles et al, 2000). It is an important aspect of relationship development, which improves performance (Schultz and Evans, 2002). In negotiations, the closer buyers and sellers are as individuals the more successful the outcome will be (Tarver and Haring, 1988). Both parties exchange information through verbal and non-verbal means in order to make judgements about competence and trustworthiness. This information is then used to determine the levels of performance expected as part of the agreed solution.

Study session 9 briefly introduced the communication process (see figure 9.1) and discussed the sending and receiving of messages in the context of negotiations. The process was highlighted as quite complex and three different tasks were identified in terms of preparing to negotiate:

- The content of the message – what will be conveyed.
- The structure of the message – how it will be dealt with.
- The style of the message – its presentation.

During the negotiation, it is evident that the types of issue being discussed have an influence on the negotiation outcome. For example, in relational situations the process of communication influences the outcome by:

- maximising return within larger time frame
- considering the needs, interests and attitudes of other side
- a non-antagonistic style
- focusing on joint gains
- concentrating on substance.

Whilst in distributive situations, it focuses on:

- maximising return from transaction
- no consideration of needs, interests and attitudes of other side
- cooperative behaviour only if it helps to achieve returns
- military style manoeuvres
- presenting strong defence against opposing tactics
- controlling the negotiation for future manipulation.

Lewicki et al (2003b) identify five typical categories of communication in negotiations:

- Offers and counteroffers: the bargaining about substantive issues which results in narrowing of the bargaining range and, ultimately, agreement.

- Information about alternatives: even when the BATNA is not revealed to the other party, it acts as a powerful influence resulting in a higher target for the party.
- Information about outcomes: how the outcome will be evaluated is best kept inside the organisation because the other party may be unhappy if you appear to have achieved a better deal than they have!
- Social justifications for mistakes made, positions taken or bad news: research suggests the more justification used, the better the outcome.
- Information about processes: a review of the negotiation process so far can be a powerful antidote to negative conflict episodes.

Learning activity 12.1

When preparing for a negotiation, how will you develop more effective communication? Remember to identify whether it is a collaborative or distributive situation.

Feedback on page 166

It is evident from this discussion that the perception of communication messages plays an important role. Perception is about making sense of the messages sent and received by the communicators. Often messages are framed according to the experience of the negotiator. This is why it is important to self-evaluate and learn from past negotiating experiences, in order to find ways of using new knowledge. Negotiators use short cuts in making decisions based on past experiences, referred to as 'decision heuristics' (although this can be problematic, see section 12.3).

A typical negotiation follows a pattern of communication (figure 12.1).

12

Figure 12.1: Pattern of negotiation communication

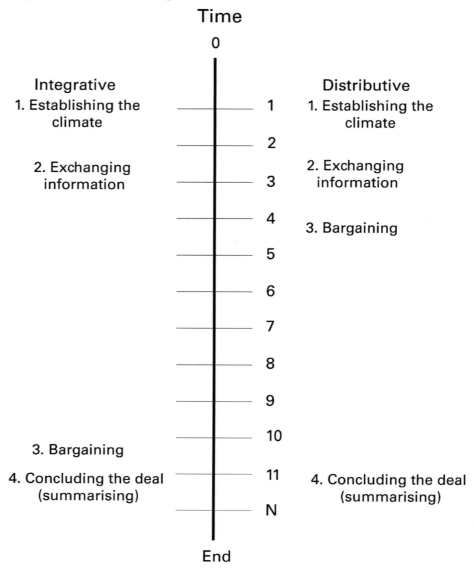

Figure 12.1 illustrates that the parties spend longer in the exchanging information phase when involved in an integrative style of negotiation than in a distributive negotiation. Other models of negotiation phases identify three distinctive types of communication, relating to the initiation, the problem solving (exchanging information) and the closing phase (Lewicki et al, 2003a). When negotiations break down, it typically happens in the first two stages.

Now attempt self-assessment question 12.1 below. Plan to spend at least 30 minutes on this, by referring back to notes from previous study sessions.

Self-assessment question 12.1

What is effective communication?

Feedback on page 167

12.2 Communication techniques

How people communicate in negotiation extends both to verbal techniques and non-verbal behaviour. There are two aspects to considering verbal behaviour: the logic of the language, that means the proposals and counter-proposals, and the more pragmatic level, relating to the meanings and style of the communication. For example, Gibbons et al (in Lewicki et al, 2003a) identify five different characteristics of threats:

- The polarity of the language used, such as positive words and negative words relating to each party's position ('this is a *generous* offer from us; you are being *unreasonable*').
- The verbal immediacy of the language which can be high or low ('this is a good offer *now…*' compared to 'you *may* want to consider this…').
- Language intensity, which incorporates feelings.
- Diversity of language in use: the range of vocabulary which conveys competence, knowledge, or inexperience.
- Power style exhibited by confident and self-assured commentary, possibly firmness and verbal domination.

Thus language can be used to command, compel, sell, persuade or gain commitment in negotiation. Outcome success depends on the negotiators' abilities to transmit and receive messages accurately.

As identified in learning activity 12.1 above, questions are a key tool in effective verbal communication. The phases of negotiation imply different types of question are likely to be asked in order to realise the deal. There are, however, a few generic techniques that can be adapted:

- Open-ended question: cannot be answered with a straight yes or no. They relate to the who, what, why, when forms. For example: 'Why do you think that?'
- Leading question: encourages the desired answer. For example: 'Wouldn't you prefer xxx?'
- Cool question: has low emotional content. For example: 'How does a reduction in price impact on standards?'
- Planned question: one the negotiator has previously prepared on a specific point, perhaps as part of a sequence. For example: 'If we were to offer you xxx, how would you react to yyy?'
- Treat question: incorporates some form of flattery. For example: 'Perhaps you would care to share your knowledge on this?'
- Window question: asks for insight into the other's perspective. For example: 'Why have you said that?'
- Directive question: gets to the point. For example: 'How much does it cost?'
- Gauging question: asks for reaction to a proposal. For example: 'Was that of interest to you?'

12

Learning activity 12.2

Using the generic question types identified in the discussion, formulate questions for each of the phases identified in figure 12.1. Identify questions

(continued on next page)

Learning activity 12.2 *(continued)*
for both the integrative and distributive approaches, in order to develop distinctive skills.

Feedback on page 167

It is somewhat more problematic when the following types of questions are asked – they tend to be less manageable in negotiation situations:

- Close-out questions: coercive, attempting to make the other party see your way. 'Surely that will lead to xxx?'
- Loaded questions: putting them on the spot. 'Is that really what you think?'
- Heated questions: high emotion. 'How can you justify such a stupid position?'
- Impulsive questions: no prior thought, usually 'off the cuff'.
- Trick questions: pretending to be genuine but are really loaded. 'What do you think of xxx? Is it of interest or are you going to go to another customer?'
- Reflective trick questions: 'I think the situation indicates the market will do xxx; would you agree?'

In contrast, non-verbal behaviour connects the negotiators together by sending the message that each is ready to receive communication transmissions. As previously highlighted, three aspects of non-verbal behaviour are particularly relevant (Lewicki et al, 2003a):

- eye contact
- body position
- encouragement.

Eye contact generally transmits the message that the individual is ready to receive a communication, is listening and thinks that the message will be important. Whilst accepting there are cultural norms which may impact on this statement, and recognising it is possible to listen without looking, this is, nonetheless, an important cue to the other party to begin. This is not to say that staring is appropriate (especially in some cultural contexts). Another cue is sent when the negotiator looks away, while making a comment, apparently for an appropriate choice of words. Thus eye contact is important from both a sending and receiving message perspective.

Body position conveys the message of being attentive. Sitting up, to attention, holding the body erect and leaning slightly forwards or towards the other party conveys a willingness to engage with the other party. On the other hand, crossing arms, bowing the head, knitting the brow and frowning can convey the message of disapproval or rejection of the other party.

Non-verbal encouragement refers to body gestures and movements. Behaviours that communicate readiness include small sounds of acknowledgment ('uh-huh', 'mmm', and so on) and give encouragement to the other party to continue speaking. Similarly, nodding or shaking the head can, respectively, act as encouragement or stop the other party in their conversation.

12

These non-verbal behaviours have been suggested to account for up to 55 per cent of communication. Table 12.2 identifies a range of examples which express different attitudes:

Table 12.2 Examples of attitudes expressed by non-verbal behaviours

Attitude	Example of non-verbal behaviour
Boredom	Stifled yawns; heavy eyes; decreased eye contact.
Deception	Poker-faced expression; evasive eye contact; body turned away; changes in voice tone.
Defensiveness	Arms crossed; palms hidden; fists clenched.
Doubt	Hand over mouth; stroking chin (beard); scratching head.
Frustration	Clenching and unclenching fists; gripping table/desk; tight mouth.
Nervousness	Swallowing frequently; licking lips; clearing throat; perspiring; biting nails.
Willingness	Leaning forwards; open palms; arms uncrossed; nodding.

Self-assessment question 12.2

Why is communicating with a different culture often difficult?

Feedback on page 167

12.3 Communication difficulties

Where the previous sections have focused on effective communication, this section reviews what happens when communication difficulties arise. First, it is important to realise that the communication process is influenced by the way people perceive the messages that are sent and received. Herein lies the problem. It is a frequent occurrence for messages to be misinterpreted by close friends and colleagues, and this can only be exacerbated when the parties do not know each other particularly well such as in a negotiation situation. Specifically in negotiation, perceptual distortion is an important preparatory and bargaining consideration. Negotiation is a process of making sense of the discussion, with individuals attempting to interpret the situation.

Figure 12.2: The process of perception

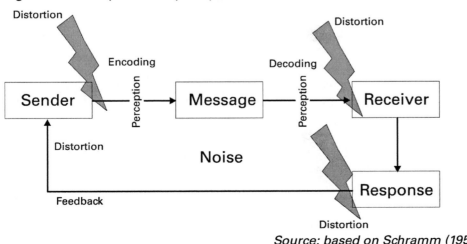

Source: based on Schramm (1955)

Figure 12.2 offers an overview of the perceptual process. It illustrates that messages are distorted when they are sent (encoded) and received (decoded), as well as when they are responded to by the receiver – a messy situation at best.

Perceptual distortion relates to the negotiators' predispositions, based on their needs, motivations and experiences. So-called 'perceptual errors' arise from stereotyping, halo effects, selective perception and projection:

- Stereotyping: in study session 1 typical characteristics of negotiators ('Rambo' and 'Mr Smith Goes to Washington') were presented as a broad generalisation about a negotiator's preferences. Once formed, stereotypes are hard to break away from.
- Halo effects; these occur when characteristics are ascribed to another person, based on the negotiator's experience of that person. Effects can be both positive or negative and can occur when the negotiator has little experience of the person. (For example: 'He just nodded so that must mean they agree.')
- Selective perception: this occurs when a single aspect of some information is identified that supports a preconceived idea, thereby reinforcing a particular view. (For example: 'She is frowning which must mean that our offer is completely unacceptable to them.')
- Projection: this occurs when negotiators assume their own view is that of the other person. The old maxim 'do as you would be done by' is an example of this in action.

Framing is another important aspect of communication. Framing is a subjective approach to making sense of situations (Lewicki et al, 2003b); frames are abstractions that individuals use to determine what something means. Types of frames relate to (Lewicki et al, 2003b):

- the views the parties hold of the substantive issues
- outcome preferences
- the parties' interests in the negotiation (their aspirations for the negotiation)
- the conflict management processes negotiators adopt
- the parties' view of the risks associated with losses and gains.

It is often the differences between the parties in their framing of the negotiation that lead to conflict. It is, therefore, important to be able to facilitate reframing in a negotiation, the first step of which is determining the underlying interests of the other party.

Reframing is about changing the other party's view (or indeed your own view) to a different perspective so that the desired outcome can be achieved, for example, by making it seem less risky. Negotiators also often have to reframe their messages based on the information that is exchanged during the negotiation process. Problems arise from the 'cognitive biases' that negotiators have about negotiating. Typical biases are:

- Irrational escalation of commitment: the negotiators stick to a specified set of actions, even when a better course of action is presented, usually because they feel they must save face.

- Mythical fixed pie; negotiator assumes the win-lose (zero-sum) situation when more integrative opportunities exist, usually because of personal interests and competitive desires.
- Anchoring and adjustments; these relate to the opening offer made, which often forms the standard (anchor) against which the outcome of the negotiation meeting is measured. Adjustments are made against the original offer. For example, the published commodity price of a product often serves as an anchor; adjustments are the concessions subsequently made.
- The winner's curse: this occurs when a settlement is reached quickly and negotiators asked questions such as: 'Could I have gained more by holding out longer?'
- Overconfidence: self-belief can lead to inappropriate or incorrect positions.
- Small samples: people tend to draw conclusions based on small sample sizes, which is often problematic.
- Self-serving bias: examples are sought that make the negotiator look good, rather than a realistic evaluation.
- Endowment effect: the value or worth of something is overestimated.
- Ignoring the other party's cognition: negotiators fail to ask the other party for their thoughts and opinions.
- Reactive devaluation: a response to a concession may be negatively charged simply because the other party made it!

Learning activity 12.3

How would you overcome difficulties presented by each of the different cognitive biases identified?

Feedback on page 168

Self-assessment question 12.3

Consider how trust is expressed and perceived in your organisational and cultural context. For example, trust can be based on performance (that is, reliance on and confidence in delivery of some product or service) or on common beliefs (for example, religious background, education or membership of a group).

Examine how perceptions of trust influence the communication process.

Feedback on page 168

Revision question

Now try the revision question for this session on page 267.

Summary

This study session has identified that communication is the means by which relationships with suppliers are developed over time. Different types of communication issue were identified for integrative and distributive situations, relating to negotiation behaviours. Three techniques were identified for improving communication.

It was identified that a typical negotiation meeting follows a pattern of exchange which includes establishing the climate, exchanging information, bargaining and concluding the deal. The time spent in each of these phases was identified to differ depending on the negotiation setting. Effective communication considers:

- the content, structure and style of messages
- the stages and phases of negotiation
- the different categories of communication
- the role of perception
- the extent of experience (personal and group).

Verbal and non-verbal communication techniques were reviewed. Verbal communication was identified to incorporate the logic and meaning of the message. Threats were said to incorporate five characteristics of language. A range of different question types were identified while other question types was identified as being less manageable. Three aspects of non-verbal behaviour were considered. These were discussed in the context of framing (and reframing) of negotiations.

Finally, difficulties in communication were identified to result from perceptual distortion, including stereotyping, halo effects, selective perception and projection. Cognitive biases that negotiators have about negotiating were also identified.

Suggested further reading

Lewicki et al (2003b) on framing and reframing, perception, cognition and communication in negotiation.

Steele et al (1989) on phases of negotiation.

Shapiro et al (2001) on probing in negotiations.

Reynolds (2003) on emotional intelligence, particularly developing self-awareness and interpersonal sensitivity.

Feedback on learning activities and self-assessment questions

Feedback on learning activity 12.1

Three key techniques can improve communication:

- Using questions: secure information on the other party's needs, interests and arguments. They can also be used to undermine the other party's

12

confidence and build power, so make sure that the questions asked are framed in the way you intended.

- Listening and reflecting: the former is passive (just being quiet), the latter is active, when the negotiator summarises what has been said. Acknowledgment is the middle of these two extremes (for example, listening noises such as 'mmmm' or 'uh-huh').
- Role reversal: actively putting yourself into the 'other party's shoes' encourages you to see the problem from their perspective and may help in reframing issues to be more attractive to them.

Feedback on self-assessment question 12.1

Your answer should state that effective communication achieves its intended aim by producing the desired response. This is likely to differ according to:

- the nature of the message – content, structure and style
- the stage and phase of negotiation
- the category of communication
- the perceptions of the receiver (and sender)
- the extent of experience of the sender and receiver of the message.

You may have also thought about:

- How the balance of power influences information exchange.
- How different relational stages may mean different content to messages, which may influence the communication process.
- The role of trust and risk.

Feedback on learning activity 12.2

Table 12.1

Integrative situation	Distributive situation
Establishing the climate 'Since we last met, xxx happened. How is that working out?' (*open-ended*)	Establishing the climate 'Shall we discuss xxx first?' (*directive, leading*)
Exchanging information 'Can you tell me your view of xxx?' (*open-ended, window, or treat*)	Exchanging information Immediate response to a comment: 'Why do you think that?' (*open-ended, window*)
Bargaining 'Was that of interest to you?' (*gauging*)	Bargaining 'Can you quote me your price if we include xxx?' (*planned, directive, cool*)
Concluding the deal 'Are there any other points we need to discuss?' (*open-ended*)	Concluding the deal 'Shall we summarise the deal we have agreed?' (*directive, leading*)

Feedback on self-assessment question 12.2

Your answer could consider the following points:

- The clarity of messages sent, and the way non-verbal behaviour can support verbal comments: there are many likely interpretations or misinterpretations of these messages, because of the differences in culture.

- The cultural biases that may exist: because of differences, one party may favour specific behaviour which differs from the approach taken by the other party.
- The use of colloquialisms (verbal) and habitual gestures (non-verbal): these may not be understood by individuals from different cultures.
- The range of experiences negotiators have of integrative and distributive settings, and the types of 'short-cuts' (decision heuristics) they use.
- Language barriers, including non-verbal behaviours.

Feedback on learning activity 12.3

- Irrational escalation: involve a facilitator who is unbiased and not involved in the situation.
- Mythical fixed pie: focus on value and benefits rather than interests and positions.
- Anchoring and adjustments: good preparation will guard against this.
- Winner's curse: do your preparation; seek independent verification of the settlement target; performance guarantees relating to the product or service also help to ensure the deal is good.
- Overconfidence: optimism is not necessarily a bad thing, but accuracy results from thorough preparation.
- Small samples: take care when generalising, especially from past experience as it is not always appropriate to use as the basis for future situations.
- Self-serving bias: a third party may be able to point out pros and cons of a particular situation.
- Endowment effect: prepare thoroughly; use a third party (expert) opinion.
- Ignoring the other party's cognition: ask them!
- Reactive devaluation: again, a third party may be able to provide some pointers for response.

Feedback on self-assessment question 12.3

Your answer could consider the following points:

- Perception is a sense-making process which enables negotiators to interpret (or misinterpret) their situation and respond to messages; so, where there is greater understanding between the parties, then perception of trust is likely to be high.
- Depending upon the familiarity with the situation, negotiators will use perception to relate to their prior experiences, as a short cut to producing an appropriate response. This is likely to mean that personal confidence in previous negotiation experiences will be important in conveying trust to the other party.
- Misperception can arise from stereotyping, halo effects, selective perception and projection. Thus if a negotiator perceives the other party to be untrustworthy, then this is likely to be conveyed in the communication process.

Study session 13
Understanding negotiation behaviour

Introduction

Building on the previous study session, this session looks at specific types of verbal negotiating behaviour and the personal traits and characteristics that lie behind these. Behavioural analysis has been used for many years by trainers as a tool for reviewing negotiation and patterns of negotiator exchange have been identified, including in a relational context. These are discussed in the first section. Patterns of conflict management are identified in the second section; and personality and negotiating styles are discussed in the third section.

> 'Silence is the worst response in some senses. Provided it is certain that the question was heard, it shows no sense of social duty or awareness of the nature of interaction... it will never be understood as meaning nothing at all.'
>
> **Joan Mulholland, on the nature, structure and rules of conversation (1991: 51)**

Session learning objectives

After completing this session you should be able to:

13.1 Define what is meant by negotiation behaviour.
13.2 Describe the nature of conflict in negotiations and explore techniques for managing conflict.
13.3 Compare and contrast different negotiation behavioural styles.

Unit content coverage

This study session covers the following topics from the official CIPS unit content document:

Statement of practice

Understand how to analyse negotiation performance.

Learning objectives

4.1 Evaluate the relative importance of verbal and non-verbal communications in negotiation situations.
- Reducing the potential for conflict
- Sales influencing tools
- The other person's perspective
- Body language
- Behavioural technologies

Timing

You should set aside about 4 hours to read and complete this session, including learning activities, self-assessment questions, the suggested further reading (if any) and the revision question.

13.1 Negotiation behaviours

Where the previous study session reviewed different types of information contained within communication messages in relation to the negotiation

13

phases, this study session reviews the types of verbal behaviour that negotiators exhibit during negotiations. This extends the discussion of those aspects relating to information content:

- offers and counteroffers
- information about alternatives
- information about outcomes
- social justifications
- information about processes.

Behavioural analytic techniques have existed since the 1950s (for example, Bales' Interaction Process Analysis). The approaches review negotiation and small group discussions and some have subsequently been adopted for negotiation skills training (for example, Huthwaite Research Group). These categories of behaviour represent all verbal communication that takes place in negotiations. Various studies into different categories of verbal behaviour have identified that some behaviours are associated with highly successful negotiators (for example, summarising, clarity testing and positive reacting, such as giving feelings), whereas others are considered to be less effective in negotiations (for example, attacking the other party or counter-proposing).

Table 13.1 provides brief examples of each of the behaviours (based on extensive review of negotiation behaviour literature). Suffice to say, it is important to understand the general category of behaviour and its use in the negotiation.

Table 13.1 Summary of negotiation behaviours

General category	Specific behaviour	Example
Scene setting behaviours	Seek situation/position –questions other party.	*'How do you view your situation?'; 'What's your view of the market at present?'*
	Situation/position – states view or opinion on an element of interest.	*'Competition in the telecommunications market is growing rapidly.'*
	'I need you' posture – promotes the other party's interests in reaching agreement.	*'No one else can supply us with this quality of product.'*
	'You need me' posture – demotes the other party's interests.	*'No one else can offer you this level of business for this product.'*
Specifying behaviours	Seek justification – used to identify reasons for stating values for issues.	*'Why do you want that?'; 'is that a problem for you?'*
	Justification – justifies an earlier statement.	*'If we are going to establish this as a potential major product line then...'; 'It's mainly due to the fact that...'*
	Seek implication – questions consequences and effects.	*'What effect does this have on your business?'*
	Problem/implied need	*'We have been losing a lot of money in this area.'*
	Seek need	*'Would it help you if...?'; 'How else might it help if...?'; 'Which of xxx and yyy is more important to you?'*
	Need	*'I need some process to keep scrap levels down.'; 'I must improve our security.'*

(continued on next page)

Table 13.1 (continued)

General category	Specific behaviour	Example
	Constraint	'We have a limited supply of 38,000 units from Japan.'; 'We do not employ on-site engineers.'
Social behaviours	Seek social	'How are your children getting on now?'
	Give social	'I recently joined a gym.'
	Interruption	Talking over someone else
Initiating behaviours	Proposing content (unspecific) about the main negotiable issues.	'We could look at an increase in volume.'; 'I can offer a reduction in payment terms.'
	Proposing content (specific)	'We could increase volume to 25,000 units.'; 'I can offer a reduction in payment terms to 20 days.'
	Counter proposals – made immediately after hearing a proposal such as those above.	
	Seek proposal	'How much do you want to pay?'; 'How many of these do you require?'
	Procedural proposal – about the conduct of the meeting.	'Tom, write the ideas on the flipchart.'; 'Can I suggest we now turn our attention to…?'
	Building – extending in a mutually beneficial way from a proposal.	'If we're going to do the distribution, why don't we take over the other distribution lines too.'; 'Let's invite supervisors to the product meeting as well, so we can save another day's fees.'
	Conditionality – proposal conditional upon another.	'If you do xxx, we can do yyy.'
Reacting behaviours	Seek reactions/feelings – asks for feedback on a previous statement.	'Was that of interest to you?'; 'How do you feel about…?'
	Supporting	'Yes, I go along with that'; 'Sounds OK to me.'
	Disagreeing	'That idea just won't work.'; 'I don't like that one bit.'
	Contrary statement	'[the competition will be in place in 12 months…] … our research suggests the competition will be in place in 6 months.'
	Personal feelings – on behalf of the individual negotiator.	'I feel disappointed.'; 'I am happy.'
	Corporate feelings – on behalf of the organisation.	'We [the company] feel.'; 'We are happy.'
	Defend/attack	'Your third point is rubbish'; Don't blame me, it's not my fault.'
	Gratuitous self-praise	'That was a good offer for you.'; 'You could easily incorporate that into your plans.'
	Retracting	'Sorry, we made a mistake with that.'; 'Unfortunately, we got that wrong.'
Clarifying behaviours	Confirming/agreeing	'[Are you saying that…]… That's correct.'; '[There has been little marketing on this brand because of its newness.]… Yes, that's the point.'
	Clarity test – clarifying issues	'Can I just check we're talking about the same thing here?', 'Can I take it we agree on this issue?'
	Incredulous test – expression of disbelief	'Are you sure we're talking about the same thing here?'; 'Do we really agree on this issue?'
	Rational test – seeks to rationalise an earlier point (tactic used to cast doubt)	'How do you reconcile that with your earlier statement?'; 'Can you explain how that equates with…?'

13

(continued on next page)

Table 13.1 *(continued)*

General category	Specific behaviour	Example
	Summarising	*'We have agreed (a) to take legal action, (b) to take it before May and (c) to issue a holding writ.'*

Source: derived from Harwood (2002)

Learning activity 13.1

Examine the behaviours in table 13.1 and identify which you think are likely to be more successful, respectively, in integrative and distributive negotiations. Justify your answers.

Feedback on page 178

In fact, patterns of these behaviours vary at different stages of relationship development (Harwood, 2002), as highlighted in table 13.3.

Table 13.3 Negotiation behaviours at different stages of relationship development

Early stage relationship	Mid stage relationship	Partner stage relationship
Small number of issues discussed	Greatest number of issues discussed	Wider exploration of issues discussed
Fewer procedures at the meeting observed		More procedures at the meeting observed
Some conditions	Greatest number of conditions	Few conditions
High scene setting	Less scene setting	High scene setting
Less justifying	More justifying	Some justifying
High supporting of the other party	Lowest supporting of the other party	Highest supporting of the other party

Self-assessment question 13.1

Briefly describe five different types of verbal behaviour.

Feedback on page 179

13.2 Conflict behaviour and styles

Conflict arises when the parties are focused on the same goal, such as price, where the supplier wants to achieve as high a price as possible, and the purchaser as low a price as possible. Often conflict has negative connotations, which are:

- Processes are competitive, which may lead to further escalation.
- Misperception and bias exist.
- Negotiators get emotional (irritated, angry and frustrated) as conflict escalates.
- Issues become blurred.

13

- Thinking becomes rigid.
- Differences are magnified.
- Conflict escalates.

As highlighted in section 9.3, however, there are certain benefits to conflict:

- Discussion leads to greater awareness of problems which may enhance problem solving.
- Conflict challenges current practice, potentially highlighting poor practice.
- Withstanding conflict tests and then builds relationships among colleagues.
- Promotes self-awareness and awareness of others.
- Enhances personal, including psychological, development, as ways are sought to overcome conflict style and preferences.
- Can be stimulating and fun; adds to the 'spice of life'.

What makes conflict more difficult to manage is the way the parties view the other party's outcome in relation to their own. For example, when the other party's outcome is considered as important as the purchaser's, then the approach to negotiation focuses on problem solving; where the outcome for both is unimportant, then there may be little point in negotiating at all! Five styles of conflict management have been identified (Lewicki et al, 2003b):

- Integrating (problem solving or collaborating): both parties' outcomes are important. Used when issues are complex; brainstorming leads to better solutions; commitment from both is important; one party cannot solve the problem alone.
- Obliging (accommodating or yielding): when it has been identified that it is important for the other party to achieve their outcome, but less so for the organisation. It is typically used when: the organisation is wrong, or is weak; future relationship is important; issue is more important to the other party.
- Dominating (competing or contending): parties pursue their own self-interests and adopt a style which incorporates threats and intimidation. The approach is typically used where: the issue is not important to them, but is to you; it could be costly to you; it may be necessary to overcome particular behaviour of the other party; a speedy decision is needed.
- Avoiding (inaction): used when issue is trivial; when negative interaction is likely to be the result.
- Compromising: half-hearted attempt at problem solving. Used when: goals are mutually exclusive; temporary solution is needed; integrating or dominating styles have not been successful.

13

Learning activity 13.2

Read the scenario below. Recommend a style of conflict management that may be appropriate for the purchaser.

Xenon Supplies Limited and Yorktel (the purchaser) have a relatively short trading history. Recently, Yorktel have identified that a part of the delivery from Xenon is not being made on time, although it is not causing any

(continued on next page)

Learning activity 13.2 *(continued)*

problems in Yorktel's production processes at the moment. Nonetheless, it needs to be put right, and quickly. There are no clear indications of why there is a delay, and the supplier is being evasive.

Feedback on page 179

A further conflict management option is the involvement of facilitators. Figure 13.1 presents an overview of available approaches:

Figure 13.1: Resolving conflict through facilitators

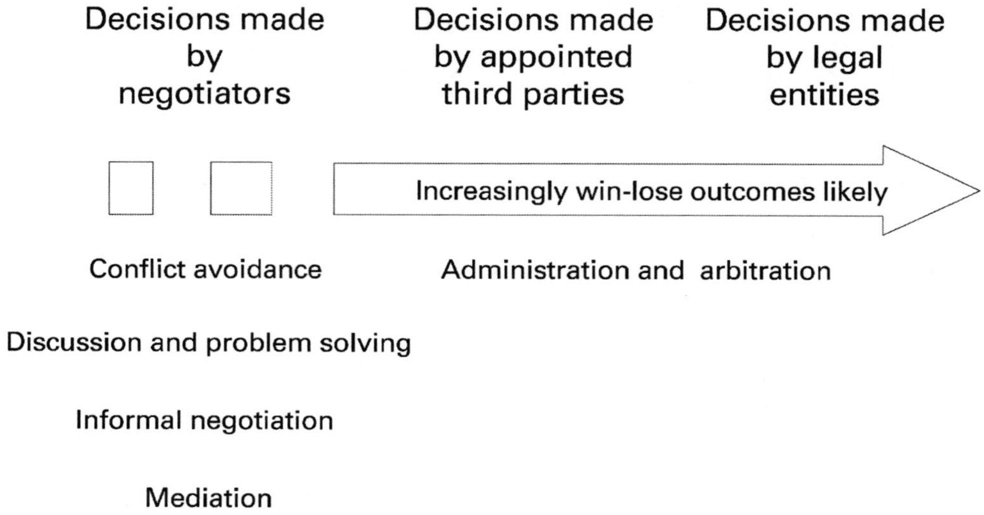

Decisions made by negotiators

Decisions made by appointed third parties

Decisions made by legal entities

Increasingly win-lose outcomes likely

Conflict avoidance

Administration and arbitration

Discussion and problem solving

Informal negotiation

Mediation

Source: based on Moore (1996) in Lewicki et al (2003a)

When the other party is being 'difficult', then one approach is worth mentioning in particular: Ury's (1991) 'breakthrough approach', reviewed in Lewicki et al, (2003b). This five-step technique aims to help both parties regain control (usually of their composure) in the negotiation. Steps are:

1 Do not react but mentally distance yourself from the discomforting tactics being employed.
2 Disarm the other party by listening carefully, acknowledging the points being made and providing them with your views – a positive response to their negative behaviour.
3 Reframe the negotiation by asking open-ended and problem-solving questions, again do not respond to their negative behaviour but be open and direct.
4 Give them a 'yes-able' offer by involving them in the solution building process and being aware of their implicit needs.
5 Make saying 'no' problematic for them by letting them know you have a good BATNA. Allow them to explore the consequences of it, and focus on the advantages of a deal with you. Incorporate plans for implementation in the agreement.

Self-assessment question 13.2

Identify three ways to manage conflict.

Feedback on page 179

13.3 Behavioural styles

Another aspect of behaviour relates to the negotiator's personal characteristics, traits, attitudes, habits, beliefs and values. These equate to the negotiator's concept of self, otherwise known as personality. It is believed that personality influences negotiation behaviour as well as impacts on the ways people perceive, and distort, messages.

This is important to understand because of the nature of reciprocation in negotiation. It is, for example, generally accepted that a closer match between individuals results in longer-lasting relationships. In the words of Pullins et al (2000): 'cuddly people are better!' Reciprocity of behaviour results in development of trust, risk-taking, balance of power, fairness and flexibility. These are influenced by, and in turn influence, the nature of the negotiation and the stylistic approaches of the individuals engaged in the process.

Thus an understanding of the personality of the other individuals can result in negotiating behaviours being flexibly employed. This is the basis of many negotiation skills training courses. Personality traits are, not surprisingly, difficult to modify because of their embeddedness within individuals. Various traits are recognised table 13.4.

Table 13.4 Personality traits

	Strengths	Weaknesses
Thinker: precision- and detail-oriented	Good communicator, deliberate in approach, prudent, evaluative, objective, rational, analytical, seeks information.	Indecisive, cautious, serious, rigid, controlling.
Intuitor: innovative	Imaginative, creative, intellectual, ideological, conceptual, involved.	Unrealistic, devious, out-of-touch, dogmatic, impractical, poor listener.
Feeler: sensitive to others, emotional, reads people well	Persuasive, empathetic, introspective, emotive, traditional values.	Impulsive, manipulative, sentimental, subjective.
Senser: action-oriented, decisive, high energy	Pragmatic, assertive, objective, direct.	Impatient, status-seeking, lacking trust in others, unable to delegate.

Source: adapted from Futrell (2002), originally based on Jung

Two often cited values of negotiators are logic and emotion. Logic relates to rationality. The discussion in section 9.4 on game theory, highlighted that in business negotiators rarely act completely rationally because of personal emotive preferences, such as a need to act with fairness, or a desire to deliberately mislead the other party, or simply that they have identified different goals, such as long-term versus short-term perspectives (Herbig, 1991).

Emotion has been identified as having both a positive and negative effect on negotiations. Positive emotions can improve the decision-making process; create positive feelings towards the other party; and encourage persistence in negotiation. On the other hand, negative emotions can lead to

13

a competitive situation; result in an escalation of conflict; and create a desire for retaliation.

As a strategic behaviour, emotion can be used to manipulate the other party, as highlighted in a number of the previous study sessions. The ability to regulate emotions has also been identified as a strategic behaviour. This will be reviewed further in study session 15.

There is also a range of other behaviour models which use different patterns of behaviour. For example, Shapiro et al (2001) identify negotiation preferences for extroverts, pragmatists, analysts and amiables (see table 13.5 which incorporates elements of emotion and logic.

Table 13.5 Negotiator styles

Type	Description	Dealing with the behaviour
Extrovert	Outgoing, impulsive, energetic, likes to tell stories.	Do not use attacking behaviour or sarcasm; listen and allow them to talk – they seek attention.
Pragmatist	Takes charge, focused, business-like, neat and tidy, competitive.	Do not give in easily; stand your ground; let them think you've lost.
Analyst	Logical, cautious, process driven, unemotional.	Slow to their pace; act predictably; use past successes to support your ideas; use their principles as the basis for agreement.
Amiable	Casual, open, conforming, reserved, tentative, good listener, wants to be liked.	Focus on people issues; avoid impatience; build the relationship; don't rush them.

Source: based on Shapiro et al (2001)

Learning activity 13.3

Which personality trait or negotiator style describes your preferred approach to negotiating? Examine why this is the case.

Feedback on page 179

The discussion on behaviour now turns to fairness. Albin (1993) identifies four aspects which are important in negotiation:

- Structural fairness: the make-up of the negotiation situation. For example: are all the parties affected by the outcome present and/or fully represented? Are the links between issues accurate or adequate? Are the rules and codes of conduct equally favourable? Are the physical arrangements suitable for all (accessibility of location and communications)?
- Process fairness: how the parties relate to each other in the negotiation process. How does fair treatment affect the procedures they use to reach agreement? How is that agreement is subsequently implemented?
- Procedural fairness: the specific mechanisms of reaching agreement, for example, reciprocity (tit for tat).

- Outcome fairness: post-negotiation evaluation of the agreement reached.

Recognising that these elements are not mutually exclusive, it would appear fairness is integral to the negotiation process. Furthermore, fairness is indefinably linked with trust, particularly if information exchanged during a negotiation is accepted as truthful and the parties act honourably towards each other before, during and after the event (Peters and Fletcher, 1995).

Self-assessment question 13.3

What are the pros and cons of each of the negotiation behavioural styles? How do logic and emotion relate to these styles?

Feedback on page 180

Revision question

Now try the revision question for this session on page 268.

Summary

This study session has reviewed verbal negotiating behaviour. Six broad categories were defined, and the way they may be used in integrative and distributive negotiation settings was discussed:

- scene setting behaviours
- specifying behaviours
- social behaviours
- initiating behaviours
- reacting behaviours
- clarifying behaviours.

Different patterns of behaviour were identified at different stages of relationship development.

The nature of conflict was discussed and negative connotations reviewed. Five styles of conflict management were identified. The breakthrough approach was discussed in relation to overcoming conflict and a five-step technique reviewed.

Discussion on personality identified a number of character traits. The roles of logic and emotion within these traits were also discussed. Logic was identified as being influenced by fairness, deceit and the goal preferences of the parties. Emotion was identified as having both a positive and negative impact on negotiation. Finally, a review of fairness as a behavioural trait identified differences relating to the structure, process, procedure and outcome of negotiations.

13

Suggested further reading

Lewicki et al (2003b) on negotiating with difficult people, negotiating behaviours and mood and emotion.

Reynolds (2003) on emotional intelligence, particularly developing self-awareness and interpersonal sensitivity.

Shapiro et al (2001) on negotiating with difficult people, and different negotiation behavioural preferences.

Steele et al (1989). See section called 'eyeball to eyeball', where authors review personal dimensions to negotiation ('cold and warm' styles) and business dimensions ('hard to get' and 'easy to get' deals).

Feedback on learning activities and self-assessment questions

Feedback on learning activity 13.1

See table 13.2 for feedback.

Table 13.2

General behaviour category	Integrative approach	Distributive approach
Scene setting behaviours	Helps to establish a climate of openness when used to generate information for integrative use, problem solving, and developing understanding on underlying interests	Can be used to establish or confirm power ('you need me'); or to generate information for later use distributively.
Specifying behaviours	Can be used to develop further detail on interests and positions ('why xxx?'); also to identify difficulties and problems as part of problem solving and information exchange.	Can be used tactically by negotiators to buy time (by asking questions to get the other party talking) before moving to the bargaining phase.
Social behaviours	Can be used to develop the relationship between the individuals in the negotiation.	The same as for integrative situations.
Initiating behaviours	Procedural proposals are used more than other bargaining behaviours because there is greater openness about the process of the negotiation itself.	Bargaining behaviours are used extensively in distributive situations; counter proposals indicate that you have not listened to the other party's offer before making one of your own.
Reacting behaviours	These are characteristic of openness at both personal and corporate levels. Questioning behaviour is used to generate better understanding of the other party's response; supporting behaviour is used to draw the other party into further disclosure.	Can be used tactically to communicate dissatisfaction with a comment or offer. Tactical supporting can be used to generate information for subsequent use. Defend/attack is aggressive adversarial behaviour; self-praise can be extremely irritating to the other party!
Clarifying behaviours	Used to test understanding of discussion – even if one party summarises, then there is greater clarity between the negotiators. This may have the effect of	Testing (incredulous, rational) can both be used tactically to cast doubt on the other party's comments.

(continued on next page)

Table 13.2 *(continued)*

General behaviour category	Integrative approach	Distributive approach
	conferring power on to the other party. Testing is also a behaviour that is used to communicate active listening.	

Feedback on self-assessment question 13.1

List any from the behaviour categories (or the specific behaviours themselves):

- scene setting behaviours
- specifying behaviours
- social behaviours
- initiating behaviours
- reacting behaviours
- clarifying behaviours.

Feedback on learning activity 13.2

Recommended approach is dominating because it appears that the issue is relatively trivial and yet it could become problematic. The supplier also appears to be being difficult. A further approach could take into account the relational aspects, although it is not well developed as yet. Thus a secondary approach could be compromising.

Feedback on self-assessment question 13.2

Your answer could include any three of the following:

- integrating (problem solving or collaborating)
- obliging (accommodating or yielding)
- dominating (competing or contending)
- avoiding (inaction)
- compromising.

Feedback on learning activity 13.3

You may favour one or more of the behavioural styles discussed (thinker, intuitor, feeler, senser; extrovert, pragmatist, analyst, amiable) because of your role in the organisation, your previous negotiating experiences or your career path and broader educational experiences. Some people are considered to be natural communicators and others need to work a bit harder to achieve the same impact.

It is well known, however, that successful negotiators are able to adapt their approach and styles to different circumstances and, therefore, where you identify a preference for mainly one behaviour, you may want to consider how you can develop your competence in other approaches (by looking for opportunities to practice, for example).

13

There are also a number of personality trait modeling tools that exist (for example, Myers-Briggs) which you can use to develop understanding of your behavioural preferences, although these are outside the scope of this study session.

Feedback on self-assessment question 13.3

Refer to table 13.4. Varying degrees of both logic and emotion exist in all the behavioural styles identified! Emotion can sometimes be used as a tactic to coerce the other party into conceding, whereas logic will appeal to those who are more analytic in their approach. Shapiro et al, for example, identify that where emotion is used tactically, it is important to identify the specifics of the emotional content (such as anger or insult) and then deflect it by finding out why or by focusing on key issues. Previous discussion has also identified that emotion can also be used to positively reinforce the situation – as a means of responding to the other party (supporting, corporate or personal feelings).

Characteristics of successful negotiators

Introduction

This study session extends the discussion on negotiator behaviour beyond the examination of verbal behaviours to discuss what makes some negotiators better than others. First, the characteristics of successful negotiators are reviewed; then the discussion examines how competences can be developed. Finally, the role of teams in negotiations is discussed.

Session learning objectives

After completing this session you should be able to:

14.1 Describe the characteristics of successful negotiators.
14.2 Identify how negotiation competences can be developed.
14.3 Explore the role of teams in negotiations.

Unit content coverage

This study session covers the following topics from the official CIPS unit content document:

Statement of practice

- Explain the different approaches required when negotiating in different settings.
- Understand how to analyse negotiation performance.

Learning objectives

4.2 Identify and explain how to apply the attributes of a good negotiator to effective negotiations.
- Interpersonal sensitivity
- Characteristics of a skilled negotiator
- The emotionally intelligent negotiator
- How to improve negotiation capabilities

Timing

You should set aside about 5 hours to read and complete this session, including learning activities, self-assessment questions, the suggested further reading (if any) and the revision question.

14.1 Characteristics of successful negotiators

Notwithstanding the differences in skills and competences that reflect professional expertise in industries, successful negotiators exhibit a range of

'You can make a decision because you are told to or are pressured to by others or by public opinion. You can make decisions in a routine fashion according to some signal. You can make decisions based not on the facts of the matter but on your sense of style.'

Edward de Bono, commenting on the values people hold and the choices they make (2005)

14

skills that enhance their effectiveness in negotiation. Research conducted by Raiffa (1982) highlights the important characteristics of negotiators (see table 14.1). This research was used as the basis for more recent research into how negotiators perceive the skills and competences of the other party (Harwood, 2002), which highlights some differences in rankings.

Table 14.1 Important characteristics of effective negotiators

Level of importance	Characteristics in rank order (Raiffa, 1982)		Characteristics in rank order (Harwood, 2002)	
Considered to be *very* important	1	preparation and planning skill	1	verbal expression
	2	subject knowledge of negotiation content	2	judgement and general intelligence
	3	clarity of thought under pressure	3	clarity of thought under pressure
	4	verbal expression	4	subject knowledge of negotiation content
	5	listening skills	5	open mindedness and tolerance
	6	judgement and general intelligence	6	integrity
	7	integrity	7	listening skills
	8	persuasiveness	8	attractive personality
	9	patience	9	respected by the other party
	10	decisiveness	10	negotiating experience
Considered to be important	11	respected by the other party	11	preparation and planning skill
	12	problem solving and analytic abilities	12	internal organisation and communication
	13	self-control	13	trusting temperament
	14	emotional intelligence	14	self-control
	15	persistence and determination	15	persistence and determination
	16	ability to exploit power to achieve objective	16	ability to exploit power to achieve objective
	17	understanding of the other party's needs and interests	17	patience
	18	leadership (own team)	18	decisiveness
	19	negotiating experience	19	problem solving and analytic abilities
	20	personal confidence	20	debating skill
	21	open-mindedness and tolerance	21	personal confidence
	22	competitiveness	22	competitiveness
	23	internal organisation communication	23	understanding of the other party's needs and interests
	24	debating skill	24	persuasiveness
	25	willingness to risk being disliked	25	compromising temperament
	26	ability to take on different negotiating roles	26	rank within the organisation
Considered to be *unimportant*	27	rank within the organisation	27	emotional intelligence
	28	tolerant of uncertainty	28	ability to take on different negotiating roles
	29	non-verbal behaviour	29	non-verbal behaviour
	30	compromising temperament	30	tolerant of uncertainty
	31	attractive personality	31	willingness to risk being disliked
	32	trusting temperament	32	willingness to take high business risks
	33	willingness to take high business risks	33	leadership (own team)
	34	willingness to employ force	34	willingness to employ force

It is interesting to see in the later research how the ranking of behaviours reveals the nature of collaboration in modern supplier-purchaser contexts: the top 10 behaviours relate to mutual respect in personal interactions (such as, attractiveness of individuals, ability to tolerate one another, listening skill, integrity, judgement and expertise – see table 14.1). This is also reflected in

14

the elevated role of trust in the later research and the need for competence in engaging with internal colleagues.

Learning activity 14.1

From your own experience, identify the characteristics you exhibit which are considered to be highly important.

Feedback on page 190

Research by Rackham (1978) compared successful negotiators with less successful counterparts. Although based on labour negotiators, this research is considered to have much credibility in a business context. He identified characteristics at the pre-negotiation, the negotiation meeting and post-negotiation review stages (summarised in table 14.2).

Table 14.2 Rackham: characteristics of successful negotiators

Pre-negotiation stage	• Evaluated more outcome options for the issues to be discussed. • Spent longer looking for common ground. • Considered the longer-term consequences. • Used ranges for issues. • Did not plan to negotiate issues sequentially.
Negotiation meeting	• Did not offer immediate counter proposals. • Did not overstate the benefits of their terms. • Did not verbally attack the other party. • Asked more questions, especially to test understanding of the other party's points. • Summarised frequently in order to enhance clarity. • Did not undermine their position through weak justifying behaviours.
Post-negotiation stage	• Reviewed the negotiation to identify what they had learned from it.

Source: Adapted from Rackham (1978a and b) and Lewicki et al (2003b)

14

Success has also been linked to personality traits, as briefly outlined in study session 13. The following factors associated with personalities have been identified:

- extroversion
- agreeableness
- conscientiousness
- emotional stability
- openness.

Of these, the first two, extroversion and agreeableness, have been found to achieve less successful outcomes because the negotiators tend to focus on their own positions – quite simply, they just keep talking! High levels of motivation have, however, been found to diminish this effect (Barry and Friedman, 1998). Where negotiations are complex, such as in an advanced stage relationship, then success has been attributed more to general intelligence than personality traits (Lewicki et al, 2003a).

Gender differences have also been found to influence outcomes. Tactical ploys may have different effects when used by men and women; they may be perceived differently and used differently. Kolb and Coolidge (1991) identified four ways that women and men approach negotiation differently:

- Relational view of the other party: women tend have a broader view of the relational context, relate to perceptions of individuals involved in the negotiation, express emotions and feelings. Men are more task-oriented and pragmatic.
- The role of negotiation: women view negotiation as part of a relationship with another party. Men see negotiation as a separate behaviour.
- Control: empowerment is used by women so that all parties build their power base. Men use power to achieve their own goals.
- Problem-solving dialogue: women seek clarity through interaction with others. Men use dialogue to convince the other party, and use tactical ploys accordingly.

It is worth commenting, however, that stereotyping by gender should be avoided; it is inappropriate to generalise for all men or all women.

Self-assessment question 14.1

Reflecting on the personality traits identified in table 13.4, consider which of the characteristics of successful negotiators from table 14.2 are likely to be associated with each type of person:

- Thinker: precision- and detail-oriented
- Intuitor: innovative person
- Feeler: sensitive to others, emotional, reads people well
- Senser: action-oriented, decisive, high energy.

Feedback on page 190

14.2 Developing negotiation competences

It is suggested that to be successful, negotiators require three primary competences (see also table 14.1):

1 cognitive ability
2 emotional intelligence
3 perspective-taking ability.

Cognitive ability relates to the ability to reason, make decisions, process information, learn and adapt to change in the face of new information or dynamic circumstances. Negotiation often requires complex problem solving and, therefore, negotiators with greater mental capability will achieve more successful negotiation outcomes. This is because negotiators are able to move the other party towards an outcome that favours both parties by getting them to recognise the joint gains.

Emotional intelligence involves perception, comprehension and regulation of emotion (Lewicki et al, 2003a). This capability is important because it provides negotiators with subtle insights into the other party's thinking processes and, therefore, provides opportunities for extracting information and solving problems. Reynolds (2003) suggests those negotiators who have emotional intelligence are self-aware, emotionally resilient, motivated, sensitive to others, intuitive and have integrity and influencing abilities. These enable the negotiator to move the negotiation forward and develop commitment from the other party.

Perspective-taking ability relates to how negotiators make sense of and respond to the other party's argument, that is, the other party's viewpoint. Previous study sessions have highlighted the importance of considering the other's perspectives in order to prepare for negotiation. Ability to consider the other party in this way has been found to lead to higher achievement levels for both parties in negotiation (Lewicki et al, 2003a).

Learning activity 14.2

Consider a recent negotiation and examine how personal competences impacted on the processes and outcome.

Feedback on page 191

As stated in previous study sessions, negotiation experience can have a direct influence on the success of negotiations. Experience enables negotiators to use short cuts to frame and reframe negotiation. This helps to focus attention on issues that are identified as being important, enabling the parties to use tactics with a degree of predictability (although a danger has been highlighted that not all situations can be extrapolated from past experience). This is particularly relevant where negotiators who have generated experience in distributive settings begin work in a new relational context.

Experience draws on the ability to learn – and unlearn and relearn! Learning is the process of acquiring knowledge which has the potential to change behaviour (Huczynski and Buchanan, 2001). These changes in behaviour constitute a 'learning curve' which relates to:

- perceptual abilities
- reflective abilities
- information processing abilities
- personal motivations.

Kolb (1984) identified a 'learning cycle' which illustrates how learning takes place based on previous experience (see figure 14.1).

14

Figure 14.1: Learning cycle

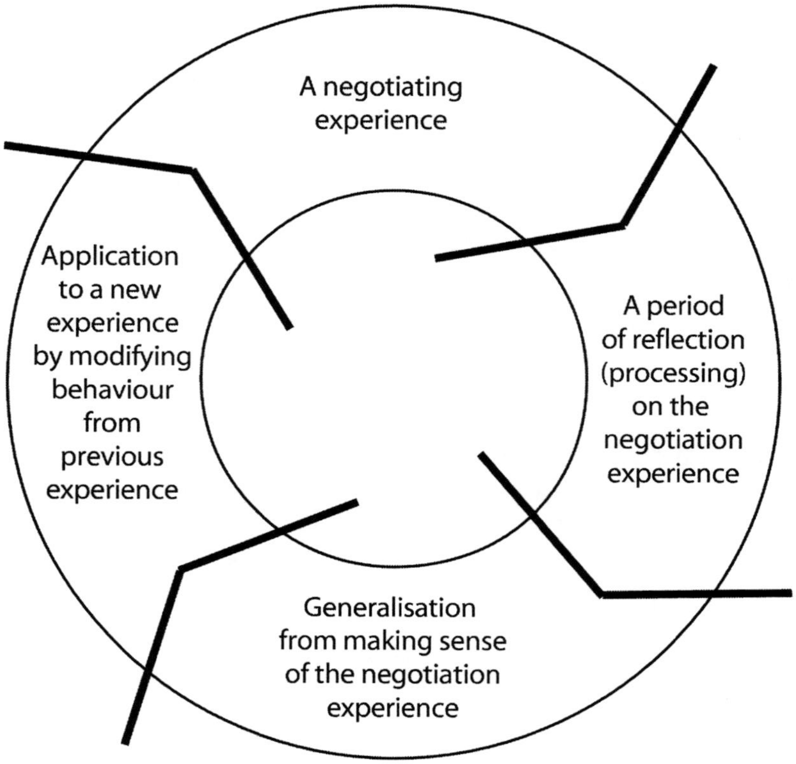

Source: adapted from Kolb (1984)

The model identifies that the learning process is based upon a real-life negotiation experience (rather than a practice negotiation or a simulation) which is followed by a period of reflection. Subsequently, the process of reflection leads to some broad generalisations about the experience; for example, open behaviour leads to reciprocation from the supplier, or a personal attack leads to retaliation. The application stage of the cycle is the point at which negotiators take their cumulative experiences and apply them to a new situation. Experience is built up over time by continuous learning.

Research also suggests that people have only so much capacity for knowledge, which requires them to unlearn and relearn. Poell et al (2000) suggest that a learning 'elite' is created, with individuals divided into those who continually engage with learning and those who are less enthusiastic. Thus successful negotiators will be those who are continually reflecting on their experiences and applying their knowledge to new situations.

Self-assessment question 14.2

Compare and contrast the personal competences associated with successful negotiators.

Feedback on page 191

14.3 Negotiation teams

Negotiation teams are more likely to achieve collaborative outcomes than individual negotiators – even when only one side negotiates as a team

(Thompson et al, 1996). This is because there is a much higher level of information exchange which leads to greater clarity between the two parties. Teams may also, however, be more competitive than individuals in their ability to achieve a favourable distributive outcome. This is due to the parties' perceptions of power, especially where one side is made up of a single negotiator.

Not surprisingly, another important aspect when considering the use of teams is the impact on negotiating processes. For example, where teams are made up of individuals who are familiar with one another, if not friends, then there is obviously much greater cohesion among the members. In turn, this enhances the prospects of a successful outcome because the individuals are more focused on the outcome, rather than in developing a relationship with each other. Conversely, friendship between members can be detrimental to the outcome (Lewicki et al, 2003a) because it may interfere with the ability of the team to pursue an optimal outcome for fear of spoiling a relationship.

Important considerations for negotiating teams are:

- What happens if there is no agreement because of the increased complexities associated with a team approach?
- How will decisions be made? What decision rules will be used?
- Is a chair or facilitator required to oversee the negotiation? Should this be a neutral third party, or an individual from one of the parties?

These questions provide clarity for the negotiation which is likely to result in a better outcome because of the parties' perceptions of fairness in the process adopted.

Of course, there is a difference between an individual in a team and the roles within the team. For example, an individual negotiator may perceive him- or herself to be more important than the collective team, in which case, it is argued that a team cannot perform effectively. Teams are effective when members take on the values of the team as their own. This can be particularly difficult in distributive negotiation settings, where the outcome is transactional (one-off) and the resource given to a team approach limited. Nonetheless, effective teams can be formed over time and deployed in appropriate situations. Huczynski and Buchanan (2001) summarise the factors that contribute to team cohesion:

- Small size: enhances group success.
- Threat external to the group: develops team member satisfaction.
- Stable membership: improves 'productivity'.
- History of success: encourages conformity.
- Exclusiveness: teams develop their own, exclusive and distorted 'language' which members accept and learn to speak.
- Sharing common goals: increases cooperation among members.
- Interactivity: opportunities lead to greater interactivity.
- Status: individuals agree their status within the group, which enhances power over members.
- Attractiveness of the group.
- Rewards, when perceived as being fair.

14

Benefits of teams are that they:

- Identify and solve problems more effectively.
- Increase product quality, that is, the negotiation outcome.
- Enhance performance.
- Achieve better relationships.
- Increase participation within the buying and selling organisations.

Raiffa (2002) argues that individuals may contribute to negotiation teams because they add to the decision-making process or may usefully support the agreement reached. Team structures operate along a number of dimensions that confer identity on the group, providing order and reducing ambiguity. These have been identified (Huczynski and Buchanan, 2001) as:

- Power: relating to the power balance between members, the control of the team (group) and the relationships between individuals within it. Power is often considered to be exerted by the team leader through the ability to reward individuals, influence them to undertake tasks and reinforce behaviour by presenting a role model.
- Status: relating to leadership, where power is exerted through expertise and authority.
- Liking: the feelings individuals have for one another in the team.
- Communication: the way information is exchanged between members.
- Role: the expectations members have of their position within the team.
- Leadership: who leads, how they are appointed and how individuals relate to the leader within the team.

Of special interest for negotiation is the role individuals assume within negotiating teams. A team role relates to the preferences of an individual to behave in a particular way, which is often associated with their function within an organisation (for example, a purchaser, a financial advisor, a production worker, and so on). Two key functions within a negotiating team have already been identified: the leader and the facilitator or chair. Clearly, the leader takes control of the team in all phases of negotiation; the facilitator or chair acts out the role within negotiation meeting. Other functions in the negotiation meeting may include:

- a summariser, whose function it is to restate the discussion in order to enhance clarity for the two parties
- experts and specialists, who may be asked to contribute with their particular knowledge on a substantive issue
- an observer, who sits outside the negotiation and acts as an 'informant' in order to draw out the lessons from the negotiation.

Learning activity 14.3

When you negotiate as part of a purchasing team, what function do you typically perform: leader, chair, summariser, expert/specialist, observer? Examine why this is the case, and how you could take on any of other functions identified in the discussion.

Feedback on page 191

14

Lewicki et al (2003a) advise that team negotiations should be managed at the pre-negotiation and negotiation meeting phases. At the pre-negotiation phase, decisions need to be made on the following:

- Who will negotiate – the participants.
- Whether there are any coalitions between the participants (within or between teams) that may influence the achievement of an outcome.
- The roles individuals within the team will take.
- The consequences of no agreement for the individuals.
- How the final decision will be made, and who will make it.
- How the agenda will be constructed, based on the contributions of one, some or all of the team.

At the negotiation meeting phase, management should comprise:

- Appointment of a chair to act as facilitator to the negotiation.
- Restructuring of the agenda based on both parties' input.
- Providing a wide range of information and perspective from the parties, and ensuring that information is adequately used.
- Ensuring the decision rules are discussed and managed between the two parties.
- Agreeing an outcome, including implementation of the deal.

Self-assessment question 14.3

Define and briefly describe the functions of the five different team roles.

Feedback on page 192

Revision question

Now try the revision question for this session on page 268.

14

Summary

This study session has reviewed those characteristics that make some negotiators better than others. A list of characteristics identified a top ten which includes verbal expression, general intelligence, listening skills, integrity, clarity of thought under pressure, subject expertise, respect, experience and open-mindedness. These were identified as being relevant particularly to integrative situations. Other research was discussed that identified particular behavioural aspects at the pre-negotiation, negotiation meeting and post-negotiation review phases. Personality traits and gender differences were also reviewed.

Cognitive and perspective-taking abilities and emotional intelligence were also discussed in the context of developing negotiation competences. It was identified that the post-negotiation review phase is particularly important in the learning cycle as it provides the opportunity to reflect upon experience, which subsequently informs future negotiations.

Finally, negotiation teams were reviewed. It was identified that it is important to clarify the processes by which team decisions will be made in negotiations. Factors that influence the success of teams were discussed in relation to the cohesion of members. Functions of negotiation team members were identified and reviewed.

Suggested further reading

Lewicki et al (2003b) on individual characteristics of negotiators and team approaches to negotiation.

Reynolds (2003) on emotional competency in negotiation – a short checklist.

Feedback on learning activities and self-assessment questions

Feedback on learning activity 14.1

Are the characteristics you identified similar to those in table 14.1? How do you compare to the rankings, including in the newer research?

You may want to reflect further on whether the behaviours to be better for collaborative or distributive situations.

Feedback on self-assessment question 14.1

See table 14.3 for answer.

Table 14.3

Thinker	Good communicator, deliberate in approach, prudent, evaluative, objective, rational, analytical, seeks information.

- Evaluated more outcome options for the issues to be discussed.
- Spent longer looking for common ground.
- Considered the longer-term consequences.
- Used ranges for issues.
- Asked more questions, especially to test understanding of the other party's points.
- Summarised frequently in order to enhance clarity.
- Did not undermine their position through weak justifying behaviours.
- Reviewed the negotiation to identify what they had learned from it.

Intuitor	Imaginative, creative, intellectual, ideological, conceptual, involved.

- Evaluated more outcome options for the issues to be discussed.
- Did not plan to negotiate issues sequentially.
- Did not overstate the benefits of their terms.
- Reviewed the negotiation to identify what they had learned from it.

(continued on next page)

Table 14.3 *(continued)*

Feeler	Persuasive, empathetic, introspective, emotive, traditional values.

- Did not plan to negotiate issues sequentially.
- Did not verbally attack the other party.

Senser	Pragmatic, assertive, objective, direct.

- Evaluated more outcome options for the issues to be discussed.
- Considered the longer-term consequences.
- Used ranges for issues.
- Reviewed the negotiation to identify what they had learned from it.

Feedback on learning activity 14.2

You should have considered the role of any of the three competences identified: cognitive ability, emotional intelligence and perspective-taking ability. You may also have examined how you gained experience in negotiating which enabled you to develop your skills and competences in particular areas (see table 14.1). If this is the case, then you should examine your abilities in relation to each of the stages of negotiation identified (preparation through to implementation phases).

Feedback on self-assessment question 14.2

Answers should examine each of the three competences:

1 cognitive ability
2 emotional intelligence
3 perspective-taking ability.

Feedback on learning activity 14.3

Most negotiators have a preferred function within a team negotiation:

- leader, facilitator/chair;
- summariser;
- expert/specialist; observer.

Some may take on more than one function (or, if acting as an individual negotiator, will take on all the functions identified).

The reasons for preferred functions include:

- There is an existing strong leader, such as a manager or individual with considerable knowledge of the situation who assumes the leadership for the particular situation.
- Your experience limits you to a particular function, such as an expert or specialist; or your knowledge is highly relevant to the current situation, making you a leader.
- Team members have negotiated together before and have developed expertise in the functions they assumed previously.
- Team members are looking to develop their negotiating competences by assuming different functions, perhaps by acting as 'critical friends' to one another.

14

Feedback on self-assessment question 14.3

- Leader: manages the team, leads the preparation.
- Facilitator/chair: may be a neutral person from one of the organisations, or a third party.
- Summariser: supports the leader by reviewing the current situation in a negotiation meeting. This role also functions to provide a break, which can be used to relieve tension or refocus the discussion.
- Expert/specialist: is used for narrow areas of focus in a negotiation to discuss technicalities.
- Observer: is a non-participant but contributes especially at the post-negotiation review phase.

Developing questioning skills

Introduction

Asking questions is a fundamental human behaviour – and asking the right questions at the right time constitutes effective negotiation skills! The previous study sessions have identified the communication process and the different types of negotiating behaviour. Specific types of questions have also been reviewed.

This study session builds on this by further explaining how questions can be linked together in order to achieve the goal. First, the role of effective questioning in negotiation is reviewed. Discussion then follows on how to develop a trusting environment. Finally, there is discussion of the way negotiators may prepare to respond to questions from the other party.

'Effective questioning is essential to you as a manager or executive if you want to have your ideas accepted and implemented, just as it is the crucial tool of the salesperson.'

Tom Lambert, commenting on using questions to influence others (2003: 180)

Session learning objectives

After completing this session you should be able to:

15.1 Explain the role of effective questioning in negotiation.
15.2 Link questions together to develop an environment of trust.
15.3 Prepare for dealing with questioning from the other party.

Unit content coverage

This study session covers the following topics from the official CIPS unit content document:

Statement of practice

Apply a range of negotiation theories in order to achieve set outcomes.

Learning objectives

4.3 Evaluate the effect of effective listening and questioning skills in the negotiation process.
 • Different types of questions
 • Effective listening
 • Timing of questions

15

Timing

You should set aside about 5 hours to read and complete this session, including learning activities, self-assessment questions, the suggested further reading (if any) and the revision question.

15.1 Using questions

This study session builds on study session 12, particularly section 12.2, which listed the types of question that may be used. In other sessions goals have been identified for negotiation which require negotiators to uncover facts, distinguish positions and interests, and explore implicit and explicit needs. Study session 13 identified a broad range of verbal behaviours that negotiators use in negotiations and study session 14 identified how more successful negotiators use these behaviours, including questions.

Questions are used in a number of ways:

- to ask for information
- to inquire
- to verify or validate why something is so
- to query a point
- to interrogate, interview, cross-examine
- to request something is undertaken.

Negotiation behaviours which are explicitly worded as questions seek to elicit some response from the other party. They were identified as:

- seek situation/position
- seek justification
- seek problem/implication/need
- seek social
- seek proposal, including a procedural proposal
- seek reactions/feelings
- seek by testing understanding.

When sequenced together, some of these behaviours have been used to lead the other party to a greater understanding of their situation. Such a technique is common in selling and one particular strategy is noteworthy in the negotiation context: Huthwaite's 'SPIN'® approach (Rackham, 1987) ('Change Behaviour, Change Results' specialist, Huthwaite Research Group Limited, trading as Huthwaite International. Huthwaite International: http://www.huthwaite.co.uk. SPIN® is a trademark of Huthwaite Research Group Limited trading as Huthwaite International and is registered in many countries throughout the world). This strategy uses questions to first establish the current situation by asking 'situation' questions, then following these up with 'problem' questions in order to establish the difficulties the other party is experiencing in their current situation. Subsequently, 'implication' questions seek to establish the consequences of the problems the other party are experiencing. Finally, questions are asked that test whether certain solutions would be of interest to them, these are 'need-payoff' questions. In fact, this is a logical approach in negotiation to problem solving, because it enables both parties to establish whether an explicit need can be met. Table 15.1 gives some examples of the approach.

Table 15.1 The 'SPIN'® approach

Question (Purchaser)	Response (Supplier)
'So, how are you coping with the price of gas going up?' (*situation* question)	'It means we will have to increase our prices generally.' (situation response)
'Is that causing a problem with any of your customers?' (*problem* question)	'Well, not just now, but it could put a few of the smaller ones off if it continues.' (a problem)

(continued on next page)

Table 15.1 *(continued)*

Question (Purchaser)	Response (Supplier)
'Are you considering switching to oil as an alternative?' (*situation* question)	'We may have to.' (further situation)
'Will that be difficult with your production as it is?' (*problem* question)	'Dealing with waste is going to be a trade-off; so yes, it is likely to cause us a few difficulties.' (another problem)
'What will that mean for your customer base?' (*implication* question)	'The smaller customers are most likely to be affected by the increases in prices, but we have so many of them that if they start to fail, it means we will have to find new customers.' (an implied need – they need to maintain the small customer sales to cover costs)
'So, if we were to increase our order volume above our contracted levels, would that be of interest?' (a *need-payoff* question)	'We would have to look at our schedules and establish how we would accommodate the increase but it is certainly something we would like to do.' (explicit statement that volume increase is a negotiable option)

Cycles of this subtle approach can be useful because they enable the parties to generate alternatives which may be used to reach a win-win outcome.

Some authors advocate 'probing' the other party, although this is a more coercive technique in a negotiation context. Shapiro et al's (2001) strategy ('WHAT') seeks information in a prioritised format by 'digging':

- First, questions seek to identify *what* is important, what else is important, which is the most important, and why it is the most important.
- Then, a *hypothetical* question ('what if…') is asked in order to draw the other party into a conversation.
- *Answers* are then given by using further questions to elicit even more information (although this can be destructive if used to the extreme).
- Finally, further information is probed by '*tell* me more…'

Questions are a powerful tool because, as Mulholland (1991) states, a direct response is unavoidable – unless, that is, the respondent chooses not to answer the question! Remember, however, that a supplier is likely to be asking questions, too – for example, Lambert (2003) comments that a salesperson expects to spend no more than 40 per cent of the time talking, and the rest of the time listening to the purchaser.

Learning activity 15.1

SPIN© is a technique more typically associated with sales. Explain how the technique can be used effectively in a purchasing context.

Feedback on page 200

Finally, questions can be framed in different styles (see also study session 12):

- Open-ended: cannot be answered with a straight yes or no, for example: 'Why do you think that?' They relate to the who, what, why, when forms.

15

- Leading: implies an answer, for example: 'Wouldn't you prefer xxx?'
- Cool: with low emotional content, for example: 'How does a reduction in price impact on standards?'
- Planned: one the negotiator has previously prepared to ask, for example as part of a sequence: 'If we were to offer you xxx, how would you react to yyy?'
- Treat: incorporates some form of flattery, for example: 'Perhaps you would care to share your knowledge on this?'
- Window: asks for insight into the other's perspective, for example: 'Why have you said that?'
- Directive: gets to the point, for example: 'How much does it cost?'
- Gauging: asks for reaction to a proposal, for example: 'Was that of interest to you?'

However questions are used, they must be responded to for best effect either by acknowledgement, support (using verbal and non-verbal behaviour), or further request for information.

Self-assessment question 15.1

Consider a scenario where you are presenting an important idea to a supplier whose support you want. Identify the types of question you could ask to gain support for the idea. Explain why they would work.

Feedback on page 201

15.2 Questions for developing trust

Creating a trusting climate is not simply a matter of exchanging all available information, for example, negotiators may feel they have given away critical and confidential information which may ultimately reduce their competitive advantage. In developing trust, Pruitt and Carnevale (1993) identify that appropriate feedback (a response) is fundamental. This is the 'give and take' in any exchange. For example, providing some information encourages reciprocation, although it need not be on key issues. Thus, since negotiating parties often have differing priorities for issues, asking questions is a useful tactic enabling information to be given on an issue which may be highly relevant to the buyer but of less strategic importance to the seller. Questions may also be linked together, depending on the negotiation context, in order to develop a trusting environment.

Raiffa (1997) suggests that trust results from 'full, open, truthful exchange', or 'FOTE', stating: 'some adversaries who hate each other and would not trust each other in real life may nevertheless know so much about each other that it's senseless not to tell the full truth during negotiations... [they are] dubbed intimate enemies'. The extent of truthful exchange will, therefore, influence trust. Negotiators often need to resolve this 'dilemma of trust' (Lewicki, 1983) by establishing the true priorities and intentions of their counterparts; however, in so doing they are generally cautious, if not deceitful, about revealing their own priorities and intentions.

15

Parties reciprocate trusting behaviour and so build an integrative climate (Walton and McKersie, 1965). Hence, early open and non-threatening behaviour will engender trust and cooperation in the other party which is more likely to continue during the negotiation, even if a deadlock occurs (Lewicki et al, 2003b). Importantly, trust may also be indicated by acting flexibly to reach a mutually satisfactory agreement (Pruitt, 1995).

Questions that may be used to help refocus on an integrative solution include (Lewicki et al, 2003b):

- 'What are the important issues for you?' This type of question identifies priorities which may provide an opportunity for logrolling.
- 'What can I do to help you achieve xxx?' This may help to identify cost-cutting opportunities.
- 'Why is that important to you?' This may help to identify underlying interests and needs which enable bridging solutions.

These questions can also be used in preparing for negotiation:

- What issues are important to me? And the other party? (logrolling)
- How does my offer impact on them? (cost cutting)
- What are our respective priorities for the deal? (bridging)

Detecting lies is also important. Lewicki et al (2203b) summarise a number of tactics which can be used to uncover deception. Examples are:

- Intimidation: using criticism, accusations, indifference in order to provoke an admission.
- Bluffing: using a lie to make the other party believe they have been discovered in their deception.
- Prodding: asking for further information; keeping them talking may mean they reveal the lie.
- Self-disclosure: revealing something in order to get the other party to reveal something in return.
- Direct approach: asking outright ('tell me the truth').
- Silence: making it uncomfortable for the other party to keep quiet.

Although recognising the tactic may be difficult, options are to ignore it, ask questions, respond in a similar way, or 'call' the tactic by indicating awareness of the behaviour.

15

Learning activity 15.2

Review the following types of question discussed in section 15.1 and evaluate how they may be used to develop trust:

- open-ended
- leading
- cool
- planned.

Feedback on page 201

Bartos (1995) suggests flexibility applies differently in distributive and integrative negotiations. In distributive negotiations, it is about making concessions, whereas in integrative negotiations, it is the readiness to engage in the search process (Druckman and Mitchell, 1995). Thus questions are likely to be different when demonstrating a flexible approach. Flexibility is often implicit in dealings with parties on issues concerning: resolution of differences; compromise of interests; adjusting positions; reciprocation; understanding another's views; revealing mutually satisfactory solutions; reframing problems; bundling of proposals; and embracing new methods or processes.

Flexibility is characterised by change which may have both short- and long-term consequences. It is witnessed in altered behaviours, objectives, plans or walk-away positions; abandoned bargaining stances; controlling strategies or activity patterns (Lambert and Heston, 1995). Flexibility, must, therefore, involve some notion of the speed of change as well as the degree of change, that is, the 'rapidity' and 'significance' of change.

Greater flexibility occurs when the possibility of future negotiation exists. It can also be derived from the preparation and planning which has been undertaken prior to face-to-face interaction, resulting in a more flexible approach once negotiations commence. Conversely, adherence to predetermined strategies may also result in less flexibility.

It is generally assumed that flexibility is beneficial to negotiating parties: 'Flexibility... leads to more stable and acceptable agreements, reached more rapidly and involving greater benefits to all...' (Lambert and Heston, 1995). Being inflexible, which frequently has negative associations, may also imply stability and commitment because the pace of change is slow which, in turn, is likely to lead to lasting agreements and thorough resolutions.

It is obviously important that timing of flexible behaviour is appropriate. It has been found to be most successfully employed where initial firmness is later followed by flexibility. Pruitt (1995) has identified six common tactics of 'firm flexibility':

- Concede to a point.
- Hold on a position while seeking to recompense the other party.
- Hold on important issues and concede on less important issues.
- Hold on interests but find ingenious ways to achieve them.
- Hold on important issues and abandon less important issues.
- Hold on interests only if the other party's appear less important.

Flexible behaviour indicates a desire to reach a mutually satisfactory agreement while firmness discourages exploitation. This is an important factor in building trust between the parties (Pruitt, 1995).

Self-assessment question 15.2

You are entering a negotiation with a supplier that you know prefers to use distributive tactics, even though you want to be more integrative (and

(continued on next page)

Self-assessment question 15.2 *(continued)*

long-term) in your approach. What are the problems associated with being flexible, and how might they be overcome?

Feedback on page 202

15.3 Tough questions

Invariably, the other party will ask questions that are difficult to answer! First, attempt learning activity 15.3 below.

Learning activity 15.3

Consider a recent negotiation, how well prepared were you to answer the questions you were asked? What questions were 'surprises' and why?

Feedback on page 202

Lewicki et al (2003a) identify a number of question types that are potentially difficult to deal with:

*   Ultimatums: where you are given a take it or leave it scenario. ('If I have an alternative, would you take or leave my offer?')
*   Unreasonable deadlines: where you are given limited options and little time to think about your answer. ('Why can't we agree this today?')
*   Highball or lowball tactics: where the offer is unreasonable but nonetheless makes you re-evaluate your position.
*   An impasse: where the other party demands a conclusion, or else…
*   Creating indecision: casting doubt in the mind of the other party. ('If you don't accept my offer, how do you know you'll get a better offer from someone else?')
*   Comparability: where you are not certain whether the offer matches that made to others ('Do you think our current offer is fair?')
*   Coercive tactics: where you are pressurised and manipulated to accept the offer made. ('Are you feeling pressured by your colleagues on this one?')

By considering how likely it is that the other party will use these types of question, then negotiators will be prepared to respond in a way that does not undermine their outcome preferences.

Self-assessment question 15.3

What steps can you take to anticipate more effectively the types of question you will be asked in a negotiation?

Feedback on page 202

15

Revision question

Now try the revision question for this session on page 268.

Summary

This study session has identified how questions are used. It first identified why questions are asked and then reviewed verbal negotiation behaviours. It was stated that when sequenced together, some of these questions can be used to develop an effective negotiation strategy. The SPIN© approach can be useful because it provides alternatives which may be used to reach a win-win outcome. WHAT seeks information in a prioritised format by probing the other party.

The nature and means of creating a trusting climate were reviewed, wherein asking questions was identified as a useful tactic. Questions may be linked together, depending on the negotiation context, in order to develop a trusting environment, and establish the priorities and intentions of the other party. Trust leads to reciprocation and cooperation which is more likely to continue during the negotiation, even if a deadlock occurs. In this context, flexibility was identified as an implicit means to reaching a mutually satisfactory agreement while firmness discouraged exploitation.

Finally, a number of question types that are potentially difficult to deal with were reviewed. It was stated that considering the likely question patterns of the other party leads to more effective and thorough preparation for negotiation.

Suggested further reading

Lewicki et al (2003b) on questioning, including in tough negotiations.

Shapiro et al (2001) on questioning ('probe, probe, probe') the other party.

Review study sessions 12, 13 and 14 on verbal behaviour, framing and characteristics of successful negotiators.

Feedback on learning activities and self-assessment questions

Feedback on learning activity 15.1

Your answer should consider the following points:

- Provides an opportunity to understand the other party – asking questions generates information.
- Communicates that the purchaser is interested in other party's situation.
- Helps to identify how a win-win can be reached.
- Identifies strengths and weaknesses in other party's approach by defining the nature of the problems they have and the implications of these.

- Defines the nature of the payoffs the other party is seeking and so provides an indication of their bargaining ranges.

Feedback on self-assessment question 15.1

Because the issue is important, you may identify that an integrative approach should be used.

An ideal sequence of commentary would be:

- It is important first to identify the objective that is common to you both and confirm its primary focus in the negotiation. A question such as, 'How are you coping with xxx?' helps to set the scene for the bargaining because it is open-ended and encourages information exchange; you could respond by offering your view. This is better than starting with, 'Which of x or y is affecting you more?' because it discourages open information exchange beyond the immediate options.
- 'Can you comment on why that's important to you?' This is specifying behaviour, which is again open, seeking justification for a statement about some position. This is preferable to, 'I assume that's because of xxx?' which is closed and seeks justification by confirmation.
- 'How do you feel about our offer of zzz?' This openly asks for emotive feedback, rather than a question such as, 'Can you confirm your support for that suggestion?' which is closed and generates no further insight into reactions beyond 'yes' or 'no'.
- 'How could we both benefit from that?' This is openly asking for feedback which relates to positions and interests, rather than 'That would be better for you because...?' which is closed, and has the potential to annoy the supplier (because you are telling them their business).

For further examples of questions, revisit study session 13 on verbal negotiation behaviours.

Feedback on learning activity 15.2

Your answer should consider the following points:

- Open-ended questions enable the other party to give more information than closed, which is a useful technique for empowering the other party, and encouraging them to trust you with their thoughts.
- Leading questions may also incorporate your own opinions, thus giving the other party the opportunity to demonstrate their trust by accepting your lead.
- Cool questions do not give emotion, which limits their effectiveness in developing trust.
- Planned questions can be used tactically to develop trust by linking specific questions together.

Other questions may similarly add to or detract from the development of trust between the parties.

15

Feedback on self-assessment question 15.2

This is a typical scenario where the purchaser and the supplier have a different view of how things should proceed; you are mismatched in your approach even though your goals may be common. Your options are:

- To ignore their distributive behaviour in the hope they will desist.
- Call them on their behaviour: you know what they are doing and why, so you may embarrass them into more appropriate behaviour.
- Respond similarly with distributive behaviour, although this may result in escalation and deadlock.
- Ask for them to improve their behaviour in order to achieve an outcome.

By showing flexibility in your behaviour, you may undermine your position in the negotiation. You should consider the following:

- The negotiation setting, or context, will require different approaches in order to achieve goals. For example, flexibility may be an important consideration where an integrative outcome is sought, but less relevant to a distributive situation. Therefore, when the approaches being used are mismatched, your actions need to communicate your intentions (a clear BATNA will help you in this because it keeps you focused).
- The range of tactics to be employed need to be consistent with your intentions.
- The competence, experience and preferences of the individuals involved must remain focused.
- Will being flexible undermine the position of the negotiator? This will depend on the sources of power identified in the negotiation.
- Will the other party reciprocate with flexible behaviour?

Feedback on learning activity 15.3

Questions were only surprises because you had not anticipated they would be asked. This means your preparation was inadequate in terms of your understanding of the other party, their likely strengths and weaknesses, the opportunities they have elsewhere and their likely positions and interests. You may also have underestimated the individuals involved and their personal motivations in relation to the negotiation with you and your organisation. Another consideration may, of course, be the relative experience you have of dealing with the other party, or in negotiating.

By identifying the specific questions that you were unprepared for, you can develop an action plan for subsequent negotiations.

Feedback on self-assessment question 15.3

Effective preparation and planning is the key to this, as highlighted in this section. Study session 12 also looked specifically at this from the perspective of becoming a more effective communicator. Aspects identified related to:

- The use of questions to generate information on the other party's needs, interests and arguments.

15

- Being sure to listen carefully and reflect upon what is being said.
- Role reversal as a means of actively putting yourself into the 'other party's shoes' in order to see the problem from their perspective.

You may also have considered role-playing responses as part of your preparation activities for different scenarios. For example:

- How to respond in a way that gives you more time to think before giving an answer to a question: for example, using questions to buy time. ('Or have you thought about xxx?')
- How to respond without committing yourself to an answer: for example, acknowledging you have heard but then moving the discussion on. ('That's an interesting point, but let's just look at...')
- Deferring the answer to another person outside the negotiation meeting. ('That sounds interesting but I need to see if Jim agrees.')

15

Cultural dimensions in negotiations

Introduction

It is often difficult enough to negotiate with another party who shares the same cultural background but when conducting business in an international setting, these difficulties may be magnified. This study session examines the impact of cultural differences on commercial negotiations.

There are clearly as many different cultures as there are countries and regions within countries, so it is not the intention here to evaluate country by country. Instead, the dimensions of culture are reviewed which influence the negotiation and development of strategies. Then, strategic approaches to negotiation are discussed. Finally, an overview of how to plan for negotiating in an international context is presented.

'The challenge for every global negotiator is to understand the simultaneous, multiple influences of several factors on the negotiation process and outcome, and to update this understanding regularly as circumstances change.'
Lewicki et al (2003a: 405)

Session learning objectives

After completing this session you should be able to:

16.1 Discuss the nature of cultural differences and how this influences negotiations.
16.2 Develop culturally aware negotiation strategies.
16.3 Present a planning tool for preparing to negotiate with international parties.

Unit content coverage

This study session covers the following topics from the official CIPS unit content document:

Statement of practice

Explain the different approaches required when negotiating in different settings.

Learning objectives

4.4 Analyse and explain different negotiation practices in international cultures.
   • Culture and negotiation
   • Body language
   • Barriers to international negotiation

16

Prior knowledge

Study sessions 1 to 14

Timing

You should set aside about 6 hours to read and complete this session, including learning activities, self-assessment questions, the suggested further reading (if any) and the revision question.

16.1 Cross-cultural negotiations

Hendon et al (1996) state that culture impacts on all areas of an international negotiation: the motivations the parties have to enter the negotiation, the process of the negotiation meeting, the outcomes achieved, the traditions and values that underlie the agreement, and the specific situational conditions within which the negotiation takes place. In fact, cultural differences and similarities impact on all negotiations – it is characteristic of human interaction. What makes culture a special consideration in negotiation is when the supplier and purchaser are not familiar with the cultural context. As Hendon et al state: 'when you are negotiating with someone from your own country, it is often truly possible to expedite communications by making reasonable cultural assumptions. The situation reverses itself when two cultures are involved.'

Culture is a 'total communication framework' and includes:

- shared meanings, values and beliefs
- group and ethnic orientation
- judgement and opinion on good and bad
- language.

Without an intimate understanding of these aspects, misperception and distortion in communication is certain. Information that contains significant cultural meaning is avoided or misinterpreted in favour of a more familiar meaning.

Lewicki et al (2003a) identify two key factors that influence cross-cultural negotiations: the macro-environment and the immediate context. The macro-environment comprises a number of aspects:

- the political and legal context
- the role of international economics
- the nature of government and bureaucracy
- how political stable the country is
- the ideology of the people, whether they are individualistic or collectivist
- the negotiation setting or approach.

The immediate context includes the relative bargaining power, levels of conflict, relationships and outcome preferences, which all influence the negotiation. Thus, in preparing for a negotiation with a party from a different cultural context, it is especially important to consider the range of factors that influence the negotiators.

Learning activity 16.1

Discuss how to communicate effectively with individuals with different cultural backgrounds. Consider both verbal and non-verbal behaviour.

Feedback on page 213

Hofstede's (1991) dimensions of culture have been well applied to cross-cultural negotiations. They are (Lewicki et al, 2003a):

- Individualism/collectivism: this represents an independent versus a team approach, where impact is likely to be on processes, outcomes and preferences for conflict resolution. Collectivist cultures (such as Pacific Rim and certain Latin American countries) favour a longer-term relationship whereas individualistic cultures (such as the UK, US and Australia) focus on the short-term, preferring to introduce new negotiators to resolve problems.
- Power distance: this relates to the acceptance of inequality in society and the use of power. High power distance cultures (Arab, Asian, South American countries) tend to defer decision making in negotiations to a leader within an organisation which results in a slow process, whereas low power distance cultures (Western Europe, US) tend to make decisions more quickly because they are made throughout the organisation.
- Masculinity/femininity: this refers to male assertiveness versus the more female concern for relationships. More masculine cultures (Japan, Austria, Venezuela, Switzerland) favour more competitive negotiations whilst feminine cultures (Taiwan, Spain, Costa Rica) prefer collaboration and compromise.
- Uncertainty avoidance: this is the extent to which structure and risk avoidance is preferred to rapid change and new situations. Those cultures that prefer structure (and are therefore more stable) tend to be high in avoiding uncertainty. Such cultures are uncomfortable with ambiguity and prefer procedures and rules to guide the negotiation process (such as Greece, Portugal and Guatemala), while others (such as Sweden, Hong Kong and Ireland) are more appreciative of less structure in the negotiation process.

Hofstede and Bond (1988) identified a fifth dimension:

- Long-term orientation: this includes work ethic and commitment, and is referred to as 'Confucian dynamism', although there has been little published on its impact in negotiations. This dimension relates to deeply rooted values and traditions. A high orientation in business may indicate non-acceptance of 'outsider' influence whereas a low orientation may indicate willingness to accept change more easily.

16

These dimensions can be further investigated for individual countries at Hofstede's website: Geert Hofstede: http://www.geert-hofstede.com/. Take time now to review the rankings of these dimensions for your own culture before proceeding with this study session.

Now attempt self-assessment question 16.1 below. Spend at least an hour on this exercise.

Self-assessment question 16.1

What are the sources of cultural difference? Describe how culture influences negotiations. Use examples from Hofstede's website to support your answer.

Feedback on page 214

16.2 Developing cultural awareness

There are two broad strategies to negotiating with a different culture: 'when in Rome, do as the Romans do' or 'business is business'. These refer to the adaptation of behaviour to the cultural setting in which negotiations are taking place. The 'when in Rome' approach suggests that taking on the other party's culture is the most effective approach. However, research suggests that only limited modifications to behaviour are satisfactory, for the following reasons:

- It is often not possible to modify behaviour closely, unless you have a very intimate knowledge of the culture.
- It is difficult to determine how much the other party will modify their behaviour, so even if you try to adapt, it is unlikely you will achieve a close match.
- Behavioural studies suggest people behave differently naturally when they negotiate with another culture, so an intimate understanding of how cultures behave may not be helpful in a cross-cultural context.

Thus it is not necessary, and is often impossible or implausible, to attempt to adopt a different culture. The primary aim is, therefore, to show respect for local values and norms by attempting to work with the differences. It is not uncommon, for example, for Americans to discuss the finer points of football (soccer) with Europeans!

The 'business is business' approach assumes that wherever you are in the world, business is a basic reality. However, research by Frances (1991) suggests moderate, rather than comprehensive, adaptations are the most effective. The rule of thumb depends on the extent of the party's familiarity with the different culture (Lewicki et al, 2003a):

- Where negotiators have low familiarity with the cultural setting and there is limited time to become more familiar, then an adviser may be useful. Advisers can act as negotiators or commentators on the negotiation. Mediators may be used to introduce the parties and act in

16

a facilitating capacity. An alternative strategy is to encourage the other party to adapt to your own culture.

- Where negotiators have moderate familiarity, the party may adapt their behaviour to match the other party's more closely. It may also be appropriate to seek adaptations from the other party so that both are consciously coordinating their behaviour.
- Where there is high familiarity, then it may be appropriate to adapt completely to match the other party, finding some common approach that meets the needs of the negotiating context. It may also be worth considering the adoption of a third culture so that both are culturally 'neutral'.

Learning activity 16.2

Compare and contrast the two different approaches to international negotiations discussed in this section. Which approach does your organisation favour and why?

Feedback on page 215

Given the different approaches discussed so far, it is evident that the use of teams will be more appropriate in some cultural situations than in others (for example, where advisers or mediators are to be used). It is also apparent that negotiations with international counterparts may be a long-term endeavour, compared to same culture situations. Furthermore, swapping negotiators during the process may cause problems, rather than resolve any difficulties. For example, Asian countries tend to make deals with individuals and so if the original negotiators are not part of the final deal, then there is a tendency for non-compliance with the contractual terms. Changing negotiators also sends the message that the party is unreliable, disorganised and cannot, therefore, be trusted (Hendon et al, 1996).

First, this highlights the importance of situational factors in selecting negotiators:

- time resource available for the negotiating process
- availability of individual negotiators throughout the negotiation process.

Secondly, there are a number of important factors when selecting individual negotiators to participate:

- Status: hierarchy is important to many East Asian cultures, so sending a lower status individual to negotiate is tantamount to failure. Many cultures, however, expect negotiators to have similar authority in their dealings. What constitutes status will, however, vary with different cultural settings. For example, some countries determine status by connections with key individuals such as politicians or industrialists (for example, Mexico); others by education (such as France) and social class (UK); yet others by the respect they have within their work context (Germany) and others by age (China and Japan).

16

- Authority and decision making: while these relate to power and status, clearly without authority it will be difficult to achieve an agreement that can be implemented. It is important not only to confirm the level of authority before the negotiation but also to evaluate this throughout the process. Some cultures prefer to diffuse their authority among a number of individuals (for example, the Chinese). This limits the level of authority that individual negotiators have which, in fact, enhances the power of negotiators because it provides a means for offering to save face. This becomes difficult when trying to determine which of the other party's negotiating team has the final decision-making authority! In such situations, defining the leader is often difficult. For example, in some cultural settings (such as with the Japanese) the decision maker may be only a peripheral team member but carries the final decision because his view represents that of the organisation. Thus it must not be assumed that the team will be made up of similar individuals to your own.
- Size of team: some cultures send large teams (Chinese and Japanese) others prefer small teams, or even individual negotiators (US). There are pros and cons with each approach, depending on the situation. Team members, as previously discussed, bring individual and collective expertise to the negotiating table. Tasks can be divided between team members, which may be beneficial because different tasks can be performed simultaneously during the negotiation. This is not possible where teams negotiate with individuals. Obvious difficulties relate to coordination and consensus building among team members. Often cost is also a factor in sending negotiating teams to foreign countries.

Self-assessment question 16.2

What factors should be considered when negotiating with a different culture? Use examples to support your answer (from Hofstede's website).

Feedback on page 215

16.3 Preparing for cross-cultural negotiations

According to Acuff (1997), there are a number of key problems that negotiators must be able to deal with in a cross-cultural negotiating context:

- Overcoming 'culture shock': negotiators typically go through four phases of adjustment to a new cultural setting: excitement and anticipation, awakening, disillusionment and realisation.
- Dealing with your boss: because of the protracted nature of the negotiation, your boss may be unhappy with status reports on progress, especially when it is perceived that very little has been achieved other than social interaction.
- Dealing with the negotiation team: negotiator may have to deal with escalating costs, with personality issues and disagreements among team members, and with building the team approach for negotiation.

- Resolving ethical issues: bribery and payments made to individuals to speed up or guarantee desired outcomes may be commonplace in some cultures; or the giving of gifts may be seen as a good way to build relationships. In other cultures, however, these are viewed as evidence of corruption (refer to CIPS Personal Ethical Code which articulates a code of conduct for dealing with these issues).
- Venue: costs and culture shock are key problems to negotiating in a foreign country.

Additional factors (Acuff, 1997) that need consideration for negotiation are:

- Pace of negotiation.
- Negotiating strategies: opening offer, BATNA, presentation of issues including level of detail and formality, concession patterns, conflict resolution processes.
- Role and emphasis of personal relationships.
- Decision-making process, including authority, team roles, interests and positions of individuals.
- Contractual and administrative aspects, including bureaucracy, detail, need for an advisor, detail of agenda.

Now attempt learning activity 16.3 below. Spend at least 30 minutes on this activity.

Learning activity 16.3

Consider a scenario where a supplier from a different culture is clearly offended by your comment: 'Let's review your numbers again; I can't seem to make them add up to mine.'

How can the problems of dealing with different cultural settings be overcome?

Feedback on page 215

Hendon et al (1996) recommend a number of dos and don'ts for cross-cultural negotiations:

- Do plan effectively. Know the culture; know the limits to the information you want to disclose to the other party; ensure the team know what they are doing! It is also useful to prepare for the tactics the other party is likely to use, so take time to research this aspect thoroughly.
- Do undertake preliminary work with advisers, mediators or others who are familiar with the cultural context and who may act as a go-between. This will help to build the relationship with key individuals before the main negotiators attend a face-to-face meeting.
- Do take time to learn the local language, or employ an interpreter; if the latter, learn how to use one effectively!
- Do use visuals (diagrams, drawings and photographs or copies of key documentation) to support the communication process in the

16

negotiation meeting; pictures are easier than words to understand (but beware imagery is not offensive).

- Do use time effectively. Be prepared for a longer negotiation process and take care not to reveal return plans as they may be used against you.
- Do use ethnic origin individuals with care. Most people are loyal first to their original culture and second to their citizenship but where an individual has been 'acculturated' into an organisation and country, then it is possible they may have lost touch with subtle and key cultural overtones.
- Do be aware of longer-term implications of the negotiation and agreement reached. In some contexts the agreement reached is the first stage of a continuing relationship.
- Do not be intimidated into reaching an agreement; this is especially true if you have identified your BATNA.
- Do be aware that the other party's approach to negotiating may be different. Take care, therefore, not to assume the tactics you use are perceived in the same way by them.
- Do know your BATNA – sunk costs are irrelevant.

Now attempt self-assessment question 16.3 below. Spend around 30 minutes on this question.

Self-assessment question 16.3

Summarise a list of dos and don'ts in preparing for cross-cultural negotiations.

Feedback on page 216

Revision question

Now try the revision question for this session on page 268.

Summary

This study session has reviewed the nature of culture and examined some of the key issues that influence the negotiation process. Firstly, culture was identified as comprising four aspects: shared meanings, values and beliefs; group and ethnic orientation; judgement and opinion on good and bad; and language. Two key factors were highlighted as important in developing an appropriate approach to negotiation: the macro-environment and the immediate negotiating context.

Hofstede's work identified five cultural dimensions which can be used to determine the approach to negotiating:

- individualism/collectivism
- power distance
- masculinity/femininity

- uncertainty avoidance
- long-term orientation.

Two strategic approaches to negotiating were discussed: 'when in Rome' and 'business is business'. The selection of a strategy will depend on the extent to which the negotiating team is familiar with the other party's cultural context. It was identified that a moderate adaptation strategy can be highly effective. Important considerations for team selection were also reviewed.

Finally, discussion focused on how to plan for cross-cultural negotiations, especially on overcoming five common difficulties, including culture shock, selection of venue, ethical considerations, team approach and management of the boss. A plan of important dos and don'ts was considered.

Suggested further reading

Acuff (1997) reviews the negotiation approaches for a range of different countries/regions; compare the UK with Latin America, for example.

Lewicki et al (2003b) on global negotiations.

Geert Hofstede: http://www.geert-hofstede.com/,Geert Hofstede's Cultural Dimensions provides many examples of the cultural dimensions for different countries.

Feedback on learning activities and self-assessment questions

Feedback on learning activity 16.1

Language is inherently complex because words common in one language often have no direct translation. Examples include 'fair play', which is common in the UK and US, but has no equivalent in other countries; similarly, the closest translation of individualism in Japanese is 'selfishness'. More specifically, the word '*muda*' means 'waste' in Japanese and is a term often used in Lean Supply and JIT, but it also has a more negative meaning ('wasteful and parasitical'). In countries where natural resources are scarce and self-reliance a priority, waste is seen more negatively than in some westernised countries.

Considerations of verbal behaviour:

- Use of argumentation and listening, which is often the most effective technique.
- Role of evidence to support a position.
- Use of emotion and logic.
- Process of consensus building, or decision making.
- Development of relationships among the negotiating parties.
- Role of status and protocol.
- Use of translators and interpreters to inform the other party.

In contrast, non-verbal behaviours are used less consciously, and are instead habitual and routinised. Seven categories of non-verbal behaviour have been

16

identified (Hendon et al, 1996) which collectively communicate messages to the other party:

- Body language: gestures, body movement, facial movement, eye contact.
- Vocal noises (listening noises), tone and volume of voice.
- Touching behaviours.
- Use of personal space, often referred to as proxemics.
- Use of time.
- Physical appearance: clothing and jewellery.
- Artifacts associated with the negotiator: a car, desk ornaments, photographs, and so on.

Given the diverse mix of verbal and non-verbal behaviours, negotiators must ensure they are prepared for differences when meeting face to face with the other party. It is evident that messages are constructed from a range of behaviours, so a negotiator must be 'culturally aware' of their own behaviour so as not to anger, insult or embarrass the other party, unless that is intended.

Feedback on self-assessment question 16.1

As the discussion has highlighted, there are four main cultural dimensions to consider:

- individualism/collectivism
- power distance
- masculinity/femininity
- uncertainty avoidance.

And one further dimension:

- long-term orientation.

These are likely to influence negotiations in different ways:

- Definition of negotiation: identifying what is negotiable and when negotiation occurs.
- Selection of negotiators: culture means that seniority, expertise, gender, age, experience and status are likely to be viewed another way in a different country.
- Protocol: formality, style, language, introductions, respect for personal physical space will be viewed differently.
- Communication (verbal and non-verbal): each country has its own norms and expectations and it is all too easy to anger, insult or embarrass the other party if cultural conventions are not adhered to.
- Time: respect for and use of time.
- Risk propensity: some cultures tend to be more conservative, and negotiators may require considerable information before making decisions; others are more entrepreneurial in their approach to negotiation.
- Teams or individual negotiators: the decision-making processes differ.
- Nature of agreements made: whether agreements are viewed as formal and enforceable by law or just a general intention is often down

16

to cultural difference. In some countries, for example China, legal decisions may be made by political leaders on the basis of personal connections, rather than by trained judges,

- Change: attitudes towards change (for example, in process or protocol, or post-negotiation follow-up) may differ depending on a society's view of its traditional values.

Feedback on learning activity 16.2

'Business is business' assumes parties have limited time and/or no inclination to adapt their behaviour. This may be appropriate for a shorter-term relationship or one-off transaction, or where the parties have deliberately chosen to retain their own cultural identity because of a lack of familiarity with the other party's culture.

'When in Rome' assumes there is more time available and the other party is important and, therefore, adaptation may be beneficial to achieving a satisfactory outcome. This may be appropriate for a longer-term relationship or where repeat interactions are likely. Adaptation is considered to be desirable because there is a high level of joint understanding between the parties, possibly because there may be a developed relationship.

Other factors may relate to resource allocations, negotiator experience, risk taking, outcome preferences, knowledge, ignorance and capability.

Feedback on self-assessment question 16.2

Your answer should include the following:

- Extent of familiarity with the cultural context.
- Knowledge of the other party: is it a developed relationship, a one-off situation?
- The risks associated with not achieving a deal, including the organisation's BATNA.
- Time available to the party, for the whole negotiation process.
- Research into the different culture: negotiating preferences, cultural style and overtones.
- The availability of advisers and mediators – or, at least, an experienced individual to participate.
- Use of team: size, make-up, status of members, familiarity with team members and negotiation experience/competence/skill, commitment of individuals to team and the negotiation.
- Preferred levels of authority conferred upon team members.
- Resource implications for the negotiation, including costs associated with sending large negotiating teams.

Feedback on learning activity 16.3

The scenario indicates that the supplier may have lost face because you have questioned the details of their offer. It may also be that the individual (or team) perceives other issues to be more important and that you are attempting to undermine their position. Of course, it may be that you are

16

indeed attempting to exert pressure on their position; or it may be that you genuinely do not understand how their numbers have been reached.

Issues to consider in overcoming these problems:

- Culture shock: find a mentor to coach you in the cultural overtones, language and behavioural norms; plan to be flexible and patient with yourself in the new setting; do not judge people; recognise that you will pass through the four phases of adjustment; plan to take the lessons you learn back.
- Dealing with the boss: emphasise the slower pace of negotiating; educate on what to expect; identify the key factors within the contract.
- Teams: limit team size; clarify roles, responsibilities and intended outcomes; ensure all are skilled and competent.
- Ethical issues: ensure your behaviour is legal; keep your boss informed; consider investing in community projects as an alternative to direct payments.
- Venue: do not divulge your return journey details; allow time to recover from jet lag; do not be tempted to agree unless it is inside your acceptable range.

Feedback on self-assessment question 16.3

Table 16.1 Dos and don'ts of cross-cultural negotiation

Dos	Don'ts
• Be well prepared.	• View the other party strictly from your own perspective.
• Identify clear objectives.	
• Know your BATNA.	• Coerce.
• Get to know the other party before the negotiation.	• Ask for politically or culturally sensitive concessions.
• Follow protocol.	• Avoid the other party's priorities.
• Understand cultural sensitivities.	• Use language that will confuse the other party.
• Know the decision-making process.	
• Identify the specifics of the deal.	• Disagree with members of your own team.
• Become familiar with the negotiation style to be used.	• Circumvent levels of authority within the other party's organisation.
• Take care with time deadlines.	• Ask for a decision they cannot make.

Source: derived from Hendon et al (1996)

16

Telephone negotiations

Introduction

Negotiating by telephone is a fundamental reality for purchasers in a modern business environment but it presents some real challenges. This study session first identifies some of the key differences between conducting telephone negotiations and face-to-face negotiations. Difficulties are reviewed and, finally, considerations for conducting effective negotiations by telephone are presented.

'Sheer geography means you don't meet people, you don't work face to face, you need different forms of communication.'

Jeff Beal, director of GPA Recruitment, commenting on the soft skills needed by purchasers to be effective communicators in a modern business environment (2004: 23)

Session learning objectives

After completing this session you should be able to:

17.1 Identify the key differences between conducting telephone negotiations and face-to-face negotiations.
17.2 Identify the difficulties that are encountered in telephone negotiations.
17.3 Prepare a plan for conducting effective negotiations by telephone.

Unit content coverage

This study session covers the following topics from the official CIPS unit content document:

Statement of practice

Explain the different approaches required when negotiating in different settings.

Learning objectives

4.5 Analyse and explain the features of effective negotiation by telephone and email.
  • Factors affecting telephone negotiation
  • Factors affecting email negotiation
  • Good practice when negotiating by telephone/email

Prior knowledge

Study sessions 1 to 16

17

Timing

You should set aside about 4 hours to read and complete this session, including learning activities, self-assessment questions, the suggested further reading (if any) and the revision question.

17.1 Telephone negotiations

Begin by attempting learning activity 17.1 below.

Learning activity 17.1

Compare and contrast personal experiences of face-to-face and telephone negotiations. What was easier to deal with over the telephone?

Feedback on page 224

Discussion in previous study sessions has shown the embeddedness of language, culture and discourse between negotiators. Language provides meaning; it is a device for understanding when communicating with another party and may be used to build a relationship (Mulholland, 1991). Non-verbal behaviour, however indistinctive, has also been highlighted as communicating meaning to another party. When negotiating by telephone, however, much of the non-verbal behaviour is lost, which increases the potential for misunderstandings, misperceptions and, generally, distortion of meanings.

An understanding of the pattern of speech is, therefore, important in telephone negotiations. Mulholland (1991) identifies that speech is structured in three phases: initial, middle, close.

The initial phase sets the tone for the subsequent negotiation and encompasses:

- Establishing or re-establishing the relationship bonds.
- Taking a role – advisor, organiser, clarifier – and allocating a role to the other party.
- Providing information about mood or attitude, and anticipating the response from the hearer.
- Speech conventions, politeness, formality, tactics to be used.

The middle phase encompasses the main negotiation. The closing phase conveys the normal conventions of speech such as some verbal signal of agreement ('OK' or 'yes' or, more formally, 'any other business?' or 'the discussion is now closed').

Patterns of speech are developed by taking turns to speak – after all, only one person can be effectively heard at once over the telephone, and silence is

17

difficult to interpret when there are no other cues, such as facial movement. Considerations for turn taking include:

- Speaking is a socially important act.
- Anyone 'present' for the negotiation is entitled to speak.
- Speaking for a long time denies the other person an opportunity to participate in the conversation, thus speakers should not 'hold the floor' for too long.

Silence can communicate that individuals are comfortable with each other, or the complete opposite, even disapproval or distance. It may be used to build antagonism and can be a tactical ploy. Hesitation in a response can indicate uncertainty or might convey a considerable effort of thought (which may be irritating to a hearer who processes information quickly).

When the speaker has finished their speaking turn, they may send a message that they are ready for another person to take over:

- The grammatical construction may indicate that a sentence has been finished and the point has been fully expressed, for example: 'The delivery we are anticipating is ten working days from order date'. Interrupting such an expression may well be perceived as impolite.
- The tone of voice may lower in pitch or slow in pace.
- The speaker may appear to have run out of things to say, for example: 'and so on...'
- A question may be asked such as, 'What do you think?'; this can be emphasised when used in conjunction with a person's name: 'John, what do you think?'

The speaker may want to continue a point, which can be signalled by:

- Stating that the forthcoming comments have a number of parts ('I have three comments on that...').
- Holding off the other person by saying, 'just a minute...' or, 'I'm not quite finished yet.'
- Constructing the sentence in a way that communicates there is more to come. For example, one could say, 'because our new production line is not fully functional, we are reluctant to take on new *business*,' rather than saying, 'our new production line is almost *functional*, but we need to take care not to overload our existing *teams*, although they are prepared to work *overtime*.' The italicised words indicate places where the hearer could believe the comment to be finished.
- Not pausing for breath.

To claim a speaking turn, it is possible to:

- Identify the speaker's end point and then speak quickly in the pause.
- Interrupt the speak (over-speak)
- Begin over-speaking hesitantly which may cause the speaker to stop and listen while the comment is restated.
- Make supportive noises ('uh-huh', 'umm') which, because they suggest agreement, may cause the speaker to stop.
- Reciprocate a question to encourage further discussion.

17

Listening is also a key activity in telephone negotiation. Mulholland states that around 60 per cent of speech interaction is spent on listening. Listening involves two key components: hearing and interpreting (see section 14.2 on the learning cycle). Interpreting the speech necessarily involves understanding the meaning of what is being said – which can be a particular challenge in a cross-cultural context as highlighted in study session 16. Indeed, study session 12 identified three forms of listening: passive, acknowledgement and active.

Active listening is where the receiver of a message indicates their interpretation by restating the message in their own words, for example:

Negotiator A: 'I felt we achieved very little at our meeting last week.'

Negotiator B: 'You were very disappointed with the outcome.'

Athos and Gabarro (1978) identified five different active listening responses which Lewicki et al (2003a) state can be used in a negotiation to encourage the other party to give information about their priorities, interests, opinions, and so on:

- Put more emphasis on listening than speaking.
- Respond to personal points, such as feelings and beliefs, rather than abstract points.
- Allow the speaker to lead the conversation process.
- Seek to clarify the speaker's thoughts and feelings rather than putting words into their mouth by suggesting how they feel.
- Respond to feelings that are expressed.

One factor which influences the success of a telephone negotiation relates to who initiates the call. It is evident that a call is made for some purpose and the caller will expect that to be the focus of the conversation. Unless previously set up, and to some extent planned, the purpose of the call is hidden from the receiver. However, a successful outcome is likely to depend on how well prepared the receiver is to respond. Notwithstanding this, the caller would not have placed the call if they did not want interaction with the other person. It is clear from this that giving the other party advance warning of your call will lead to a better outcome.

Self-assessment question 17.1

List five key considerations for telephone negotiations.

Feedback on page 224

17

17.2 Dealing with telephone negotiations

As with face-to-face negotiation, telephone negotiations need to be carefully prepared in order to achieve the desired goals. In terms of interaction between the negotiators, issues are broadly similar except that the degree of an individual's involvement in a telephone discussion tends to be lower than when the parties are face to face (Lievrouw and Finn, 1990). A more recent investigation by Purdy and Nye (2000) looked at different communications media (face-to-face, videoconferencing, telephone and computer-mediated communication) and found the most effective means in terms of outcome efficiency, time taken and satisfaction of the parties, was face-to-face interaction. These authors also found that face-to-face interaction was more likely to result in collaboration between the parties.

It has been suggested that approximately 10 to 15 per cent of time is spent on the telephone with another party (Mulholland, 1991) with an average duration of call between two and eight minutes. Much of this time is spent on gathering information but particular strategies need to be thought through carefully. This is especially true when closing a call because a common response by the other party is to raise a new topic ('whilst I have you on the 'phone, can we discuss xxx?') which you may not want to respond to.

There are a number of strategies to close a call:

- A pre-closure comment, signalling the conversation is near and end: 'One last point…'
- A comment indicating the conversation is closed: 'That is all I needed to speak to you about today.'
- An indication that closure is imminent: 'Well, I have kept you talking for long enough now.'
- Question close: 'Is that OK for you?'

Learning activity 17.2

How might the following difficulties, often encountered in telephone negotiations, be overcome?

1 premature close
2 no feedback
3 misperception.

Feedback on page 224

Other difficulties that apply to telephone negotiations relate to listening skills. Hearing a message is sometimes difficult because of background 'noise'. This may be because of physical interference, such as the air conditioning in the office or signal failure of a mobile telephone. Alternatively, it may be because of strongly held opinions, dislike for the other person, and preconceived ideas about the outcome, which means the hearer does not receive the whole message. Furthermore, inadequate cognitive abilities may mean the message is heard but not understood. Thus there are two distinct problems associated with listening (Mulholland, 1991):

- Selective listening, where only some information is received and the 'blanks' are filled in by the hearer, causes serious distortion of the overall message.

17

- Adaptive listening, where an idea relates so well to the experiences and context of the hearer, that they weave it into their own thoughts and cannot disentangle the new idea from the original. This causes the hearer to make potentially erroneous assumptions about the idea presented in the message.

The speaker must, therefore, ensure that sufficient information is provided and not 'too much'. This will require listening for indications that messages have been received. Clues to this lie in the responses made, such as those outlined in this section and section 17.1.

Mulholland (1991) suggests a number of techniques to improve listening skills:

- Translate the key ideas and terms used into your own words.
- Reduce the speaker's message to its basic idea.
- Remove emotive words from the utterance and identify if there is an underlying rationality to the message.
- Identify the main points from the surrounding rhetoric, and prioritise them.
- Decide the purpose of the utterance; use the negotiation behaviours identified in study session 13.
- Try to identify if there are missing components to the message and whether this is deliberate.

Self-assessment question 17.2

Summarise the difficulties that may be encountered in telephone negotiations.

Feedback on page 225

17.3 Planning for telephone negotiations

First, attempt learning activity 17.3 below. Use the discussion in the previous two sections as the basis for your answer. Spend at least 30 minutes on this exercise.

Learning activity 17.3

List factors that are identified as good practice for the effective management of telephone negotiations.

Feedback on page 225

The modern business environment means it is not always possible to negotiate face to face. However, the difficulties associated with conducting telephone negotiations may outweigh the perceived benefits, even if costs in engaging in face-to-face meetings are high. There is great potential for miscommunication which needs to be thoroughly understood in order to overcome this significant problem.

There are advantages to telephone negotiations, however, which are worth bearing in mind (Casebolt, 1995):

- It is easier to say 'no' because you are more distant from the receiver.
- It is faster than face-to-face negotiation; in fact, discussion has highlighted that the longer the discussion is, the more likely the key issues will be lost in the volume of information.
- It is more direct because the parties stick to the point and tend to be more impersonal; as a consequence, negotiations tend to be more competitive.
- It is easier to close the conversation.
- It forces you to listen, because once a point has been made, the other party needs to respond to you.

Self-assessment question 17.3

Review the role of telephone negotiations.

Feedback on page 226

Revision question

Now try the revision question for this session on page 269.

Summary

Telephone negotiations are fundamentally different from face-to-face negotiations because of the lack of visual cues to enhance the communication process. The review of communicating by telephone highlighted three distinct phases to conversation: initial, middle and closing, which cover aspects such as the nature of the relationship and individual roles, exchange of information and conversational formalities. Verbal cues were discussed in relation to speaking, turn taking, and replacing non-verbal behaviour, as well as listening for clues about how the discussion will proceed.

Difficulties associated with telephone negotiations were then reviewed, including how to close a call. Listening more effectively was identified as a key skill and a number of approaches to overcoming hearing distortion, such as selective and adaptive listening, were presented. Finally, the advantages and disadvantages of telephone negotiation were briefly discussed and an approach to planning for telephone negotiations presented.

Suggested further reading

Lewicki et al (2003b) on improving communication skills.

17

Steele et al (1989) on telephone negotiations.

Negotiation Academy Europe: http://www.negotiationeurope.com: a useful website for latest practitioner-oriented articles.

Feedback on learning activities and self-assessment questions

Feedback on learning activity 17.1

From the previous study sessions, it is anticipated that discussion may focus on:

- Communication medium: it is possible for messages to be distorted because of a lack of visual cues over the telephone.
- Available time: there may be less time for each negotiating episode, but more time overall because of the multiple opportunities for discussion.
- Relationship building: it is easier to build a relationship when emotive responses can be seen; however, if a relationship is not desired then the telephone means time is not wasted on this.
- Direct costs for negotiating: costs are minimised, especially when negotiating with international parties.
- Preparation time.
- Imparting bad news: this is easier over the telephone.

Feedback on self-assessment question 17.1

Your answer should include five from the following points:

- time available
- clarity of communication medium (telephone line distortion)
- listening skills, especially active listening skills
- speaking skills (ability to listen for cues)
- turn-taking competence
- turn-giving competence
- awareness of the possible meanings of words and silence
- understanding of the other party, including relationship context
- awareness of any cultural under- or overtones to the conversation
- preparation for the call, including alerting the other party to expect the call.

Feedback on learning activity 17.2

1   Providing an agenda for the telephone conversation ahead of the call using another medium (for example, by email or letter or at a previous face-to-face meeting) may ensure all the issues are covered in the discussion. Similarly, agreeing at the start of the conversation what needs to be covered may be a useful starting point.
2   Asking for feedback, response, feelings, thoughts, views when appropriate: What do you think about that?'; 'How do you feel about this so far?'
3   Questions which seek to clarify understanding may be helpful in identifying whether there are any misperceptions in what has been said:

'Can you run that past me again please?' Summaries of the discussion so far also help clarity: 'So far, we have discussed delivery, quality and unit costs; I think that leaves just warranty and servicing.'

It is important to remember that visual cues are missing in telephone negotiations, so speakers need to ensure they replace non-verbal responses (facial and body movements) with verbal ones, such as listening noises ('uh-uh' and so on). Next time you use the telephone with family or a friend, try giving no response to the other person – and see what happens!

Feedback on self-assessment question 17.2

Your answer may cover aspects relating to the telephone conversation:

- Understanding the other party, the language they use, their frame of reference and the points they make.
- Selective listening (on both sides) which means the whole message is not properly received, or will be misinterpreted.
- Hearing all the cues from the other party, and responding to them appropriately.
- Providing all the cues for the other party to respond appropriately.

They may also relate to the physical context of the call:

- Ensuring there is enough time and a conducive environment for a telephone negotiation.
- Establishing an interference-free call connection.
- Connecting to the right person in order to conduct the negotiation!

Feedback on learning activity 17.3

Your answer should cover the following points:

- Consider the phases of the negotiation; determine content, bargaining ranges, BATNA, strategy and tactics, relational setting, concession patterns and implementation. Remember it is unlikely that complex issues will be satisfactorily dealt with by telephone.
- Ensure the cultural context is accounted for in the preparation phase.
- Prepare your speaking and listening skills for telephone negotiation: including acknowledging points and active listening; also asking specific types of question and summarising to enhance clarity.
- Be aware of any colloquialisms or jargon which may be misinterpreted by the other party; find 'plain English' ways of communicating the message.
- Prepare an agenda which may act as a prompt for yourself, even if this is not provided to the other party as an aide to the negotiation. During the early part of the telephone call, this may be developed with the other party.
- Arrange in advance to speak to the appropriate person at a time when you can both give the discussion its due attention in an appropriate environment.
- Pay attention to detail and check understanding when speaking to the other party; be prepared to examine the points made.

17

- Follow-up the telephone discussion with a written summary of the outcomes agreed and send it to the other party.
- Make any personal notes on the telephone negotiation as an 'aide memoire' as well as a learning device for future.

Feedback on self-assessment question 17.3

Telephone negotiations are often seen as a useful follow-up to face-to-face meetings. Your answer should cover the following points:

- The relationship context.
- Previous experience of both parties in telephone negotiating.
- Previous face-to-face contact between the individuals.
- The topics planned for discussion and their potential influence on the parties.
- The need for visual cues to support the negotiation process, such as documentation, samples and so on.
- The type of approach used for the negotiation (distributive or collaborative).
- The range of negotiating tactics to be used.
- The availability of resources such as time, meeting space, people to support the negotiation process.
- The type of follow-up activity required, including writing up the agreement and, subsequently, the ratification and implementation of the deal.

Your answers should also consider:

- The difficulties associated with telephone negotiations such as language, lack of visual cues, possible misinterpretations.
- The role of geographic distance.
- The perceptions of the other party and the likely influence of a telephone negotiation on the outcome.

17

Internal negotiations

Introduction

Internal negotiation is complementary to the achievement of goals with external parties. The extract above indicates that purchasers must win the commitment of internal stakeholders in order to integrate their activities with the business goals. Yet, conflict between stakeholders and purchasers is commonplace, often because stakeholders do not value the role of purchasing beyond cost reduction. Thus the ability of purchasers to negotiate the internal mandate to engage in external negotiations with suppliers is key; just take a look through the vacancies pages of *Supply Management* to see how employers emphasise this.

It is clear that failure to achieve a successful outcome to an internal negotiation will surely lead to failure of an external negotiation. This is not least because a specification needs expert guidance in development but also because the deal may fail to win the commitment of stakeholders on implementation.

This study session identifies the differences and similarities between internal and external negotiations, and examines the nature of conflict in internal situations. Finally, a plan for preparing for internal negotiation is discussed.

MW: 'The business itself doesn't talk, you have to understand the people, and the people you need to talk to are the key stakeholders in the business. You have to establish who the leaders are and go and speak to them.' Response KW: 'A successful relationship is one that's two way... if it's always me knocking on the door, it's a one-way marriage'.

Comments on the soft skills needed by purchasers to enhance their influence inside an organisation (reported in *Supply Management*, 2004)

Session learning objectives

After completing this session you should be able to:

18.1 Identify the key differences in conducting internal negotiations compared with external.
18.2 Examine the difficulties that are encountered in internal negotiations.
18.3 Prepare a plan for conducting effective internal negotiations.

Unit content coverage

This study session covers the following topics from the official CIPS unit content document:

Statement of practice

Explain the different approaches required when negotiating in different settings.

Learning objectives

4.6 Identify and evaluate the key features of effective negotiation with internal customers across the organisation.

18

- Listening to the internal customer's perspective
- Rapport building techniques
- Dealing with difficult customers
- Concessions, and the impact on purchasing

Prior knowledge

Study sessions 1 to 17

Timing

You should set aside about 4 hours to read and complete this session, including learning activities, self-assessment questions, the suggested further reading (if any) and the revision question.

18.1 Negotiating mandates

In study session 11, discussion about the successful outcome of a negotiation highlighted the importance of internal negotiation in generating an achievable mandate. Implicit within each of the negotiation phases is that both parties, the purchaser and the supplier, are:

- Able to carry the mandate from their respective organisations to enter into negotiation.
- Authorised to concede on the issues discussed in the bidding (bargaining) phase.
- Formally approved by the respective buying and selling organisations to close a deal and, subsequently, to act upon it.

Thus internal negotiation is important for decision making and problem solving, as well as managing conflict resulting from the inevitable differences in opinion on the bases for engaging external suppliers. It is also, however, important for team negotiations, as discussed in study session 14. In a procurement context, where the role of purchasing is as a facilitator to the business, it is a fundamental skill, because more effective internal negotiation means that external negotiations can enhance business value. It is, in essence, about the internal alignment of support and resources.

Morse (2005) identifies that without internal alignment, external negotiations are seriously undermined:

- Implementation may suffer because not all internal parties are ready to support the agreement reached.
- Conflict with internal colleagues, and the risk of interference from them, increases.
- Team members will not reflect consensus opinion but individual positions.
- Alienation from your internal support base may result from lack of involvement of colleagues.

18

Learning activity 18.1

Compare and contrast personal experiences of internal and external negotiations. Which was more difficult?

Feedback on page 232

A key similarity between internal and external negotiations is the complex, multi-party nature of the process. They both involve tangible resources (people, money, time) and intangible resources, such as trust, honesty and reputation. Relationships are also a prominent feature, as Morse (2005) states: 'yesterday's turf-conscious manager might be tomorrow's critical project ally.' Similarities also exist in the way the individuals involved in the negotiation may change; people move on to new jobs both within and outside the organisation.

Here also lies the key difference: agreement is a necessity, not an option. It is important, therefore, that negotiators adopt a win-win approach which is interest-based, rather than adversarial, in order that internal negotiating adds, and prolongs, value for the organisation. Morse argues that communication with internal stakeholders is especially important in developing strategies for successful internal negotiation. Communication should ensure (Morse, 2005):

- Internal colleagues are not 'surprised' with external negotiation outcomes.
- Internal colleagues are actively engaged in joint problem solving, and in preparation for external negotiations.
- Internal relationships are managed effectively so that there is open support for the external deal.

A first step is to identify the influential individuals in the internal negotiation:

- Who is interested/implicated/involved in the deal?
- Whose support is important for effective implementation?
- Who would not want the deal to be implemented?
- Who could actively support the deal?

Morse suggests it is often a good idea to work back from implementing the deal to the beginning of the process in order to identify key individuals and generate support.

Self-assessment question 18.1

Consider a scenario where a general manager has engaged a consultancy organisation and the finance manager has asked you to 'get involved'. Identify the key considerations for an internal negotiation.

Feedback on page 233

18

18.2 Internal conflict

Cohen (2005) highlights that the basic difficulty with achieving success in internal negotiation arises from the different 'world views' interested parties have. For example, marketing people view the production of a magazine in terms of sales; sales in terms of revenue generated from advertising space; purchasing in terms of cost savings for production materials bought; editorial staff in terms of stories and pictures and the publisher in terms of profitability! This amounts to functional speciality which can lead to conflict between individuals because of a 'silo mentality', whereas the overall aim is to achieve a common goal, namely to enhance the business. It is important, therefore, to recognise that those silos exist and deal with them appropriately. 'Both good information and an open mind can empower you to keep corporate tribes from waging war instead of waging peace.' (Cohen, 2005)

Learning activity 18.2

Managers are often keen on a purchasing department that is good at finding savings but generally less enthusiastic when their budget is being cut. Discuss how internal conflict can be overcome.

Feedback on page 233

Cohen identifies a number of potential steps to overcoming silo mentality:

- Remember people make up the organisation.
- Identify the people with an interest in the external negotiation.
- Identify who will make the decision to implement the outcome of the external negotiation.
- Ask colleagues' opinions about the internal people you need to negotiate with. Then consider their decision-making processes; identify the most efficient individuals; and identify their underlying motives.

Decision making by committee on multiple issues can be chaotic at best. It may, therefore, be better to review previous discussions with individuals and use the information generated from that in order to produce an agenda which can facilitate a negotiation. As previously discussed, an agenda that has been co-developed is most likely to achieve a collaborative outcome.

A further approach to resolving antagonistic behaviour is to produce rules of engagement, such as clarifying before challenging a point, or only allowing one person to speak at a time. A procedural agreement may be used to establish a relationship by, for example, specifying how decisions will be made, or how conflict will be dealt with. Clearly, the more involved the whole group is in developing the rules, the greater the chances are of success.

Conflict typically results in either a refusal to cooperate or an undermining of progress by some means away from the face-to-face negotiation. This can be dealt with by encouraging the individual's participation and, simultaneously, publicising the involvement of those that do participate. Of

18

course, such an approach may be too subtle, meaning a direct comment, albeit said with patience, may be appropriate.

Self-assessment question 18.2

'People must rely on group collaboration if each member is to experience the optimum of success and goal achievement.' Gordon (1991: 211)

'There's no doubt that purchasing has the potential to take on the role of a strategic business adviser on cost management for the whole business, but to do this, it needs to earn the respect of the rest of the organisation in order to be invited to have an opinion in the first place.' Wheatley (2005)

Considering these two quotes, briefly comment on the role of internal team development for negotiations.

Feedback on page 234

18.3 Planning for internal negotiation

First, attempt learning activity 18.3 below.

Learning activity 18.3

List the factors identified as good practice for the effective management of internal negotiations within your organisation.

Feedback on page 234

Effective negotiators prepare for external negotiation using internal resource, including the expertise of colleagues, which is deal-focused. Morse identifies a six-step plan for preparing for internal negotiations:

1   Examine the interests of those with a vested interest in the negotiation; put yourself in their shoes in order to identify their motivations and needs.
2   Build relationships, in much the same way as you would with external parties. Be transparent, share information, do not present surprises and facilitate genuine participation. Continue to communicate throughout the process.
3   Co-create with internal stakeholders; ask for their ideas.
4   Determine how internal colleagues will measure success of the external deal. Using their terms enables you to confirm success to them. Be sure to communicate your (jointly identified) BATNA, so that in the event of a pull-out internal colleagues remain supportive of your decision.
5   Develop alignment and consensus with internal resources.
6   Remember to close the internal deal before the final agreement is made in the external negotiation.

18

There is often a complex set of internal relationships that support external deals. Consensus built by matching internal and external interests results in best value for both parties and a deal that is implementable. This is, nonetheless, difficult to achieve, as highlighted by recent research (Unisys, 2004) where 47 per cent of information technology decision-makers were found to believe that inflexible purchasing processes negatively impacted on their long-term business goals and best practice.

Now attempt self-assessment question 18.3 below. Spend at least thirty minutes on this exercise.

Self-assessment question 18.3

Compare and contrast internal and external negotiations.

Feedback on page 235

Revision question

Now try the revision question for this session on page 269.

Summary

Internal negotiation is the process of obtaining the mandate to conduct external negotiations. It is about the internal alignment of support and resources so that successful implementation follows the external agreement. Its purpose is to minimise conflict with internal colleagues; to build team consensus; and to avoid alienation from internal support. Key factors in achieving a win-win for internal stakeholders were discussed.

Conflict was identified as arising from the difference in world view between negotiators and internal stakeholders, which may lead to a silo mentality. Approaches to breaking down the internal barriers were reviewed. Finally, a six-step plan for preparing for internal negotiations was presented, which emphasised the importance of understanding the individuals involved and the importance of open and honest communication with colleagues.

Suggested further reading

The Negotiator Magazine: http://negotiatormagazine.com/ contains some useful articles about internal negotiation, including that cited within this study session by Morse.

Feedback on learning activities and self-assessment questions

Feedback on learning activity 18.1

Your answer to this may depend upon the view that internal colleagues have of purchasing's role. Organisational structure, for example, may be influential here – hierarchies restrict interactions and control levels of discussion.

18

Factors that may make negotiation easier include:

- Prior relationship with individuals involved – good rapport, mutual respect and trust.
- Experience of internal negotiation.
- Experience of specific negotiating context.

Factors that may impede internal negotiation:

- History of conflict with individuals involved.
- No history of contact.
- Limited prior experience of either internal negotiation or the specific context.

It may be possible to overcome these difficulties by providing a summary of the situation from your perspective, an overview of those involved in the negotiation, and an idea of the resource implications, including a timetable. A preliminary meeting to introduce colleagues may help to establish support; regular updates may be used to show progress, including early wins. In effect, building support is achieved over time, in much the same way that a supplier relationship is built.

Feedback on self-assessment question 18.1

Your answer may have considered the following points:

- The nature of the organisation and the role of purchasing within it. If it is seen as an integrated function, then it is more likely that the general manager will accept the purchaser.
- The role of the general manager and his attitude towards purchasing. For example, if he is hostile to purchasing's involvement, then getting involved may mean identifying how to do this at an earlier stage of the buying cycle.
- The methods of communication that work best with this manager, including conflict management approach.
- The timescales involved in generating a negotiating mandate and reaching agreement with external suppliers, and the implications this has on the people that will be involved throughout the process.
- The need to use an integrative approach to negotiation, which requires that the purchaser must be familiar with the market context, as well as the appropriate tactics for success, including conflict management techniques.

Feedback on learning activity 18.2

Your answer could have identified the following points (see Morse, 2005):

- Define the boundaries of interaction between the parties before the internal negotiation, and specify any behaviour that is considered to be inappropriate.
- Negotiate with different departments, or 'silos', separately.
- Produce an agenda so that individuals have the opportunity to be well prepared.

- Make it clear that a person's behaviour is unacceptable so that they cannot reasonably continue with it.
- Confront the behaviour directly to stop it.
- There may be organisational means of dealing with inappropriate or extreme conflict; a last resort may be to refer to the law.

Feedback on self-assessment question 18.2

Teams are often said to be capable of achieving more than individuals. However, if the team is not cohesive, this may present problems in an external negotiation and will, ultimately, lead to failure. Before negotiation, therefore, team building activities may include:

- Identifying group norms – and those factors which undermine group cohesiveness.
- Enable individual group members to: articulate disagreement in a 'safe' environment; become leaders but not dominators; vent feelings; learn respect for others in the team.

Relationships between team members must be given time to develop. It is important to identify roles, as well as individual and leader expectations. Cohesiveness is built as a result of success, so an early achievement for the team is important. Effective teams are those that:

- Have clear objectives.
- Involve all team members in decision making.
- Encourage active participation, including expression of feelings.
- View conflict as healthy, leading to more creative solutions.
- Build consensus among members.
- Diagnose problems before presenting solutions.
- Respect one another's expertise.
- Hold mutual trust for members.
- Are flexible and support team development.

Mannix (2005) identifies that a new negotiating team's preparation phase should include three components:

- substantive discussion of the negotiation
- skills review of team members and assignment of team roles
- a plan for the negotiation process.

In the context of the second quotation, one aim of the team-building effort should be to 'sell' the benefits of purchasing to internal stakeholders.

You should also revisit study session 14 for a review of negotiation teams.

Feedback on learning activity 18.3

Your answer may have considered the following points:

- Organisational structure which facilitates collaboration, and is supported with widely published contact information and clearly defined responsibilities for individuals.

18

- Harmonious work environment that minimises confrontation and emphasises integration, supported by good pay and work conditions, effective management, and a healthy market context.
- Clear procurement strategy, which is supported by other functions.
- Strong interpersonal relationships between key decision-making individuals which facilitate exchanges between functions.
- Transparent processes which enable individuals to understand and participate in decision making.

Feedback on self-assessment question 18.3

Your answer should consider the following points:

- Nature of outcome differs: internal negotiation results in support; external negotiation results in substantive agreement on supplies.
- Opportunity for using different approaches (distributive versus integrative) is restricted for internal negotiations.
- Scope and nature of preparatory information differs: likely to be more detailed for internal negotiations.
- Relationship building phase important is to both (when integrative solution is sought with external party).
- Process may differ, including the means of communication, and types of negotiator behaviour.
- Power sources likely to differ.
- Questions play a key role in both in order to determine interests and needs.
- Internal negotiation complements external negotiation; without successful internal negotiation, successful external negotiation is ultimately likely to fail.

18

18

E-negotiations

Introduction

As Malhotra and Majchrzak's comment implies, technology is increasingly used as a means to facilitate business. It is often considered to be more cost effective and efficient in terms of response speed and convenience than traditional face-to-face approaches. Nonetheless, e-negotiation, which is an inherently human activity, presents some particular considerations, which are reviewed in this study session.

First, the key differences between e-negotiation and face-to-face approaches are reviewed, including consideration of the advantages and disadvantages. Subsequently, a plan for conducting e-negotiation is presented.

'Integrated into virtual workspaces, technology features now exist that enable members to stay close to their local situations while engaging in global activities critical to their company's sustainability.'

Arvind Malhotra and Ann Majchrzak (2005: 14) commenting on the role of technology in business

Session learning objectives

After completing this session you should be able to:

19.1 Identify the key differences between conducting e-negotiations and face-to-face negotiations.
19.2 Examine the types of difficulties that are encountered in e-negotiations.
19.3 Prepare a plan for conducting effective negotiations via the internet.

Unit content coverage

E-negotiation is an increasingly important aspect of negotiator skill. It is acknowledged to add a new dimension to the process of negotiation and the behaviour of negotiators, and there is, therefore, no exact match to the official CIPS unit content document. This study session does, however, cover a number of statements of practice (albeit within a technological context) including:

*   Apply a range of negotiation theories in order to achieve set outcomes.
*   Differentiate between a range of persuasion tools and techniques.
*   Explain the different approaches required when negotiating in different settings.

Prior knowledge

Study sessions 1 to 18

Resources

Access to the internet.

Timing

You should set aside about 4 hours to complete this session, including all reading, learning activities, self-assessment questions and sample assessments or examination questions.

19.1 E-negotiation defined

E-negotiation is negotiation where the internet supplements or replaces traditional face-to-face interaction, based on telecommunications technologies.

Learning activity 19.1

Compare and contrast personal experiences of face-to-face negotiations with different types of electronically mediated negotiations that you are familiar with (email, internet auctions, and so on). What aspects were easier to deal with over the internet?

Feedback on page 246

The rapid growth in technologies that facilitate exchange relationships between buyers and sellers has meant there are inevitable shifts in the way negotiations are entered into and conducted between organisations. Table 19.1 identifies examples of the multiple channels available for negotiation.

Table 19.1 Examples of multiple negotiation channels

	Automated	Human controlled
Synchronous (both parties connected simultaneously)	• internet service (e-auction) • mediated telephone call	• telephone call • online chat • collaborative tools
Asynchronous	• automated email • SMS (short messaging service) • fax on demand	• email response • traditional postal mail

Source: based on Strauss et al (2003)

Early e-negotiations were focused on price as the predominant driver, which gave rise to the internet auction (for example, eBay in a consumer context). A similar form of e-negotiation is 'state-your-price' (such as priceline.com), where the buyer issues the price they are willing to pay and suppliers make offers accordingly (Hobson, 1999). A further approach is 'person-to-computer' haggling where the computer assumes characteristics of a negotiator to make bids against you on a product or service that has been sourced by a search engine. The latter approach is aimed at those whose preferred negotiating style is to haggle (Hobson, 1999). Interestingly, these have been termed as negotiation entertainment ('negotainment', Hobson,

19

1999), and are predicated upon the inherent desire of humans to negotiate. Yet, the approaches are used widely in commercial settings.

The result of e-auctions has been an increase in buyer power which has led (for some) to a reduction in costs anywhere between 5 and 15 per cent (Abery and Glindemann, 2004). E-auctions are, however, a special form of negotiation which is often considered to be an alternative to negotiation (similar to tendering). Others point out its limited use as a purchasing negotiation tool because the seller can manipulate the balance of power. For example, in a face-to-face situation, the buyer often has a high level of power at the start of a negotiation which they perceive to diminish as their commitment to a deal increases; whereas in e-auctions some suppliers are becoming expert at exploiting bid processes late in the bidding phase (this is discussed further later in this section). Furthermore, as Young (2004) argues, its use may have the effect of 'deskilling' purchasers because it distances purchasing from strategic decisions, which require solution building and relationship management approaches with suppliers.

Nonetheless, e-auctions are now well used and increasingly complex because developments in technology facilitate exchanges on more than one issue (which was traditionally price). It can be argued that they are a form of negotiation because they meet the three criteria for negotiation: both parties may vary the terms of agreement through a bidding (or bargaining) process; agreement and conflict exist simultaneously; and, the resource is scarce (see study session 1).

There are a number of different forms of e-auction in use:

- English auctions: where successive bids raise the price until only one bidder remains (the winning bid).
- **Dutch auctions**: where the seller notifies a (high) price and then subsequently reduces the price until the 'ask' price is accepted by a buyer (which in effect is the only bid).
- Sealed bid auctions: where all bidders simultaneously place a bid which is kept secret from other bidders. The highest price wins, based on their bid (called 'first-price' sealed bid) or based on the bid of the second-highest price, where the winning bid has to match the deal of the closest bidder to them ('second-price' sealed bid).
- **Reverse** auction: where many suppliers bid for a buyer's purchase order (frequently used for large scale supply of commodities).
- Double-sided auctions: where many suppliers and many buyers bid against one another to secure a deal (often used in stocks trading).

For a detailed description of these auctions, see Ku and Malhotra (2001).

Suffice to say, technologies are evolving rapidly, resulting in new forms of auctions and variations to the basic approaches identified above. One such example, based on sealed bids and sometimes the English auction, is the proxy-bid system. This is where the party does not have to be available for the complete auction; instead, they specify their highest offer, the 'reservation price' (through an automated intelligent bidding system), and then let the system place bids until the reservation price is reached. Once this happens, the party is notified by email and given the option then to revise their reservation price.

Now have a look on the internet for any new forms of auctions being used in your own industry context. Use the following search terms in a familiar search engine:

- e-auctions
- e-bidding.

One site you may want to examine Free Market: http://www.freemarket.com/. CIPS also offer guidelines on conducting e-auctions.

The advantages and disadvantages of e-auctions can be summarised as follows (adapted from Ku and Malhotra, 2001):

Advantages

- Asynchronous exchange means that parties do not necessarily have to be present at the same time for negotiation to take place.
- They connect many buyers and sellers who would not otherwise be in a position to negotiate together. Searching can be simplified and narrowed through the power of search engines.
- They provide high levels of information, because buyers and sellers are able to 'shop around' to find the appropriate range for variables.
- Bid histories with particular buyers also provide considerable information and build up a resource for those who remain engaged with the processes.

Disadvantages

- Barriers to access, including familiarity with technology and access to the trading software may restrict e-auctions to only the most technologically developed regions of the world.
- Typically, price is the main negotiating variable, often meaning negotiation is a distributive process, rather than an integrative one which builds relationships between buyers and sellers.
- Asynchronous exchanges can increase the amount of time spent online whilst waiting for a decision on a bid.
- Credibility of buyers and sellers, as well as **online auction** sites, is often questioned; the security, integrity and reliability of deals made are important factors for consideration.

As briefly mentioned above, e-auctions can be exploited by sellers; therefore, moral, legal and ethical aspects are also worthy of consideration for e-auctions. Collusion and coordination between buyers and sellers has often been encouraged, with many e-auction sites making buyer and seller contact data freely available. It is arguable, however, whether the process is ultimately fair and transparent. For example, eBay has introduced guidelines against using 'shilling', which is the tactic of bidding up another's auction (tantamount to collusion) with the penalty of banning users should they be caught out. Those who are particularly familiar with, or have studied the use of, e-auctions, are often keen to engage in distributive tactics, such as 'sniping'. This is the placing of bids as late into the auction as possible in order to achieve a better outcome. It is, therefore, important to analyse how the other parties who are bidding against the organisation have behaved previously, in order that a bid strategy can be appropriately developed.

Monitoring the rules of auctions in which the organisation is to engage can be a heavy investment (time and effort). A further aspect of the preparation for e-auctions must be the scope of the technology itself. Considerations may include:

- Availability of flexible end point which could help to overcome sniping.
- Ability to set reservation prices, which may restrict inappropriate bidding – and is this made public or kept secret from other bidders?

More complex forms of e-negotiation within the context of commercial procurement have emerged which require different approaches: for example, using text-based communications, such as email. Whereas e-auctions tend to focus on single issue bargaining, other media enable multiple issues to be negotiated.

Text-based technologies, more than video, increase the abilities of the parties to recall and review information (because it is recorded). It has often been identified that where e-negotiation is conducted, there is more clarity in information exchanged because it enables immediate interrogation of issues that are not clear (Druckman et al, 2004). Furthermore, response speed is faster and perceptions of the negotiators indicate greater satisfaction with the medium when multiple technologies are involved, such as text and video forms. Figure 19.1 presents a continuum of technology solutions for e-negotiating.

Figure 19.1: E-negotiation technology continuum

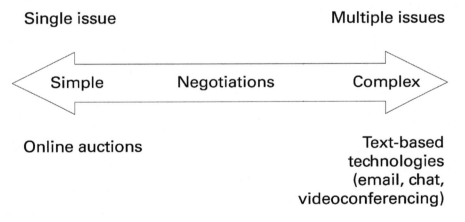

Choice of communication medium will clearly depend on the negotiation context, since, for example, e-auctions will not be appropriate for all negotiation situations. Malhotra and Majchrzak (2005) suggest that for future success, teams must make use of media that enable richer communication. In a negotiation, this leads to more information being available to the parties which creates greater common understanding and, therefore, the basis for more integrative solutions. This can be synchronous (where parties exchange information as they would in a face-to-face situation, with both being 'present' for the negotiation) or asynchronous (as described above). Rich media may include:

- electronic whiteboard application sharing
- audio- and videoconferencing

19

- central knowledge repository such as searchable threaded discussion boards
- hyperlinked documents.

Demand for e-negotiation also comes from the need for dispute resolution (Yuan et al, 2003). For example, in 2001 it was reported (Katsh and Rifkin, 2001) that 30,000 disputes between eBay buyers and sellers were being mediated by a third party supplier. Indeed, there are a number of organisations that supply online dispute resolution services; they work primarily by providing private email, chat room and messaging facilities, including videoconferencing services. The reasons for the growth of this, not surprisingly, are convenience, speed of service delivery and cost savings. (Use a search engine to look for 'online dispute resolution services'.)

Problems occur online, however, with the lack of communication efficiencies, effectiveness and emotional exchange processes that are an important and inherent part of the face-to-face negotiation process. Discussion in previous study sessions has highlighted how face-to-face interactions are often fundamental to negotiations, and that techniques that control (and therefore reduce) the flow of verbal and non-verbal signals between the parties result in a significant loss of information. Indeed, much emphasis has been placed on improving the negotiation process by developing communication skills. Of course, in a modern commercial environment, this includes non face-to-face means. The communication process will itself vary depending on the purchasing context, relationship intentions, and the technologies that support these. These issues are discussed further in section 19.2.

Self-assessment question 19.1

Consider the case of a buyer who has purchased a wide variety of product categories via e-auctions, many of which have delivered significant savings. Discuss the advantages and disadvantages of continuing to buy these products using e-auctions.

Feedback on page 246

19.2 E-negotiation behaviour

Problems have been highlighted with the communication efficiencies, effectiveness and emotional exchange processes which differentiate the online negotiation from the face-to-face process. Whilst some of the difficulties highlighted in the discussion about e-auctions can be overcome using text-based media, Thompson and Nadler (2002) identify four other important factors for consideration:

- Interpersonal rapport: the extent to which the parties are in synchrony (harmony) with one another. This is built up over time and face to face: the greater the personal understanding between the parties, then the more likely there is to be good rapport for e-negotiating. Indicators of good rapport are overtones of mutual support for one another – agreements and supporting behaviours (see study session 13).

- Coordination: where the parties may converge on agreement if they are close (within bargaining range). This is usually achieved most effectively face to face (or via telephone), because there is a greater chance to identify an opportunity for agreement.
- Information: the multiple exchanges that are most likely when there is a physical proximity between the buyer and seller. It is also the case that written forms of communication often take more effort than verbal, meaning there is a tendency to provide less information to start with because people are less proficient at writing than they are at speaking.
- Social contagion: whether similar emotive and affective exchanges are used; also whether the response time lags are similar, or the type of language used is equally direct. For example, research has indicated that some negotiators tend to be more aggressive when using text-based media than when negotiating face to face.

Learning activity 19.2

What are the difficulties with text-based negotiations, and how might they be overcome? What are the benefits of text-based negotiations?

Feedback on page 247

Where technology adds considerable benefit to e-negotiating is in facilitating the decision-making process. This goes beyond the typical roles that negotiators are familiar with:

- development of strategy and tactics
- information generation and exchange
- communication.

Often referred to as decision support tools (e-negotiation support or eNS), technology may facilitate decision making by undertaking some or all of the activities traditionally undertaken by a negotiator. Such systems run using a set of decision 'rules' which, necessarily, restrict interpersonal exchanges. Although still in a relatively early stage of development, eNS involves mapping typical negotiation activities (development of goals and strategies, tactics, and so on) to an electronic environment. As yet, the studies into relative success are incomplete and only partially reported on (Kersten and Lai, 2005).

Nonetheless, as part of the e-procurement process, the benefits of e-negotiation are (see Chemconnect: http://chemconnect.com/):

- Better purchasing decisions based more reliable (up-to-date) market data.
- Quick and cost-effective identification and qualification of new suppliers.
- Faster negotiation using online tools.
- Lower prices.

19

243

- Lower costs resulting from electronic exchange of data with suppliers so that order processing is streamlined.

Good practice for written communication (Mulholland, 1991) will also apply to e-negotiation:

- Ensure the important aspects are included.
- Establish the main proposition.
- Prepare any data needed to support your proposition.

It is also important to ensure the text is appropriately framed so that the reader can understand your points.

Self-assessment question 19.2

List five key considerations for e-negotiations.

Feedback on page 247

19.3 Planning for e-negotiating

Planning for e-negotiating includes the same basic phases as those outlined throughout the previous study sessions. First, attempt learning activity 19.3 below.

Learning activity 19.3

List factors that are identified as good practice for the effective management of different types of e-negotiations.

Feedback on page 248

Lewicki et al (2003b) identify a ten-step plan for preparing for e-negotiation:

1 Ensure a relationship is developed before the negotiation, even if this only constitutes brief small talk (Nadler, 2003). This enables the parties to visualise a 'face' behind the technology.
2 Be explicit about the process of the negotiation.
3 If there are 'observers' involved supporting either party, it is good practice to ensure everyone knows who they are and why they are there.
4 Select a medium (email, e-auction, and so on) that is the most appropriate for generating all the information needed for consideration by both parties.
5 Label emotion explicitly so that the other party understands why it is being used. Do not 'flame'!
6 Do synchronise offers and counteroffers; and if you are unsure whose turn it is, seek clarification.

19

7 Use questions to check assumptions about interests, positions, offers, proposals and so on. The lack of face-to-face communication means there is likely to be much less understanding of the other party.

8 When communicating in writing, take care not to state anything that can be used against you, and avoid taking advantage of the other party in the same way.

9 Although it is easier to use unethical tactics (because facts are often harder to establish than in face-to-face negotiation), it is best not to as written comments can be stored for later use.

10 Use an approach (integrative or distributive) that is appropriate to the medium being used. For example, it is often difficult to know when to stick to a point or make a move.

A final point is:

- Use learning points from previous experiences to enhance preparation, planning and execution of future e-negotiations.

Self-assessment question 19.3

What factors should be included in a plan for e-negotiations?

Feedback on page 248

Revision question

Now try the revision question for this session on page 269.

Summary

This study session has examined the nature and role of technology in supporting negotiations, so-called e-negotiations. Review considered the variety of e-auctions that are used in e-procurement (English, Dutch, sealed bid, reverse, double-sided) and variations of common approaches, such as proxy-bidding. Advantages and disadvantages of e-auctions were examined in some detail. Strategy and tactical ploys, such as shilling and sniping, were discussed.

Other forms of e-negotiation include the use of text-based media, such as email, chat and other collaborative (mediated) facilities. Four key considerations were identified for using text-based media: rapport building, coordination, information use and social contagion. Development of online decision support tools was also briefly commented on as beneficial to text-based forms of e-negotiating. Finally, a ten-step plan was identified as a planning aid to e-negotiation.

Suggested further reading

CIPS practice overview on e-auctions.

19

Lewicki et al (2003b) on virtual negotiations.

Feedback on learning activities and self-assessment questions

Feedback on learning activity 19.1

Your answer may have considered the following points:

- Difficulties with lack of face-to-face interaction.
- Misinterpretation of meanings with written words.
- Complications arising from storing of information provided in electronic forms.
- Ability to deal rapidly with international situations, where the parties are physically distant and where time differences may otherwise make communication problematic.
- Speed of response, compared with face-to-face negotiations.
- Ability to access new sources of supply, which would otherwise be unheard of (auctions).
- Everything is recorded, thus providing an audit trail.

Feedback on self-assessment question 19.1

Possible advantages:

- Suppliers will learn about market prices for their products and may, therefore, be keen for future business resulting in a lower purchase price.
- Refined (rationalised) specification for the product or service resulting from the purchaser's previous experience may be attractive to a broader range of suppliers;
- Shift in market dynamics may make e-auctions appropriate.
- E-auctions may facilitate the purchaser's understanding of the market context by allowing suppliers to find their own levels in the bidding process; this can be used by the organisation in their marketing of end products.
- Supplier market experience of e-auctioning may make the process more acceptable (normal) to them as time goes on.

Possible disadvantages:

- Subsequent savings from e-auctions are likely to be lower than the first; experience may influence suppliers to hold positions in reserve, and to protect information and final offer point.
- Costs associated with technology may be high, including generating sufficient experience to support the process.
- Collusion between suppliers may result in higher prices, especially where the supplies are differentiated in the market, making competitive positions imperfect (such as in the supply of services).
- Focus on issues other than price and reducing overall costs as drivers for increasing value may be limited by using e-auctions.
- High levels of preparation are required for subsequent development of the specification and any rationalisation.

Other points to note:

19

Even when purchasers have been unsuccessful in their e-auctions, they will nonetheless have learned a great deal about the supply market context, and about the bidding processes which may be used to promote success in subsequent situations. The same applies to those on the supply side too.

Feedback on learning activity 19.2

Difficulties:

- How rapport can be built when there are no face-to-face interactions and no previous trading experience. The disclosure of personal information, feelings and opinions via email may facilitate rapport building. In fact, this may be more effective than face-to-face means because some parties take instant dislike to one another – due to gender, age, physical attractiveness, and so on (Thompson and Nadler, 2002).
- Whether coordination can be achieved best through synchronous or asynchronous means. There are fewer exchanges when using text media than with face-to-face negotiation; so there is a potential for greater convergence where the parties are more closely linked, such as through synchronous exchange.
- Information exchange may be difficult to mediate because of storage and retrieval requirements; but it is probable that where both parties engage in a similar style of exchange, agreement is most achievable.
- Social contagion (following on from the previous two points): to analyse messages and then formulate responses with similar levels of emotive and affective content will be time-consuming.

Benefits:

- Greater clarity of information exchange because there is an audit trail of written information.
- Increased flexibility in negotiating because of asynchronous options.
- Lower costs than face-to-face negotiation because of lower resource requirements (time and space for conducting negotiation).
- Complements contractual relationships, because of the written nature of exchange.
- Facilitates a learning approach to the relationship because subsequent interactions build knowledge, which can be developed into a tangible resource by the parties.

Feedback on self-assessment question 19.2

Your answer should have considered five from the following points:

- Whether a relationship exists which enables the parties to enter into e-negotiation with some prior trading history and building on face-to-face exchanges.
- The goals of the e-negotiation: the complexity and type of variables to be agreed upon.
- The availability of suitable technologies to the parties involved, and user know-how for e-negotiating.
- The flexibility of e-negotiation technologies in achieving the goals set.

19

- The imperatives for information storage and retrieval (for example, compliance with the Freedom of Information Act) and the impact this may have on using text-based technology.
- Whether synchronous or asynchronous exchanges are more appropriate, with resulting implications for scheduling and the time spent on e-negotiating.
- The types of information that the parties wish to exchange; more detail can be communicated using multiple media technologies, rather than e-auctions.

Feedback on learning activity 19.3

Use the phases of negotiation as a guide to support your answer (see study session 1).

- Information about the negotiation situation will determine whether e-negotiation is the best approach for generating an appropriate deal. For example, are your likely suppliers able and willing to engage in e-negotiation?
- Evaluation of the technological solution to support e-negotiation is needed to ensure adequate flexibility. (Is it fit for purpose?)
- Use preliminary relationship building in order to establish an appropriate basis for e-negotiation where more personal interaction is not possible, especially if an integrative solution is sought.
- Consider how information generated during the negotiation will be used.

Feedback on self-assessment question 19.3

Your answer should include the following points:

- relationship context
- goals for the negotiation: for example, cost reductions
- role of a tendering process
- role of technology in supporting the negotiation
- preferences of the parties – whether technology will adequately support the negotiation process
- use of information generated
- process of reaching agreement, that is, bid making and counter-offers
- experience of the parties involved, and history of tactics used by the other party.

Evaluating personal performance

Introduction

'Make a distinction between what can be improved and when limitations will persist, no matter what we do.'

Sir Andrew Likierman, professor of management practice, London Business School, commenting on the limitations of measuring purchasing performance (2005: 24)

Likierman's comment is pertinent since the 'nature or nurture' debate ('Are people born with certain skills, or can they be taught how to develop them?') continues to influence thinking on skills development, when the key question is really how basic skills can be improved upon. Ability to reflect on experiences enables a process of learning and, in negotiations, there are some clear focuses for reflection:

- achievement of goals
- relative success of the process adopted in achieving goals
- personal (and team) effectiveness of communication.

This study session first reviews the negotiation outcome, and how this may vary when a relational outcome is sought. Finally, the role of reflection in learning is discussed.

Session learning objectives

After completing this session you should be able to:

20.1 Analyse outcome against objectives for a negotiation.
20.2 Explore the impact of personal relationship development on negotiations between the parties.
20.3 Evaluate the range of personal techniques by reflecting on performance.
20.4 Identify methods for training and development to improve negotiation techniques.

Unit content coverage

This study session covers the following topics from the official CIPS unit content document:

Statement of practice

Understand how to analyse negotiation performance.

Learning objectives

4.7 Evaluate personal effectiveness in negotiations in different contexts.

- Reflecting on performance
- Feedback mechanisms
- Looking ahead to improvement and development

Prior knowledge

Study sessions 1 to 19 (especially study sessions 12 to 16)

Timing

You should set aside about 5 hours to read and complete this session, including learning activities, self-assessment questions, the suggested further reading (if any) and the revision question.

20.1 Evaluating outcomes

Negotiations can be evaluated in much the same way as other organisational projects. Evaluation is an important activity because, as reported by the CBI (2005), some 70 per cent of deals that organisations make are sub-optimal at best, or simply bad for business! Immediate evaluation may provide rapid feedback to individuals for performance improvements; remedial actions can be implemented before problems arise between the parties; longer-term reviews can facilitate auditing; and strategic and procedural reviews can enable future business development (Maylor, 2003). Evaluation is, therefore, important for identifying where skills development is needed, what aspects of performance should be repeated and how future negotiations should be evaluated. It is fundamental to creating and sustaining a learning organisation, based on the lessons learned from activities (Senge, 1990; Pedlar et al, 1997).

This discussion suggests that improvement activities should be continuous, rather than one-off, for example post-negotiation. Furthermore, Pisano (1997) suggests that lessons from activities can be incorporated into future performance in two key ways: learning *before* doing (training and development) and learning *by* doing (outcome evaluation). Figure 20.1 illustrates the process.

Figure 20.1: Performance improvement

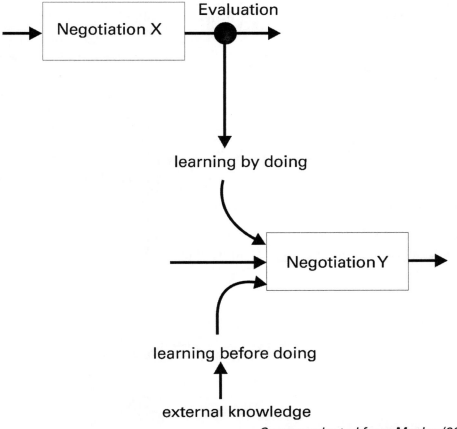

Negotiation X

Evaluation

learning by doing

Negotiation Y

learning before doing

external knowledge

Source: adapted from Maylor (2003)

Performance measurement considers the effectiveness of the outcome and the efficiency with which it is achieved (Horngren et al, 2005). Implementation of a deal is clearly the ultimate test of a successful outcome for the purchasing organisation. Evaluation of the deal concluded, however, also includes the process followed and personal performance, at individual and team levels. Table 20.1 identifies the basic criteria for evaluation.

Table 20.1 Review of negotiation

Criteria	Review
goals	evaluation against targets for each issue
financial	cost variance
human resources	team roles, motivations, skills
planning	costs, techniques used
control	basis for improvement

Discussion throughout previous study sessions has highlighted some important lessons for evaluation. Evaluation and review of negotiation should focus on:

- Processes, rather than individuals.
- Factual data, rather than opinion (memory loss may make the latter biased).
- Alternative scenario, such as: 'What if xxx had happened?'

- Problem-solving techniques, which will help more critical evaluation, rather than reaching premature conclusions.
- Evaluating cause and effect, rather than stereotyping.

There are three specific aspects that outcome evaluation needs to consider in relation to the phases of the negotiation (see figure 20.2):

1   outcome achievement
2   process appropriateness
3   personal and team communication performance.

Figure 20.2: Outcome evaluation and the phases of negotiation

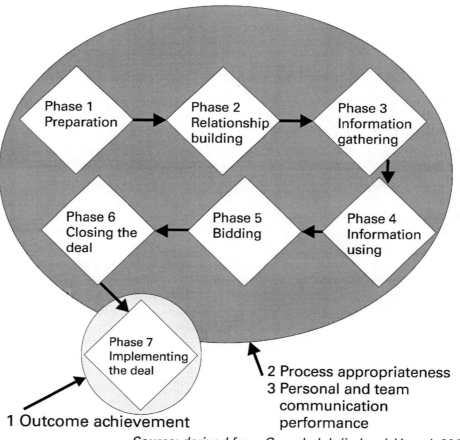

Source: derived from Greenhalgh (in Lewicki et al, 2003)

First, evaluation will consider whether goals set for the negotiation have been achieved. From a financial evaluation perspective, variance analysis calculates the variation between the final deal and the budgeted or targeted deal – a standard management accounting text will provide guidance on different forms of analysis that can be used.

The following questions may be asked in reviewing the outcome against each of the negotiation phases:

Implementing the deal phase

- Did the objectives for the negotiation remain realistic at the point of implementation?
- Were any important issues impacting on implementation left unresolved? How could they have been better dealt with?
- Have market dynamics influenced the implementation phase?

Preparation phase

- Did analysis of the market context mean that all appropriate variables were identified?
- How accurate were financial evaluations?
- Were ranges for all the variables established realistic?
- Did team members contribute appropriately to the preparation?
- Was the strategy selected appropriate to the negotiation situation?

Relationship building phase

- Did we have sufficient knowledge of the other party involved before commencing the negotiation?
- Was there an appropriate rapport between us that we could build on in the negotiation?
- Was an ethos of trust and mutuality established between the individuals and organisations before we started?

Information gathering phase

- Did we ask a range of questions?
- Did we understand the answers that were given?
- Did team members participate? Were we an effective team?

Information using phase

- Did we explore all the variables?
- Did we focus on common interests?
- Were we creative in identifying solutions to problems?

Bidding phase

- What messages were sent by the concessions we made – and were they (apparently) received as they were intended to be?

- Were proposals appropriate, and accepted by the other party?
- What impact did our tactics have on the other party?
- Were our persuasive techniques appropriate?
- Were we flexible yet firm?
- Did we use power appropriately?
- Did we trade variables effectively?

Closing the deal phase

- Did we summarise effectively?
- Did we capture the points made so that follow-up agreement was easy to write?
- Could visuals have improved the closing phase, for example, a flip chart?

When faced with a negotiation outcome failure, the review may examine the outcome in more detail, including:

- Were the goals we set realistic and achievable?
- Were we able to identify the variables they would use in the negotiation?
- Was there sufficient overlap of the parties' variables to enable agreement to be reached?
- Were priorities for their variables diametrically opposed to ours?
- Did we understand the underlying interests and motivations for their stated position?
- Were we able to convince the other party of our argument?
- Did we understand their needs? Did they understand ours?
- Could we answer all their questions?
- Did we understand their proposals?

And in the case of relational breakdown:

- How could deadlock have been prevented?
- How could we have dealt more effectively with their difficult behaviour?
- How could we have overcome the intractable position?
- How could we have behaved differently to avoid the breakdown?

This is by no means comprehensive. However, it is important to evaluate a successful outcome as well as an unsuccessful one. Lessons can be learned from both types of outcome which will improve future performance.

Self-assessment question 20.1

How does the preparation stage influence achievement of negotiation objectives?

Feedback on page 261

20.2 Relational outcome

Whilst evaluation of the organisation's outcome is important, the purchaser is only one side of a relationship – or one part of a complicated network of relationships between the purchaser and supplier, and their suppliers. Thus, without similar perceptions of the outcome for the supplier, it is likely that success will be short lived. Rackham et al (1996) identify that where the relationship is important, then developing measures of the outcome should also be a joint task. Figure 20.3 illustrates the likely impact of outcomes on relational conflict.

Figure 20.3: Impact of outcomes on relational conflict

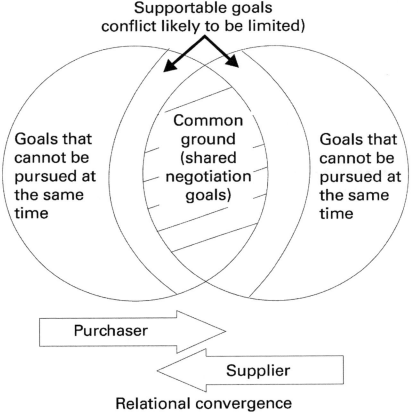

Source: adapted from Rackham et al (1996)

It can be seen that negotiation has a key role to play in bringing the parties closer together for joint value and benefit.

Learning activity 20.2

Review the negotiation approach for the different stages of a common relational development model that you are familiar with.

Feedback on page 262

So-called 'social preferences' are also an important consideration because of a basic need for fairness and equality. Indeed, research frequently identifies that negotiators value the outcome in relational terms despite the organisation's emphasis on economic payoffs (Moya, 2002).

In a relational context, trust has also been identified as important, albeit that a wide range of factors can contribute to trust, such as perceptions of reliability, credibility, honesty, integrity, openness, and the party's reputation. The relationship between trust and information exchange has been reviewed in study session 11, together with the resulting mistrust between parties who are unwilling to accept information at face value. The development of trust through information sharing is important because it exposes vulnerabilities and, therefore, provides each party with the confidence that information will not be used against them by the other party. As discussed, however, creating a trusting climate is not simply a matter of sharing all available information; for example, negotiators may feel they have given away critical and confidential information which may ultimately reduce their competitive advantage. Thus effective communication in negotiations is fundamental to achieving a successful outcome.

Self-assessment question 20.2

How does an ongoing relationship influence the approach to a negotiation?

Feedback on page 262

20.3 The value of reflection

Raiffa (1982) recommends that a checklist for negotiators includes getting yourself into an appropriate mindset by imagining that you are your own boss and your organisation is monolithic; and that you do not have to reach agreement with the other party, but that if you do, the agreement will be secure. Such an approach enables to you to visualise your intentions and subsequently reflect upon your experiences and performance in negotiations.

In study session 14, and in section 20.1, it was highlighted that experience draws on the ability to learn (and unlearn and relearn). Learning is the process of acquiring knowledge which has the potential to change behaviour (Huczynski and Buchanan, 2001). These changes in behaviour constitute a 'learning curve' which relate to:

- perceptual abilities
- reflective abilities
- information processing abilities
- personal motivations.

Kolb (1984) identified a 'learning cycle' which illustrates how learning takes place based on previous experience (see figure 20.4).

Figure 20.4: Learning cycle

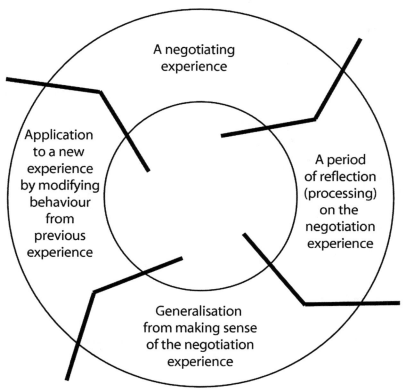

A negotiating experience

A period of reflection (processing) on the negotiation experience

Generalisation from making sense of the negotiation experience

Application to a new experience by modifying behaviour from previous experience

Source: adapted from Kolb (1984)

The application stage of the cycle is the point at which negotiators take their cumulative experiences and apply them to a new situation, such as indicated in figure 20.1. Experience is built over time by continuous learning. Successful negotiators will be those who are continually reflecting on their experiences and applying their knowledge to new situations.

Learning activity 20.3

Reflect on study sessions 12 to 16 and identify areas you feel you are weak in. Develop a personal plan to turn each of these into personal strengths.

Feedback on page 263

Reflection is itself a key skill. The ability to reflect enables learning to take place, as indicated in Kolb's cycle figure 20.4. However, a more structured framework for personal development is often appropriate. Consider how figure 20.5 may provide a more detailed structure for tackling learning activity 20.3 above.

20

Figure 20.5: Framework for skills evaluation

Source: based on Bennett et al (2000)

Communication requires:

- recognition of the organisation's work ethos
- using and developing interpersonal and organisational networks
- understanding of interpersonal styles
- awareness of the audience.

Decision making requires:

- awareness of alternatives and possible solutions
- knowledge of personal qualities and attitudes
- awareness of dependency on others and attitude to authority.

Focus on goals requires:

- contextualising to the situation
- identifying and working towards targets through the process.

Applying skills requires:

- following guidelines and instructions (the internal mandate, for example)
- evaluating, extracting and synthesising information
- thinking about future skills needed (career development).

Self-assessment question 20.3

What is the value of learning-by-doing and reflection for negotiation?

Feedback on page 263

20.4 Improvement, training and development

Negotiation is a skill and skills need to be improved and developed to keep us sharp and competitive. Evaluation and reflection are important first steps in this process of improvement and development; they provide the benchmarks against which we can measure any improvement. The terms training and development are often used synonymously, yet they are not the same thing. Training is used to enable individuals to gain or become more competent in specific job or task related skills. Development is more generic and related to helping individuals improve their personal qualities and innate abilities. It is much broader than training and focuses on longer-term career or personal needs, rather than immediate short-term tasks. Training, because of its short-term task focus, often provides almost immediate clear measurable improvements. Development can be a little more contentious than training as the benefits of broader development are often more difficult to justify as they are less obvious and immediate.

There are numerous methods for training and development and many variations on these themes. Some of these methods are formal, planned and have recognised structures and stages, for example academic qualifications through CIPS, while others can be very ad hoc and informal, for example asking for assistance from a colleague about a specific problem that is being encountered. However, some of the more common methods are considered below:

- On the job training – this takes place in the working environment and is therefore very context based and relevant to the organisation. The main problem is that there are often many distractions which can undermine or limit the effectiveness of this method.
- Shadowing – working with someone who is already skilled and knowledgeable about the task or role and picking up the basic requirements through imitation and questioning.
- Coaching and mentoring – being assigned to an established person in the organisation who will act as a guide and instructor.
- Off the job training – this takes place off-site and is usually more planned and considered because of the disruption and expense incurred. It allows the participants to focus more on the training as the distractions of the work environment have been eliminated. However, the direct relevance of this type of training can be undermined as the context becomes false.
- Workshops – practically focused events where the participants can work with experts to develop their skills to the next level.
- Seminars – discussion groups were like minded participants come together to discuss specific topics or problems with the aim of sharing experiences and know-how.
- Short courses – clearly defined programmes designed to deliver a smaller, more specific package of knowledge or skills.
- Qualifications – usually a more complex set, or mix, of training and development methods, delivered over a longer period of time with the aim of providing a broad background knowledge or framework within which the participant can gain a wide variety of opportunities for improvement.

These are rather quick and simple definitions of the more common methods for training and development.

In any organisational situation it is important to consider what the organisation needs and what the individual needs. Training and development will be much more effective when both parties are in agreement regarding these needs and also the best and most appropriate way in which they can be achieved. Training needs analysis (TNA) is the formal method used to evaluate these training needs and assess the best ways of achieving them for the organisation and the individual.

Learning activity 20.4

Review the above mentioned methods for training and development and consider which would best suit your specific needs to improve your negotiations at this time.

Feedback on page 264

Now try the following self-assessment question.

Self-assessment question 20.4

What are the values of academic qualifications for negotiations?

Feedback on page 264

Revision question

Now try the revision question for this session on page 269.

Summary

Evaluation was identified as key to understanding skills development needs, the aspects of performance that should be repeated and how future negotiations should be evaluated. Performance measurement enables evaluation of the effectiveness of the outcome and the efficiency with which it has been achieved. Thus the discussion reviewed three aspects: outcome, process and communication.

Review of the relational outcome identified that some issues are likely to be outside the domain of agreement, whilst others may be the basis of future relational development. It was highlighted that identification of common ground is especially important when evaluating negotiations within a relationship context. Review also covered the roles of trust and flexibility, as they relate to information exchange and communication skills development.

Finally, the role of reflection highlighted that learning by doing enables a negotiator to focus on particular aspects of skills development. A SWOT analysis was presented as a useful planning tool to evaluate skills and competences, whilst a further framework looked at experience and identified further considerations, such as work context.

Suggested further reading

Lewicki et al (2003b) highlight throughout their text good practice for negotiations. Pay particular attention to the discussion on framing and stereotyping as a means of personal development.

Feedback on learning activities and self-assessment questions

Feedback on learning activity 20.1

Answers may examine, but are not restricted to:

- The different categories of information identified in preparation (including financial information) may be used to draw up a checklist of factors that need to be considered, such as: the role of technology in reducing supplier costs, how the purchaser is perceived by the other party in relation to other customers of the supplier, and so on. This builds into a comprehensive preparatory action plan for gathering information that can be used to develop a strategy for the negotiation.
- Evaluate the strategic approach to the negotiation and the impact of specific tasks associated with each of the distributive and integrative methods. Examine whether a better solution to add value and benefit to the parties could have been achieved by using a different approach. This can be achieved, for example, by a debrief meeting after the negotiation.
- Examine the role of team members in preparing for the negotiation. Consider whether the tasks could have been distributed in a different way that would draw more effectively on the skills and expertise of particular individuals. Individuals can assess their own performance, or another individual's performance against a checklist of appropriate criteria.
- Identify whether the procedure adopted for the negotiation process was successful (venue, agenda, timing), and how the other party contributed to development of this. A follow-up review with the other party can be set up to solicit their views.
- Consider how your knowledge of the other party (their interests and position, alternatives, previous negotiating behaviour, cultural conventions for negotiating, and so on) impacted on your selection and use of tactics, including your ability to adapt to new information from them. 'What if…' scenarios could be set up to evaluate performance.
- How the outcome of the deal was received by internal colleagues, and whether the internal negotiation could have been better handled to facilitate acceptance of the external deal. Again, colleagues could be asked for their views.

Feedback on self-assessment question 20.1

Your answer should cover the following points:

- It is the most important phase of the negotiation because information generated at this stage informs subsequent decision making.

20

- Preparation identifies the strategy and goals for a negotiation.
- Evaluation of market data enables the identification of prioritised variables to be used in the negotiation; it also specifies ranges for those variables so that targets and resistance points are clear.
- Alternatives to negotiation can be considered, including walk-aways and BATNAs.
- It enables the preparation of the negotiating team, including the development of roles, with opportunity for skills development, if needed.
- Preparation determines the most appropriate tactics to be used in the negotiation, given an awareness of the other party and their negotiating preferences.

Feedback on learning activity 20.2

Discussion may review a model such as that used to describe the supplier-customer context (see table 20.2).

Table 20.2 Relational development model

Common relational stage	Typical relational objectives	Negotiation tone and approach
Pre-relationship	• Establish supplier potential. • Secure initial order.	• Friendly due to informal social contact. • Limited exchange of confidential information and limited trust.
Early relationship	• Penetrate supplier. • Increase volume of business.	• Liking between key individuals develops (main contacts). • Trust is still an issue.
Mid-stage relationship	• Build towards partnership. • Become main customer. • Establish preferred supplier status.	• Social interaction becomes the emphasis; trust builds rapidly. • Key information is shared, possibly through advanced technological solutions.
Partnership	• Develop spirit of partnership. • Lock in supplier.	• Profit is a focus for both parties. • Spirit of partnership and cooperation exists. • Effort on managing shared information.
Synergistic relationship	• Effect continuous improvement. • Achieve shared rewards (potential for quasi-integration).	• Systems become transparent; openness and honesty presides. • Borders between the customer and supplier become blurred; focus of interaction is on the 'end customer'.

Source: based on McDonald et al (1996); Donaldson (1996)

Feedback on self-assessment question 20.2

Your answer should have covered some of the following points:

- Satisfactory implementation of agreed contracts means potentially less need for conflict resolution or renegotiation.

- Quality of performance against contract may be maintained, or even enhanced, because of prioritised supplies, again meaning potentially less need for conflict resolution or renegotiation measures.
- Early warning of potential threats to the stability of the market or business, through intelligence exchanges between the supplier and the purchaser, enables a more thorough preparation for negotiation, fewer surprises and greater consideration of alternatives.
- Established relational exchanges mean the negotiation process may proceed with less interpersonal conflict, and greater openness and honesty, which may enhance the ability of the parties to achieve better outcomes, because of logrolling, expanding the pie, and so on.
- Trust between key individuals can potentially be transferred to new team members introduced during the negotiation phases.
- Power plays are diminished or balanced because of a perception of equality, meaning there is more open exchange.
- Perception of a win-win outcome more likely, resulting from trust, power balance, flexibility, and information exchange.

Feedback on learning activity 20.3

A good way to attempt this exercise is to undertake a personal SWOT analysis, identifying personal strengths and weaknesses and then thinking about activities that provide you with an opportunity to practise particular skills and about factors (threats) that may prevent you from practising (see table 20.3).

Table 20.3 Personal SWOT analysis

Personal strengths	Personal weaknesses
Opportunities for skills development	Threats (factors which prevent you from practising skills)

Feedback on self-assessment question 20.3

Your answer should consider the following points:

- Learning-by-doing negotiation means reflecting on real world experiences, rather than role-played or theoretical evaluations.
- Experiences, whether positive or negative, have the potential to enhance skills development. ('I won't be doing that again.' or 'That worked; I wonder if it could work in xxx situation?')
- Both logic and emotion can be considered when solving problems.

- Skills are built by handling complex issues; in fact, nothing is ever simple but it is the way that problems are broken down that simplifies them. (Refer also to the discussion on framing and stereotyping in previous study sessions, particularly study sessions 12 to 14.)
- Enhancing ability to learn (through practice and reflection) means that new ideas can be more quickly absorbed, developed and built upon.
- Innovative and creative ideas are often formed around the edges of considerable knowledge about particular aspects of business; contrary to frequent comment, creative ideas are not just 'pulled out of thin air'!

Feedback on learning activity 20.4

This will be a very personal response and there is clearly no right or wrong answer. The important thing here is to consider objectively how developed you believe your negotiation skills are, what aspects of these skills might benefit from further development and how you, as an individual, respond to different types of training and development. Depending on your level of skills and experience it might be that you already have plenty of practical experience but feel a need for a more conceptual or academic framework for these experiences. On the other hand, it might be that you feel this unit has provided sufficient academic underpinning at this stage and your needs may be more focused on practicing these skills in a dynamic environment. Here role playing with a mentor might be a safe starting point to try out your new ideals and techniques.

Feedback on self-assessment question 20.4

Your answer should consider the following debate:

It could be argued that academic qualifications for negotiations are of little value as negotiation is a skill and academic qualifications are a rather poor indicator or measure of skills. A skill that is demonstrated and tested in a controlled environment for the purpose of assessment is only really valid within that context. Under the complex and stressful conditions of a negotiation the deficiencies and limitations of those skills may become evident. One might have all the qualifications in the world and know the theories and models relating to business and negotiations, but lack the capabilities and competences to put them into practice or have had very little opportunity to develop them in a practical context. On the other hand, without these qualifications there would be no framework for evaluating or benchmarking any aspect of negotiation skills. Academic qualifications give a good idea of the underpinning knowledge that an individual has acquired and provides a framework within which they can evaluate and develop their skills and further knowledge.

Revision questions

Revision question for study session 1

Define negotiation and review its key characteristics. Discuss how these relate to the phases of negotiation.

Feedback on page 271

Revision question for study session 2

Appraise the purpose of negotiating for purchasers. Explain how the existence of a relationship with a supplier impacts on the decision to negotiate.

Feedback on page 272

Revision question for study session 3

Classify the products below using Kraljic's risk model, remembering to justify your classifications. Discuss how the model influences the negotiation process for each of the classes of product identified.

1   Semi-manufactured products where there are few suppliers.
2   Components of a commoditised product
3   Finished products where there is considerable technical expertise involved in the supplier's production for the purchaser and there is a solid relationship between the two parties
4   A support service.

Feedback on page 273

Revision question for study session 4

Preliminary discussions with two suppliers have revealed different prices for a similar product, seemingly because they have used different approaches to their calculations – this is confirmed by the suppliers when questioned.

*   Supplier A has quoted £34,500 for 3,000 units rising to £44,200 for 6,000 units, using full-cost pricing.
*   Supplier B has quoted £24,000 for 3,000 units rising to £28,000 for 6,000 units, using contribution pricing.

First, calculate the profit values for each of the suppliers using the following additional information gathered from research, which identifies the typical costs associated with supply of the product:

*   Materials and manufacture costs of £25,000 per 3,000 units rising to £30,010 per 6,000 units.

Secondly, consider that you would be willing to select one of the suppliers for a longer term supply contract. Evaluate the pricing approaches used by both Supplier A and Supplier B and comment on the approach to negotiations with each of the suppliers.

Hint: first calculate fixed and variable costs.

Feedback on page 274

Revision question for study session 5

Look at the information in table 21.2.

Table 21.2

Established breakdown of costs as quoted to the Purchaser	Supplier A £22,900 for 9,000 units	Supplier B £15,050 for 9,000 units
Materials	40%	35%
Labour	20%	25%
Production	15%	15%
Profit	25%	25%
Total	100%	100%

First, calculate the values for unit costs for both suppliers.

Secondly, comment on the approach to pricing that Supplier B appears to have used in this scenario. Explain how knowledge of this information will inform the purchaser's preparation for negotiation.

Feedback on page 275

Revision question for study session 6

Using the information below, calculate how each of the potential scenarios for price changes from your supplier will impact on demand, as identified through market research. Discuss how the results of your analysis will inform negotiations with your supplier.

Scenario 1: Price increase of 5% resulting in a decrease in demand of 15%

Scenario 2: Price increase of 3% resulting in a decrease in demand of 2%.

Feedback on page 276

Revision question for study session 7

Review the importance of having a BATNA in a negotiation. Discuss the reasons for not negotiating.

Feedback on page 277

Revision question for study session 8

List the main stages and tasks associated with (a) the competitive and (b) the collaborative approach to a negotiation.

Feedback on page 278

Revision question for study session 9

Evaluate the purchaser's bargaining power and possible sources of power in the scenarios outlined in table 21.4 below.

Table 21.4

Scenario	Degree of competition	Type of competition	Number of transactions
A	One supplier	Monopoly	Low
B	One buyer	Monopsony	Medium/high
C	Many suppliers of similar products or services	Differentiated	High
D	Few suppliers	Oligopoly	Low

Feedback on page 279

Revision question for study session 10

Briefly outline the recognised behaviour patterns of negotiators in a collaborative negotiation and a competitive negotiation. Then classify the tactics from the list below table 21.6 that are suitable for each approach.

Table 21.6

1	Expanding the pie	7	Chicken
2	Bridging	8	Intimidation
3	Lowball/highball	9	Cost cutting
4	Bogey	10	Aggression
5	The nibble	11	Logrolling
6	Nonspecific compensation	12	Snow job

Feedback on page 280

Revision question for study session 11

Review the reasons why an agreement may not always be implemented as agreed.

Then, explain why it is important for negotiators to have the agreement ratified.

Feedback on page 281

Revision question for study session 12

The process of communication is different for collaborative and competitive approaches to negotiation. Demonstrate how you would develop more effective communication for each approach.

Feedback on page 281

Revision question for study session 13

Recently, Canary Limited, a contracted long-term supplier to Marota Limited, has stated they have been hit hard by the increases in gas and oil prices. Their key account manager, Trang Hsei, says that this has impacted on production costs, with prices continuing to increase from their suppliers. Canary's managers are now concerned that their customers must support them by paying a higher prices for their products. However, Marota's new purchasing manager, Simon Kee, has all but cancelled the contract, citing a need for greater efficiency with procurement processes which results in better value for their organisation. During the renegotiation of the contract, the climate between Trang and Simon seems irretrievably damaged and tempers begin to show.

Discuss how to manage conflict in this situation and make a recommendation for adopting an appropriate style of management.

Feedback on page 282

Revision question for study session 14

Stephan's past experience of negotiating with Corinne, from Eveon Supplies Limited, has identified that she is a typical 'senser' personality. As a 'thinker' personality, Stephan has prepared to negotiate with Corinne bearing this in mind.

First, review the characteristics associated with the two personality types and comment on any gender aspects that may be important when preparing for the negotiation.

Secondly, advise Stephan on the approaches used by highly successful negotiators at the pre-meeting, meeting and post-meeting stages of negotiations.

Feedback on page 283

Revision question for study session 15

Comment on how trust may be developed by using questions effectively. Then review approaches to uncovering lies.

Feedback on page 285

Revision question for study session 16

Len-Tin Liu, from Taiwan, is negotiating on behalf of the purchaser with Hans Berhahn, a German negotiator acting for the seller. They have both lived all their lives in their respective home countries and can be described as being typical representatives of their culture.

Discuss the likely impact of their different cultural backgrounds on the negotiation.

Then, advise Len-Tin on how he should adapt his behaviour for the negotiation.

Feedback on page 285

Revision question for study session 17

A recent telephone negotiation has resulted in a less than satisfactory outcome for Juan, the purchaser for Zedos Plc. In fact, Juan was not sure he managed to get all his proposals across to Andre, Pyrmain's sales manager, and he was unclear why Andre was making some of his points. This was mainly because Andre kept over-talking and Juan struggled to get sufficient air time to make his points; when he did make a point, Andre seemed to get angry with him.

Advise Juan on how to improve his telephone negotiation with Andre. Review how Juan may improve his listening skills.

Feedback on page 286

Revision question for study session 18

Sam Volley has been successful in her negotiation with Beezees, the supplier. However, she has found considerable reluctance to support the deal inside her own organisation when she attempted to negotiate with colleagues.

Consider why this would be the case and discuss the steps she could take to produce better support for external negotiations.

Feedback on page 288

Revision question for study session 19

Tradium Corp Plc has identified key considerations for its next procurement of material from Distork, who are based some distance away:

* a need to hold detailed information for auditing and future use
* a requirement for a speedy response from Distork.

As a result, they have decided to enter into an e-negotiation using primarily email as the means to communicate.

Advise Tradium of the advantages and disadvantages of using email for negotiation. Highlight areas of good practice they should incorporate into their negotiation.

Feedback on page 288

Revision question for study session 20

Explain what aspects of a negotiation should be evaluated on completion and why.

Feedback on page 289

Feedback on revision questions

Feedback on revision question for study session 1

A definition of negotiation from the mandatory text is:

> '[a] formal process that occurs when parties are trying to find a mutually acceptable solution to a complex conflict.' (Lewicki et al, 2003)

Other definitions may be used, but these should identify common themes such as:

- existence of agreement and conflict between the parties
- bargaining process
- exchange of information
- the use of techniques of influence and persuasion
- capability of the parties to reach agreement
- existence of at least two people
- skilled use of power to achieve the outcome.

Key characteristics include:

- There are two or more parties who may be acting as individuals, as groups or organisations.
- The parties must search for a way resolve the conflict.
- The parties believe that by using influence they will achieve a better deal, rather than by accepting what is offered.
- The parties prefer to reach agreement, rather than continue to disagree.
- The parties expect to give and take, that is, modify their demands.
- Success requires management of tangibles (for example, terms of agreement) and intangibles (for example, underlying personal beliefs and values).

The phases of negotiation are:

- Preparation: identifying the important issues and goals.
- Relationship building: understanding how you will relate to the other party.
- Information gathering: learning what you need to know about (variables, other party's situation and goals).
- Information using: building the case for the negotiation.
- Bidding: the process of negotiating from initial offer towards the agreement.
- Closing the deal: building commitment from the parties.

- Implementing the deal: a post-negotiation phase. Even after the agreement is reached, there may be loose ends to clarify so there will be follow-ups to the original negotiation.

The phases of the negotiation process are characterised by different activities which can broadly be identified as: pre-negotiation activities, negotiation meeting activities and post-negotiation activities. Pre-negotiation will involve preparation and planning for the negotiation, including determining the alternatives to negotiation. The negotiation meeting will include the persuasive, issue management and bargaining approaches as well as reaching agreement. Post-negotiation involves follow-up negotiations and conflict resolution.

Feedback on revision question for study session 2

Negotiation is entered into by suppliers and purchasers when they perceive it can add value for their organisations. Value is identified as emanating from the differences between negotiators in their evaluation of a negotiated outcome. These differences enable the purchaser and supplier to create variables and attribute different values to them so that agreements may be reached.

In a supply context, value is created through differences in:

- Interests: this arises from the view each party has of the variables identified and traded; for example, a supplier of components may be more interested in the total value of the deal rather than price, whereas a purchaser may be seeking to reduce unit cost.
- Opinions: each party will have a view, for example, of the relative strategic importance of the relationship; what is important to the supplier may be less so to the purchaser.
- Risk aversion: a purchaser's need to reduce total cost of ownership may initially result in less risk being taken as it seeks to stabilise a supplier relationship.
- Different perspective: a rush order might mean quick payment from a purchasing perspective, and immediate business to a desperate supplier (which may well influence the balance of power between the parties).

A pre-existing relationship will impact on the decision to negotiate in a number of ways. These may include:

- There is a potential risk to the ongoing relationship if no agreement is reached, especially where the relationship is seen as strategically important to the organisation.
- There may be other economic consequences of the negotiation on the relationship, the costs of which may be difficult to measure where value is derived from the process. For example, benefits can relate more to savings, such as contribution towards efficiency and impact on revenue generated. Thus, in a negotiation, it is important to understand and evaluate both these constituents.
- There needs to be mutuality, that is, both parties contributing to the relationship for longevity and benefits. This relates to the 'win-win' scenario.

- Over- or under-involvement in a relationship can result in costly inefficiencies which must be corrected. This also necessitates that both parties consider the nature of interactions (or interface) between the two organisations in order to allocate appropriate resourcing.

Feedback on revision question for study session 3

Kraljic's model highlights that each category of purchase will have an impact on the bottom line (financials) according to its use and that risk is associated with supply, depending on the number or range of suppliers in the marketplace. Thus, if there are few suppliers and the impact on the organisation's financial situation is high, then the product is seen to be of strategic importance. The four classifications of products and services are illustrated in figure 21.2:

Figure 21.1: A categorisation of purchasing situations

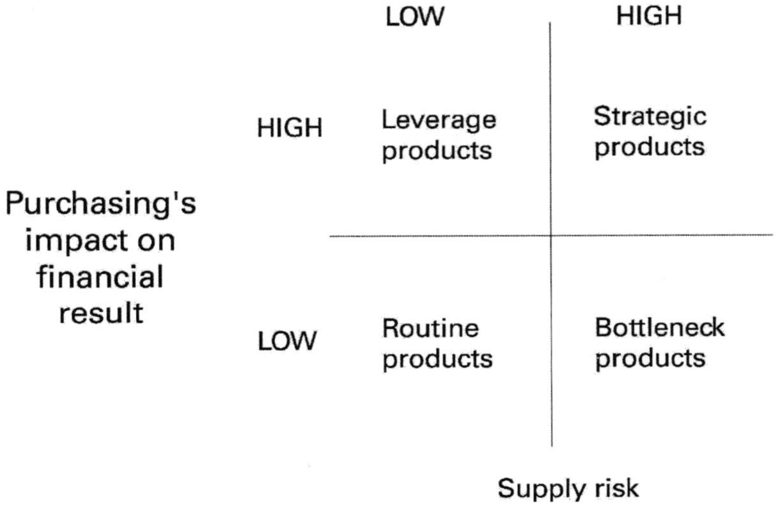

	LOW	HIGH
HIGH	Leverage products	Strategic products
LOW	Routine products	Bottleneck products

Purchasing's impact on financial result

Supply risk

Source: Kraljic (1982)

1   This indicates a high level of risk in the supply but it is not clear what the financial impact of the supply is on the purchaser. Therefore, these products may be classified as either 'strategic' or 'bottleneck'.
2   This can be said to be low risk because there are likely to be many potential suppliers of the product. Again, however, it is unclear what the financial impact of the supply is on the purchaser so these may be classified as either 'leverage' or 'routine' products.
3   This are likely to be high risk, high impact products, and are therefore classified as 'strategic'.
4   A support service is likely to be an augmented element of a semi-manufactured or even finished product, although it could also be a standalone service used by the purchaser to ensure business continuity in some way. Thus, depending on the purchasing organisation's view of how critical this service is to its processes, it could be placed in any of the quadrants.

The model influences negotiations in a number of ways:

- It simplifies the nature of the purchasing negotiation task because the activities that will be undertaken are clear.

- It enables purchasing staff to become specialised in negotiations according to classification.
- It identifies a clear link between purchasing and financial management of the organisation, therefore, enabling the identification of negotiating variables associated with pricing.

Feedback on revision question for study session 4

Full-cost pricing uses total costs (fixed and variable costs) as the basis for calculations with a percentage then added on for profit. Contribution pricing uses the variable costs only; it does not consider fixed costs. Cost calculations for the proportions of costs that may be fixed and variable are shown as follows table 21.1:

Table 21.1

	Production volume (units)	Total costs (materials and manufacture)
Production level a	3,000	£25,000
Production level b	6,000	£30,010
Difference (b - a)	3,000	£5,010
Variable cost	£5,010÷3,000 = £1.67 per unit	
(Difference in costs ÷ Difference in volume)		

At 3,000 units, total variable (materials) costs are: 3,000 x £1.67 = £5,010

If total costs are £25,000 then fixed costs are: £25,000 - £5,010 = £19,990

At 6,000 units, total variable (materials costs) are 6,000 x £1.67 = £10.020

Thus, analysis of indicative prices from Supplier A, reveals that their profits are:

At 3,000 units, £34,500 – £25,000 = £9,500 profit value

At 6,000 units, £44,200 – £30,010 = £14,190 profit value

Whereas, for Supplier B, because they are using an approach to pricing that excludes fixed costs, their profit is:

At 3,000 units, £24,000 – £5,010 = £18,990 profit value

At 6,000 units, £28,000 – £10,020 = £17,980 profit value

However, if Supplier B were to use full-cost pricing, then profit would be:

At 3,000 units, £24,000 – £25,000 = £1,000 shortfall in covering costs

At 6,000 units, £28,000 − £30,010 = £2,010 shortfall in covering costs

Thus, Supplier B's use of contribution pricing, based on variable costs only may be misleading, even though there is a proportionally higher level of profit included in their pricing. Contribution pricing is often used as a short-term marketing strategy, typically with 'loss leaders' and one-off deals and may be considered by suppliers when:

- Fixed costs are already covered by other customer orders.
- They have capacity to make and supply the order.
- The order will generate goodwill, such as from future orders and, potentially, a long-term relationship.
- The impact of the order on other customers is limited. Suppliers would not want to lose goodwill from their existing customers should they find out a cheaper price has been offered to another organisation, who may be a competitor.

For the negotiation with Supplier B, therefore, the purchaser needs to determine how a longer term supply will impact on their organisation and pricing of the product. Currently analysis indicates Supplier B could not cover typical costs associated with supply if full-cost pricing is used, although for a one-off purchase, they may be the preferred supplier because they are cheaper (assuming cost is the main negotiating variable under consideration). Where ongoing supply is sought, then their current approach is unlikely to result in a stable relationship between the parties because it may lead to the supplier going out of business!

With regard to Supplier A, there is clearly a high proportion of profit included in their price. This may well be the basis for a negotiation, depending on what your research indicates are appropriate profit levels.

Feedback on revision question for study session 5

Unit costs for each supplier (see table 21.3):

- Supplier A = £22,900÷9,000 = £2.55 per unit
- Supplier B = £15,050÷9,000 = £1.67 per unit

Table 21.3

Established breakdown of costs as quoted to the Purchaser	Supplier A £22,900 for 9,000 units	Supplier B £15,050 for 9,000 units
Materials	£1.02	£0.58
Labour	£0.51	£0.42
Production	£0.38	£0.25
Profit	£0.64	£0.42
Total unit cost	£2.55	£1.67

The pricing approach a supplier could use would reflect one of three main strategic objectives:

- volume sales
- profitability
- competitive parity.

In this scenario, both suppliers appear to have similar levels of profit built into their cost models, indicating a degree of competitive parity.

However, supplier B appears to be pursuing a strategy of volume sales (prices may be considered to be too different from supplier A for there to be parity). Supplier B may be attempting to achieve sales growth or be sure to secure the purchaser's business. In the negotiation, the purchaser therefore needs to confirm:

- Whether the price includes all important aspects (which are similar to supplier A).
- Whether, if the supplier is to become a contracted supplier over a longer term, their costs are sustainable.

It is important to understand the pricing approach used because it enables the purchaser to:

- Evaluate the volume of sales or sales revenue required to cover costs.
- Compare prices to direct competition.
- Evaluate prices should they change over time and therefore identify the volumes required to offset the changes.
- Identify the rate of return from products at different price levels.

This contributes to the preparation for negotiation by:

- Identifying the range of variables, including components of prime costs and breakdown of labour.
- Leading to evaluation of transfer costs associated with implementing any deal agreed upon with the supplier.
- Setting ranges for price and other variables in a negotiation.
- Enabling profit to be used as a variable, either competitively or collaboratively, to achieve outcome benefits for the organisation (and the other party).

Feedback on revision question for study session 6

This question aarequires analysis of the price elasticity of demand. Calculate elasticity of the two prices as follows:

Price elasticity = (% change in quantity demanded) ÷ (% change in price).

Scenario 1: 15 ÷ 5 = 3 (elastic)

Scenario 2: 2 ÷ 3 = 0.67 (inelastic)

Where the answer is over 1 then the product's demand is said to be price elastic. Thus, a 5% increase in price (scenario 1) will negatively impact on demand for the product whereas a lower % increase (scenario 2) will have little impact on demand for the product.

Thus, the purchaser should emphasise the importance of a lower price increase if volume of supplies is to be maintained, or reduce volume to reflect the lower demand from a higher price. Other factors may be worth consideration. For example, the purchaser will be less sensitive to price fluctuations where:

- The supplies represent a small part of the purchaser's costs
- Failure of the supplies may carry a high cost for the purchaser
- Contributory effectiveness of the supplies leads to high cost savings
- A quality strategy is being pursued by the purchaser
- Design or differentiation is a major factor in the purchasing decision
- Profitability is high and supply costs can easily be borne.

Finally, market research into elasticity of demand may be worth further investigation, for example, where market conditions are changing. Elasticity can be determined using information such as:

- Expert judgment, where opinions from knowledgeable individuals may enable estimation of demand from changes in pricing.
- Customer surveys, which may predict reactions to pricing fluctuations.
- Experimenting with price, using either simulation or field testing.
- Econometric studies, using extensive market data, such as retail data.

Feedback on revision question for study session 7

BATNA is an acronym for 'best alternative to a negotiated agreement'. It is the development of an alternative option to negotiating with a supplier. It is otherwise known as a 'walk-away' position, although this is the resistance point for a negotiable issue – the point at which the party will not negotiate further. Both parties will have identified BATNAs before entering a negotiation.

BATNAs are a source of power to the negotiators during the negotiation. They reinforce the bottom line and, in effect, curtail 'bad' judgment by providing another solution. A BATNA also protects by providing clarity in any agreement. Difficulties arise with BATNAs because there may be few alternatives to reaching agreement with a supplier, particularly if there is an established relationship and the supplies are strategically important to the purchaser. Problems with BATNAs include:

- They may limit the ability to respond to new information gleaned during the negotiation.
- They may inhibit creativity, especially in the joint exploration of issues, because the bottom line is predetermined by one party.
- The BATNA may be set unrealistically high making itdifficult to change.

An alternative to negotiation is not to negotiate. Conditions for not entering a negotiation may be:

- When you could lose everything you have. Choose another option rather than negotiate.
- When you are at maximum production capacity.
- When the demands being made on you are unethical.
- When you are not interested in achieving an outcome (because you have nothing to gain).
- When you do not have the time to negotiate as you would want to.
- When you cannot trust the other party in the negotiation. (How could you subsequently trust them to implement the agreed solution?)
- When waiting will improve your overall position.
- When you are underprepared to negotiate.

Feedback on revision question for study session 8

(a) The competitive approach.
   Preparation includes:
   - Identification and prioritisation of the variables and likely positions of both your organisation and the other party.
   - Production of negotiation ranges.
   - Design of the most appropriate concession patterns, given the likely stance of the other party.

   Negotiation tasks are summarised as:
   - Obtain information about the other party's resistance point: at what stage will they leave the table? What are their real needs?
   - Manage the other party's impressions: the aim is to not reveal your own position while encouraging them to accept a preferred view.
   - Modify the other party's perceptions, so that an issue may seem more or less attractive.
   - Manipulate the costs of delay and termination of the negotiation: research suggests most distributive negotiations are agreed close to the point when one of the parties must leave the table because of a deadline.

   Stages of the competitive negotiation are illustrated in figure 21.3:

Figure 21.2: Typical stages of a competitive negotiation

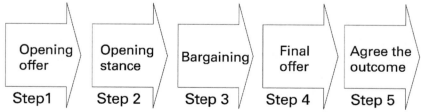

| Opening offer | Opening stance | Bargaining | Final offer | Agree the outcome |
| Step 1 | Step 2 | Step 3 | Step 4 | Step 5 |

Source: based on Lewicki et al (2003a)

(b) The collaborative approach.
   Preparation focuses on:
   - nature of the relationship
   - intentions of the parties to reach a collaborative outcome
   - variables and how these are prioritised
   - concession patterns
   - zone of agreement.

The negotiation tasks for a collaborative situation are fundamentally different from those of a competitive situation:

- Create a flow of information between the parties, so that solutions can be jointly developed.
- Try to understand the real needs and objectives of the other party; focusing on preferences and interests will achieve this.
- Work on common ground and mutual goals; this helps to minimise the differences between the parties.
- Search for solutions that meet both parties' needs; recall that the outcome of the negotiation is that both parties achieve a win-win.

Stages of the collaborative negotiation are illustrated in figure 21.:

Figure 21.3: Typical stages of a collaborative negotiation

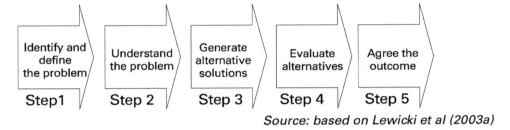

Source: based on Lewicki et al (2003a)

Feedback on revision question for study session 9

Refer to table 21.5.

Table 21.5

Scenario	Purchaser's bargaining power	Possible sources of power
A	Low	Supplier's: information and expert; resource control (reward) Purchaser's: location (possible); personal
B	High	Exact opposite of above
C	Medium/high	Supplier's: information and expert, resource control (reward); legitimate (performance, reputation) Purchaser's: information and expert, resource control (reward); legitimate (performance, reputation)
D	Low	Supplier's: information and expert; resource control (reward); legitimate (performance, reputation) Purchasers: information and expert; legitimate; location (possible); personal

Relevant aspects of power may be:

Information and expert power:

- Information is accumulated and used to support positions as facts, arguments and viewpoints.
- Exchange of information leads to a common definition of the situation.
- Expert is someone who has gained credibility as a source of specific information.
- It relates to the trustworthiness of the provider.

Resource control (reward)

- Power results from the ability to allocate, distribute and create resource scarcity, that is, the ability to reward.
- The most important resources are those which have greatest influence on the target: for example, money, supplies, time, equipment, critical services, human resource.

Legitimate power

- The usual sources are social structure, for example, birth, election or entitlement.
- Legitimate authority is respect for the holder's position.
- Derivatives of power from authority are reputation and performance.
- Reputation is image, which is shaped by accomplishments, that is, performance.

Location (within the structure)

- This means power by virtue of the position held within an organisational structure.
- The more central, critical and relevant an individual is to organisational communication, the more powerful the individual.
- The greater discretion, that is, flexibility, the individual has over who receives information, the more powerful he or she is.
- Power is also derived from the support of others as a result of visibility in negotiations.

Personal power

- This converts to influence.
- Attractiveness (friendliness and personal charisma) is used to establish a personal relationship, and softens the process of negotiation
- A component of friendliness, emotion combines with persistence and leads to assertiveness and determination, which may be unexpected in a negotiation situation.
- Integrity of character, that is, personal values and ethics, assures the other party any agreement reached will be adhered to.
- It is persistent and tenacious in creative pursuance of goals.

Feedback on revision question for study session 10

Recognised behaviour patterns of negotiators for each approach are table 21.7:

Table 21.7

Collaborative	Competitive
• Maximises returns for organisation. • Focuses on common interests. • Understands merits objectively. • Uses non-confrontational debating techniques.	• Maximises tangible resource gains. • Makes high opening demands. • Uses threats, confrontation and argumentation. • Manipulates people.

(continued on next page)

Table 21.7 *(continued)*

Collaborative	Competitive
• Open to persuasion on substance. • Oriented to qualitative goals.	• Not open to persuasion. • Oriented to quantitative and competitive goals.

Tactics for each approach are table 21.8:

Table 21.8

Collaborative		Competitive	
1	Expanding the pie	3	Lowball/highball
2	Bridging	4	Bogey
6	Nonspecific compensation	5	The nibble
9	Cost cutting	7	Chicken
11	Logrolling	8	Intimidation
		10	Aggression
		12	Snow job

Feedback on revision question for study session 11

It may not always be possible to implement an agreement because:

- The market may have changed between the time of the agreement and its implementation, which has an impact beyond the control of the supplier and purchaser.
- The purchaser's objectives set at the time of the negotiation were unrealistic.
- The supplier was unable to achieve the agreed objectives.

Ratification is the process of approving, endorsing, confirming or otherwise permitting the agreement to proceed to implementation. It is important to have negotiations ratified because there is less likelihood of internal conflict and stronger support for the detail of the agreement reached, if it matches closely the needs of the interested parties. Implicit within negotiations are that negotiators carry the mandate to enter into negotiation; that they are authorised to concede on the issues discussed in the bidding (bargaining) phase; and, that they are formally approved by the respective buying and selling organisations to close a deal and, subsequently, to act upon it. If they are not, then negotiations will ultimately fail.

Feedback on revision question for study session 12

Effective communication achieves its intended aim by producing the desired response. The following considerations are important:

- The nature of the message – content, structure and style.
- The stage and phase of negotiation.
- The category of communication.
- The perceptions of the receiver/s (and sender/s).
- The extent of experience of the sender and receiver of the message.

Techniques for improving communications are:

- Using questions – which may be designed to secure information on the other party's needs, interests and arguments, or to undermine the other party's confidence and build power.
- Listening (and reflecting) – which can be passive (just being quiet) or active (when the negotiator summarises what has been said).
- Role reversal – actively putting yourself into the 'other party's shoes' which means seeing the problem from their perspective and may help in reframing issues to be more attractive to them.

Examples of questions for different stages of the negotiation for each approach are set out in table 21.9:

Table 21.9

	Collaborative	Competitive
Establishing the climate	'Since we last met, xxx happened. How is that working out?' (*open-ended*)	'Shall we discuss xxx first?' (*directive, leading*)
Sharing information	'Can you tell me your view of xxx?' (*open-ended, window, or treat*)	Immediate response to a comment 'Why do you think that?' (*open-ended, window*)
Bargaining	'Was that of interest to you?' (*gauging*)	'Can you quote me your price if we include xxx?' (*planned, directive, cool*)
Concluding	'Are there any other points we need to discuss?' (*open-ended*)	'Shall we summarise the deal we have agreed?' (*directive, leading*)

Feedback on revision question for study session 13

Conflict often has negative connotations:

- Processes are competitive, which may lead to further escalation.
- Misperception and bias exist.
- Negotiators get emotional (irritated, angry and frustrated) as conflict escalates.
- Issues become blurred.
- Thinking becomes rigid.
- Differences are magnified.
- Conflict escalates.

As highlighted in study session 9, however, there are certain benefits to conflict:

- Discussion leads to greater awareness of problems which may enhance problem solving.
- Conflict challenges current practice, potentially highlighting poor practice.
- Withstanding conflict tests and then builds relationships among colleagues.
- Conflict promotes self awareness and awareness of others.
- It enhances personal, including psychological, development, as ways are sought to overcome conflict style and preferences.
- It can be stimulating and fun – it adds to the 'spice of life'.

Simon and Trang need to regain control of themselves in the negotiation. The following steps would help:

- Do not react but mentally distance yourself from the discomforting tactics being employed.
- Disarm the other party by listening carefully, acknowledging the points being made and providing them with your views – a positive response to their negative behaviour.
- Reframe the negotiation by asking open-ended and problem-solving questions. Again do not respond to their negative behaviour but be open and direct.
- Give them a 'yes-able' offer by involving them in the solution building process and being aware of their implicit needs.
- Make saying 'no' problematic for them by letting them know you have a good BATNA. Allow them to explore the consequences of it, focus on the advantages of a deal with you, and incorporate plans for implementation in the agreement.

Five styles of conflict management have been identified (Lewicki et al, 2003b):

1 Integrating (problem solving or collaborating): both parties' outcomes are important; used when issues are complex. Brainstorming leads to better solutions; commitment from both is important; one party cannot solve the problem alone.
2 Obliging (accommodating or yielding): used when it has been identified that it is important for the other party to achieve their outcome, but less so for the organisation. Typically used when the organisation is wrong or is weak; when future relationship is important; when issue is more important to the other party.
3 Dominating (competing or contending): parties pursue their own self-interests and adopt a style which incorporates threats and intimidation. The approach is typically used where the issue is not important to them, but is to you; when it could be costly to you; when it may be necessary to overcome particular behaviour of the other party; when a speedy decision is needed.
4 Avoiding (inaction): used when issue is trivial; or when negative interaction is likely to be the result.
5 Compromising: a half hearted attempt at problem solving. Used when goals are mutually exclusive; when a temporary solution is needed; when integrating or dominating styles are not successful.

The most appropriate style for Simon to adopt depends on how important the supplier is to the purchaser. The case indicates that Canary are an important supplier, and certainly their assignment of a key account manager would indicate that Marota are important to them. As such, it may be appropriate to use a more integrated approach in order to jointly problem solve. If, however, Marota are considered to be the more powerful party in the scenario, then a dominating approach may be justified.

Feedback on revision question for study session 14

Characteristics associated with the two negotiator types are:

	characteristics
Thinker – precision and detail oriented	Good communicator, deliberate in approach, prudent, evaluative, objective, rational, analytical, seeks information.

- Evaluated more outcome options for the issues to be discussed.
- Spent longer looking for common ground.
- Considered the longer-term consequences.
- Used ranges for issues.
- Asked more questions, especially to test understanding of the other party's points.
- Summarised frequently in order to enhance clarity.
- Did not undermine their position through weak justifying behaviours.
- Reviewed the negotiation to identify what they had learned from it.

Senser – action oriented, decisive, high energy	Pragmatic, assertive, objective, direct.

- Evaluated more outcome options for the issues to be discussed.
- Considered the longer-term consequences.
- Used ranges for issues.
- Reviewed the negotiation to identify what they had learned from it.

Research suggests different approaches to negotiating may be adopted by men and women. These include:

- The view of the relationship between the two parties: women tend have a broader view of the relational context, relate to perceptions of individuals involved in the negotiation, express emotions and feelings. Men are more task oriented and pragmatic.
- The role of negotiation: women view negotiation as part of a relationship with another party. Men see negotiation as a separate behaviour.
- The levels of control: empowerment is used by women so that all parties build their power base. Men use power to achieve their own goals.
- The problem-solving dialogue: women seek clarity through interaction with others. Men use dialogue to convince the other party, and use tactical ploys accordingly.

The scenario gives little context in which to judge gender aspects. Corinne's personality type (senser) would suggest that these may apply to only a limited extent in the consideration of longer-term consequences. Gender differences may be acknowledged but should be applied with caution.

Approaches used by highly successful negotiators are:

Pre-negotiation stage	- Evaluate more outcome options for the issues to be discussed. - Spend longer looking for common ground. - Consider the longer-term consequences. - Use ranges for issues. - Do not plan to negotiate issues sequentially.
Negotiation meeting	- Do not offer immediate counterproposals. - Do not overstate the benefits of their terms. - Do not verbally attack the other party. - Ask more questions, especially to test understanding of the other party's points.

- Summarise frequently in order to enhance clarity.
- Do not undermine their position through weak justifying behaviours.

Post-negotiation stage
- Review the negotiation to identify what they have learned from it.

Feedback on revision question for study session 15

Trust may be developed by using question aatypes such as:

- Open-ended questions: these enable the other party to give more information than closed questions. It is a useful technique for empowering the other party, and encouraging them to trust you with their thoughts.
- Leading questions: these may also incorporate your own opinions, which gives the other party the opportunity to demonstrate their trust by accepting your lead.
- Planned questions: these can be used tactically to develop trust by linking specific questions together.

Approaches used to uncover lies include:

- Intimidation: using criticism, accusations, indifference in order to provoke an admission.
- Bluffing: using a lie to make the other party believe they have been discovered in their deception.
- Prodding: asking for further information; keeping them talking may mean they reveal the lie.
- Self-disclosure: reveal something in order to get the other party to reveal something in return.
- Direct approach: ask outright ('Tell me the truth').
- Silence: makes it uncomfortable for the other party to keep quiet.

Feedback on revision question for study session 16

The two negotiators are from completely different cultural backgrounds. Culture is, therefore, likely to impact on their negotiation in a variety of ways. For example, culture is a 'total communication framework' and includes:

- Shared meanings, values and beliefs
- Group and ethnic orientation
- Judgment and opinion on good and bad
- Language.

There are four main cultural dimensions to consider:

- Individualism/collectivism: this will influence whether one or both use a team approach or negotiate as individuals on behalf of their organisations. Taiwan is more collectivist than Germany, which favours individualistic approaches, indicating Len Tin is likely to involve more people in the decision-making process than Hans.
- Power distance: this relates to the acceptance of inequality in society and use of power. A high power distance will influence how they make

decisions in the negotiation: if they defer decisions to a leader within an organisation that will mean a slow process; in a lower power distance context, decisions may be made by the negotiator, resulting in a quicker decision. Since Taiwan has a higher power distance score than Germany, this could indicate a preference for taking longer to reach agreement, and a potentially frustrating time for Hans.

- Masculinity/femininity: this refers to male assertiveness versus the more female concern for relationships. Taiwan is more feminine and favours a relational outcome, with a longer-term focus. Len Tin will make decisions from a group perspective, based on collaboration, whereas Hans will favour assertion in reaching agreement.
- Uncertainty avoidance: this is the extent to which structure and risk avoidance is preferred to rapid change and new situations. Both countries have similar scores for uncertainty avoidance, indicating that both negotiators are likely to adapt slowly to change, once agreement has been reached.

In considering whether Len-Tin should adapt his behaviour, it would be important to identify the extent of his familiarity with the German cultural context, and also whether Hans has experience of negotiating with Taiwanese buyers. If Len-Tin has some experience then adaptations may be possible; if not, then moderate adaptation may be most effective:

- Where the negotiators have low familiarity with the cultural setting, then an adviser may be useful where there is limited time to become more familiar. Advisers can act as negotiators or commentators on the negotiation. Mediators may be used to introduce the parties and act in a facilitating capacity. An alternative strategy is to encourage the other party to adapt to your own culture.
- Where the negotiators have moderate familiarity, the party may adapt their behaviour to more closely match the other party's. It may also be appropriate to seek adaptations from the other party so that both are consciously coordinating their behaviour.
- Where there is high familiarity then it may be appropriate to adapt completely to match the other party, finding some common approach that meets the needs of the negotiating context. It may also be worth considering the adoption of a third culture so that both are culturally 'neutral'.

Feedback on revision question for study session 17

Ways in which Juan could improve the quality of his telephone negotiation:

- He should first provide an agenda for the discussion ahead of the call, using another medium (email or letter notification or previous face-to-face meeting) in order to give Andre the opportunity to prepare. Alternatively, he may get Andre to agree the content of the discussion at the start of the conversation.
- He should ask for feedback on his comments in order to gauge how Andre is receiving the messages.
- He could ask questions which seek to clarify understanding between them, which may also be helpful in identifying whether there are any

misperceptions in what has been said (for example, 'Can you run that past me again, please?').
- He could periodically summarise the discussion to maintain focus and give greater clarity to both parties.

Juan could practise his skills for signalling to the other speaker that he wants to continue making his point. Signals can include:

- Stating that the forthcoming comments have a number of parts ('I have three comments on that...').
- Holding off the other person by saying, 'Just a minute...' or 'I'm not quite finished yet...'
- Constructing sentences in a way that communicates there is more to come, such as: 'Because our new production line is not fully functional, we are reluctant to take on new *business...*', compared to: 'Our new production line is almost *functional*, but we need to take care not to overload our existing *teams*, although they are prepared to work *overtime...*'. The italicised words indicate points where the other person might identify the end of the comment.
- Not pausing for breath.

Juan could practise the way he claims a speaking turn by:

- Identifying an end point and then speak quickly in the pause.
- Interrupting Andre – over-speaking.
- Beginning to over-speak hesitantly, which may cause Andre to stop to listen while Juan restates the comment.
- Making supportive noises ('uh-huh', 'umm') which, because they seem to agree with Andre, may cause him to stop.
- Reciprocating a question aato encourage further discussion.

To improve his listening skills, Juan may need to establish Andre's priorities, interests, opinions, and so on. He should:

- Give more emphasis to listening than speaking.
- Respond to personal points, such as feelings and beliefs, rather than abstract points.
- Allow Andre to lead the conversation process.
- Seek to clarify Andre's thoughts and feelings rather than putting words into his mouth by suggesting how he feels.
- Respond to feelings that are expressed.

There are a number of techniques by which Juan can improve his listening skills:

- Translate the key ideas and terms used into his own words.
- Reduce Andre's message to its basic idea.
- Remove emotive words from what's been said – and identify if there is an underlying rationality to the message.
- Identify the main points from the surrounding rhetoric, and prioritise them.
- Decide the purpose of what has been said.
- Try to identify if there are missing components from the message and whether this is deliberate.

Feedback on revision question for study session 18

If internal agreement of the parties implicated by the agreement is not achieved, then the external negotiation can be undermined, as implied in the scenario:

- Implementation may suffer because not all internal parties are ready to support the agreement reached.
- Conflict with internal colleagues and the risk of interference from them increases.
- Team members will not reflect consensus opinion but individual positions.
- Alienation from the internal support base may result from lack of colleagues' involvement.

A first step would be to identify those influential individuals in the internal negotiation:

- Who is interested/implicated/involved in the deal?
- Whose support is important for effective implementation?
- Who would not want the deal to be implemented?
- Who could actively support the deal?

Factors that may impede internal negotiation:

- History of conflict with individuals involved.
- No history of contact.
- Limited prior experience of either internal negotiation or the specific context.

It may be possible to overcome these difficulties by providing:

- a summary of the situation
- an overview of those involved in the negotiation
- an idea of the resource implications, including a timetable.

Sam may also want to set up a preliminary meeting to introduce colleagues in order to help to establish support. She could also undertake regular updates on progress, including on early wins and overall progress.

Importantly, Sam needs to understand that building support is achieved over time, in much the same way that a supplier relationship is built.

Feedback on revision question for study session 19

Advantages of using e-negotiation may be seen as:

- Faster than face-to-face negotiation.
- Lower prices than travelling to a negotiation.
- Lower costs by electronically exchanging data with suppliers so that order processing can be streamlined.

Problems occur online, however, with the communication efficiencies, effectiveness and emotional exchange processes that are an important and inherent part of the face-to-face negotiation process. Difficulties arise from impediments to the flow of verbal and non-verbal signals between the parties, which can result in a significant loss of information.

Good practice for e-negotiation may be:

- Ensure the important aspects are included.
- Establish the main proposition.
- Prepare any data needed to support your proposition.

Important factors for consideration using e-negotiation:

- interpersonal rapport between the parties: indicators of good rapport are overtones of mutual support for one another – agreements and supporting behaviours.
- levels of coordination: the parties may converge on agreement if they are close (bargaining range).
- exchange of information: this may be lower than face-to-face negotiation and will take more effort to manage, because people are less proficient at writing than they are at speaking.
- exchange of emotions: negotiators may be more aggressive when using email than face to face.

Feedback on revision question for study session 20

There are three aspects that outcome evaluation needs to consider in relation to the phases of the negotiation:

1   outcome achievement
2   process appropriateness
3   personal and team communication performance.

Specifically, evaluation and review of negotiation should focus on:

- Processes, rather than individuals.
- Factual data, rather than opinion (memory loss may make the latter biased).
- Alternative scenarios, such as: 'What if xxx had happened?'
- Problem-solving techniques, which will enable a more critical evaluation, rather than reaching premature conclusions.
- Evaluating cause and effect, rather than stereotyping.

These should be evaluated because they may impact on the success of future situations and have an influence on any ongoing relationship with the other party. For example:

- Satisfactory implementation of contracts agreed means potentially less need for conflict resolution or renegotiation.
- Maintenance of quality performance (or even enhanced quality) against contract, because of prioritised supplies, again meansn potentially less need for conflict resolution or renegotiation measures.
- Early warning of potential threats to the stability of the market or business, through intelligence exchanges between the supplier and the

purchaser, enables more thorough preparation for negotiation and consideration of alternatives (that is, there are fewer surprises).

- Established relational exchanges mean the negotiation process may proceed with less interpersonal conflict, greater openness and honesty, which may enhance the ability of the parties to achieve more successful outcomes because of logrolling, expanding the pie, and so on.
- Trust between key individuals can potentially be transferred to new team members introduced during the negotiation phases.
- Power plays are diminished or balanced because of a perception of equality, meaning more open exchange.
- Perception of a win-win outcome is more likely, resulting from trust, power balance, flexibility, and information exchange.

Evaluating negotiation outcomes provides the benefits of reflecting on experience:

- Experiences, whether positive or negative, have the potential to enhance skills development.
- Skills are built on handling complex issues – in fact, nothing is ever simple but it is the way that problems are broken down that simplify them; thus, reflection on problem solving is useful.
- Enhancing the ability to learn through reflection means that new ideas can be more quickly absorbed, developed and built upon.
- Innovative and creative ideas are often formed around the edges of considerable knowledge about particular aspects of business, so reflection can lead to new ideas.

References and bibliography

This section contains a complete A-Z listing of all publications, materials or websites referred to in this course book. Books, articles and research are listed under the first author's (or in some cases the editor's) surname. Where no author name has been given, the publication is listed under the name of the organisation that published it. Websites are listed under the name of the organisation providing the website.

Abery, J and C Glindemann (2004) 'The ten nuggets of e-wisdom', *Supply Management*, 10 June, pp 22–6.

Acuff, FL (1997) *How to negotiate anything with anyone anywhere around the World*. New York: American Management Association.

Albin, C (1993) 'The role of fairness in negotiation', *Negotiation Journal*, 9, 3 (Jul), pp 223–44.

Alessandra, T (2004) 'Sixteen commonsense listening tips', *The Negotiation Magazine*

Ambrosini, V (1995) 'Researching tacit knowledge: an empirical methodology', *British Academy of Management Annual Conference*, Doctoral Track. Sheffield: 11–13 Sept.

Aranachalam, V and WN Dilla (1995) 'Judgment accuracy and outcomes in negotiation: a causal modelling analysis of decision-aiding effects', *Organizational Behavior and Human Decision Processes*, 61, 3 (Mar), pp 289–304.

Athos, AG and JJ Gabarro (1978) *Interpersonal behavior: communication and understanding in relationships*. Englewood Cliffs, NJ: Prentice Hall.

Axelrod, R and WD Hamilton (1981) 'The Evolution of Co-operation', *Science*, 211 (March), pp 1390–6.

Baiman, S, MV Rajan and C Kanodia (2002) 'The role of information and opportunism in the choice of buyer-supplier relationships', *Journal of Accounting Research*, 40, 2, 247–87.

Ballantyne, D, M Christopher and A Payne A (2000) *Relationship Marketing: Bringing Quality, Customer Service and Marketing Together*. London: Butterworth-Heinemann.

Barrat, C (2005) 'Day-rate dilemma', *Supply Management*, 5 June, p 21.

Barry, B and R Friedman (1998) 'Bargaining characteristics in distributive and integrative negotiations', *Journal of Personality and Social Psychology*, 74, pp 345–59.

Bartos, OJ (1995) 'Modelling distributive and integrative negotiations', *The Annals of the American Academy of Political and Social Science*, 542, (Nov), pp 48–60.

Bazerman, MH (2002) *Judgment and managerial decision-making*, 5th edition. New York: John Wiley and Sons.

Bazerman, MH and MA Neale (1983) 'Heuristics in negotiation: Limitations to effective dispute resolution' in Bazerman, MH and R J Lewicki (1983) *Negotiating in Organizations*. London: Sage Publications.

Beal, J (2004) in 'Cover story: Pushing the right buttons', *Supply Management*, 18 March, pp 20–6.

Bennett, N, E Dunne and C Carre (2000) *Skills development in higher education and employment*. Buckingham: The Society for Research into Higher Education and Open University Press.

Bennett, PG (1995) 'Modelling Decisions in International Relations: Game Theory and Beyond', *Mershon International Studies Review*, 39, pp 19–52.

Blaney, D (2005) 'Constructive criticism', *Supply Management*, 9 June, p19.

Bok, S (1978) 'Lying: moral choice in public and private life', New York: Pantheon, In Bazerman MH and RJ Lewicki (1983) *Negotiating in Organizations*. London: Sage Publications, p 73.

Boles, J, T Brashear, D Bellenger and H Barksdale Jnr (2000) 'Relationship selling behaviors: antecedents and relationship with performance', *The Journal of Business and Industrial Marketing*, 15, 2–3, pp 141–153.

Brams, SJ (1990) *Negotiation Games: Applying Game Theory to Bargaining and Arbitration*. New York: Routledge.

Brewster, C (1989) *Employee Relations*. London: MacMillan Education Limited, pp 125, 162.

Butler, J K (1995) 'Behaviors, Trust and Goal Achievement in a Win-Win Negotiating Role Play', *Group and Organization Management*, 20, 4 (Dec), pp 486–501.

CAPS Research: http://www.CAPSresearch.org/

Casebolt, JM (1995) 'Taming your telephone', *Physician Executive*, Apr, 21, 4.

Cohen, SP (2005) 'Cross-silo negotiation' The Negotiation Skills Company Inc: http://www.negotiationskills.com

Colman, AM (1995) *Game Theory and its Applications in the Social and Biological Sciences*, 2nd edition. London: Butterworth-Heinemann Ltd.

Czinkota, MR (2000) 'International information cross-fertilization in marketing: an empirical assessment', *European Journal of Marketing*, 34, 11–12, pp 1305–14.

Davenport, T (1994) 'Saving IT's soul: human centred information management', *Harvard Business Review*, 72, March–April, pp 119–31.

De Bono, E (2005) *The six value medals*. London: Vermilion.

DeCormier, R and D Jobber (1998) The Counsellor Selling Model: Components and Theory, *The Journal of Selling and Major Account Management*, 1, 2, pp 22–40.

Department of Trade and Industry: http://www.dti.org.uk

Donaldson, B (1996) 'Industrial marketing relationships and open-to-tender contracts: cooperation or competition?' *Journal of Marketing Practice: Applied Marketing Science*, 2, 2, pp 22–33.

Donaldson, B and T O'Toole (2002) *Strategic market relationships*. Chichester: Wiley and Sons.

Donohue, WA with R Kolt (1992) *Managing Interpersonal Conflict*. London: Sage Publications, pp 88–166.

Dougherty, V (1999) 'Knowledge is about people, not databases', *Industrial and Commercial Training*, 31 (7), pp 262–6.

Doyle, DP (2002) *Cost control: a strategic guide*. London: CIMA Publishing.

Druckman, D and C Mitchell (1995) Flexibility in negotiation and mediation, *The Annals of the American Academy of Political and Social Science*, 542 (Nov), pp 10–23.

Druckman, D, JN Druckman and T Arai (2004) 'e-Mediation: evaluating the impacts of an electronic mediator on negotiating behavior', *Group Decision and Negotiation*, 13, pp 481–511.

Drummond, G and J Ensor (2003) *Strategic marketing planning and control*, 2nd edition. Oxford: Butterworth Heinemann.

Dwyer, FR, PH Schurr and S Oh (1987) Developing Buyer-Seller Relationships, *Journal of Marketing*, 51 (Apr), pp 11–27.

Fisher, R and W Ury (1981; 1991) *Getting to yes*. London: Arrow Business Books.

Ford, D (1980) 'The development of buyer-seller relationships in industrial markets', *European Journal of Marketing*, 14 (5/6), pp 339–54.

Frances, JNP (1991) 'When in Rome? The effects of cultural adaptation on intercultural business negotiations', *Journal of International Business Studies*, 22/3, pp 403–28.

293

Futrell, CM (2002) *Fundamentals of selling: customers for life, 7th ed.* London: Irwin McGraw Hill.

Gadde, L-E and H Hakansson (1993) *Professional Purchasing.* London: Routledge.

Gordon, JR (1991) *Organizational behaviour*, 3rd edition. New York: Allyn and Bacon.

Gronroos, C (1997) 'Value-driven Relational Marketing: from Products to Resources and Competencies', *Journal of Marketing Management*, 13, pp 407–19.

Gummesson, E (2002) *Total relationship marketing.* London: Butterworth Heinemann.

Harsanyi, JC (1980) 'Measurement of social power in n-person reciprocal power situations', *Essays on Ethics, Social Behavior, and Scientific Explanation.* London: D Reidel Publishing Company, pp 162–203.

Harwood, T (2002) 'Business negotiations in the context of strategic relationship development', *Marketing Intelligence and Planning*, 20, 6, pp 336–48.

Harwood, T (2002) *Negotiations in buyer-seller relationships*, PhD Thesis, De Montfort University.

Hawes, JM, KE Mast and JE Swan (1989) 'Trust earning perceptions of sellers and buyers', *Journal of Personal Selling and Sales Management*, IX (Spring), pp 1–8.

Hendon, D and R Hendon (1989) *How to Negotiate Worldwide: A Practical Handbook.* Aldershot: Gower Publishing Company Limited.

Hendon, DW, RA Hendon and P Herbig (1996) *Cross-cultural business negotiations.* London: Quorum Books.

Herbig, PA (1991) 'Game Theory in Marketing: Applications, Uses and Limits', *Journal of Marketing Management*, 7, pp 285–98.

Hobson, CA (1999) 'E-negotiations: creating a framework for online commercial negotiations', *Negotiation Journal*, 15, 3, pp 201–18.

Horngren, CT, A Bhimani, SM Datar and G Foster (2005) *Management and cost accounting*, 3rd edition. Harlow: Prentice Hall Financial Times.

Huczynski, A and D Buchanan (2001) *Organizational behaviour*, 4th edition. London: Financial Times/Prentice Hall.

Jennings, D (2004) 'Contracts: how words become law', *Supply Management*, 1 Apr, pp 32–3.

Johnston, RW (1982) 'Negotiation strategies: different strokes for different folks', *Personnel*, Mar–Apr, 59, pp 36–45.

Kaplan, RS and DP Norton (1992) 'The balanced scorecard – measures that drive performance', *Harvard Business Review*, Jan–Feb, pp 71–9.

Katsh, E and J Rifkin (2001) *Online dispute resolution: resolving conflicts in cyberspace*, San Francisco, CA: Jossey Bass.

Kersten, GE and H Lai (2005) 'Satisfiability and completeness of protocols for electronic negotiations', *Internet Research Papers INR* 01/05.

Klein, A (2004) 'Three steps to excellence', *Supply Management*, 1 Apr, pp 22–5.

Kolb, D and GG Coolidge (1991) 'Her place at the table: a consideration of gender issues in negotiation', in Rubin JZ and JW Breslin eds, *Negotiation theory and practice*. Cambridge, MA: Harvard Program on Negotiation, pp 261–77.

Kolb, DA (1984) *Experiential Learning*. New Jersey: Prentice Hall.

Kraljic, P (1982) 'Purchasing must become supply management', *Harvard Business Review*, Sept–Oct, pp 109–17.

Ku, G and D Malhotra (2001) 'The online auction phenomenon: growth, strategies, promise and problems', *Negotiation Journal*, 7, 14, pp 349–61.

Lambert, RD and AW Heston (1995) 'Flexibility in international negotiation and mediation', *The Annals of the American Academy of Political and Social Science*, 542 (Nov), pp 213–18.

Lambin, J-J (2000) *Market-driven management*. London: Macmillan Business.

Lax, D and J Sebenius (1986) *The manager as negotiator: bargaining for cooperation and competitive gain*. New York: Free Press.

Lewicki, RJ (1983) 'Lying and deception: a behavioral model', in Bazerman, MH and RJ Lewicki (1983) *Negotiating in Organizations*, London: Sage Publications, pp 68–90.

Lewicki, RJ, B Barry, DM Saunders and JW Minton (1997) *Essentials of Negotiation*, 2nd edition. Boston MA: Irwin McGraw-Hill.

Lewicki, RJ, B Barry, DM Saunders and JW Minton (2003a) *Negotiation*, 4th edition. London: McGraw Hill Irwin.

Lewicki, RJ, B Barry, DM Saunders and JW Minton (2003b) *Essentials of Negotiation*, 3rd edition. London: McGraw Hill Irwin.

Lievrouw, LA and TA Finn (1990) 'Identifying the common dimensions of communications: the communications systems model' in Varey, RJ (2002) *Relationship marketing: dialogue and networks in the e-commerce era*. Chichester: John Wiley and Sons.

Likierman, A (2005) 'Performance measurement', *Supply Management*, 7 July, pp 20–4.

Lysons, K (2000) *Purchasing and supply chain management*, 5th edition. London: Financial Times Prentice Hall.

Malhotra, A and A Majchrzak (2005) 'Virtual workspace technologies', *Sloan Management Review*, Winter, 46, 2, pp 11–14.

Mannix, EA (2005) 'Strength in numbers: negotiating as a team', *Negotiation*, 8, 5, Harvard Business School: http://hbswk.hbs.edu/item.jhtml?id=4940&t=negotiation.

Masterson, R and D Pickton (2004) *Marketing: an introduction*. London: McGraw Hill.

Maylor, H (2003) *Project Management 3rd ed.* London: Financial Times/Prentice Hall.

McDonald, M, B Rogers and D Woodburn (2000) *Key customers: how to manage them profitably*. Oxford: Butterworth Heinemann.

Monczka and Morgan (2000) in Gadde, L-E and H Hakansson (2001) *Supply Network Strategies*. Chichester: John Wiley and Sons.

Moore, C (1996) *The mediation process: practical strategies for resolving conflict*. San Francisco, CA: Jossey Bass.

Morley, I and G Stephenson (1977) *The Social Psychology of Bargaining*. London: George Allen and Unwin Limited, p 26.

Morse, R (2002) Internal negotiations: supporting the external deal, *Negotiator Magazine*, http://negotiatormagazine.com/subject_index.html#internal.

Morse, R (2005) 'Internal negotiations: strategies for negotiating with difficult people...', *Negotiator Magazine*

Moya, LH (2002) Social preferences for negotiated outcomes, *Carnegie Mellon University*.

Mulholland, J (1991) *The language of negotiation*, London: Routledge.

Murray JS (1986) 'Understanding Competing Theories of Negotiation', *Negotiation Journal*, 2 (Apr), pp 179–86.

Murray, J (2004) 'Murray's law: just what are the terms of your contract?' *Purchasing*, 9 Dec, pp 24 C2–4

Nadler, J (2003) 'Legal negotiation and communication technology: how small talk can facilitate e-mail dealmaking', *Social Science Research Network Collection*

Nalebuff, BJ and AM Brandenburger (1996) *Co-opetition: The New Win/Win Game Theory Approach to Business*. London: Harper Collins.

Neale, MA and MH Bazerman (1991) *Cognition and Rationality in Negotiation*. Oxford: Maxwell Macmillan International.

Neslin, SA and L Greenhalgh (1983) 'Nash's Theory of Co-operative Games as a Predictor of the Outcomes of Buyer-Seller Negotiations: An Experiment in Media Purchasing', *Journal of Marketing Research*, XX (Nov), pp 368–79.

Nuata, D and J Hoekstra (1995) 'Effective Choice in the Single-Shot Prisoner's Dilemma Tournament', *Theory and Decision*, 39, pp 1–30.

Payne, A and P Frow (1997) 'Relationship marketing: key issues for the utilities sector', *Journal of Marketing Management*, 13, pp 463–77.

Pedlar, M, J Burgoyne and T Boydell (1997) *The learning company: a strategy for sustainable development*, 2nd edition. London: McGraw Hill.

Peters, LD and KP Fletcher (1995) 'The role of trust in facilitating information exchange', *Proceedings of the Annual Conference Making Marketing Work*. Bradford: University of Bradford, II, pp 606–15.

Phatak, AV and MM Habib (1996) 'The dynamics of international business negotiations', *Business Horizons*, May–June, pp 30–8.

Pisano, GP (1997) 'Knowledge, integration and the locus of learning: an empirical analysis of process development', *Strategic Management Journal*, 15, pp 85–100.

Poell, RF, GE Chivers, FJ van der Krogt and DA Wildemeersch (2000) 'Learning-network theory: organizing the dynamic relationships between learning and work', *Managing Learning*, 31(1), pp 25–50.

Polzer, JT (1996) 'Intergroup negotiations: the effects of negotiating in teams', *Journal of Conflict Resolution*, 40, pp 678–98.

Porter, ME (1985) *Competitive strategy*. London: Free Press.

Pruitt, DG (1995) 'Flexibility in conflict episodes', *The Annals of the American Academy of Political and Social Science*, 542 (Nov), pp 100–15.

Pruitt, DG and PJ Carnevale (1993) *Negotiation in Social Conflict*. Buckingham: Open University Press.

Pullins, EB, CP Haugtvedt , PR Dickson, LM Fine and RJ Lewicki (2000) 'Individual differences in intrinsic motivation and the use of cooperative negotiation tactics', *The Journal of Business and Industrial Marketing*, 15, 7, pp 466–78.

Purdy, JM and P Nye (2000) 'The impact of communication media on negotiation outcomes', *International Journal of Conflict Management*, 11, 2, pp 162–87.

Putnam, R (1988) 'Diplomacy and domestic politics: the logic of two-level games', *International Organization*, 42, pp 427–60.

Rackham, N (1987) *Making Major Sales*. Aldershot: Gower Publishing.

Rackham, N and J Carlisle (1978a). 'The effective negotiator, part II: planning for negotiation', *Journal of European Industrial Training*, 2, 7, pp 2–5.

Rackham, N and J Carlisle (1978b). 'The effective negotiator, part I: the behaviour of successful negotiators', *Journal of European Industrial Training*, 2, 6, pp 6–11.

Rackham, N, L Friedman and R Ruff (1996) *Getting partnering right: how market leaders are creating long-term competitive advantage*. London: McGraw Hill.

Raiffa, H (1982) *The art and science of negotiation*. Cambridge, MA: Belknap Press of Harvard University Press.

Raiffa, H (1997) *Lectures on Negotiation Analysis*. Cambridge MA: Program on Negotiation at Harvard Law School.

Raiffa, H (2002) Negotiation analysis: the science and art of collaborative decision-making. London: The Belknap Press of Harvard University Press.

Reichheld, F (1996) The loyalty effect: the hidden force behind growth, profits and lasting value. Boston, MA: Harvard Business School Press.

Reichheld, FF and WE Sasser Jnr (1990) 'Zero defections: quality comes to services', *Harvard Business Review*, Sept–Oct, pp 105–11.

Reynolds, A (2003) *Emotional intelligence and negotiation*. Lymington: Tommo Press.

Rich, MK (2000) 'The direction of marketing relationships', *Journal of Business and Industrial Marketing*, 15, 2/3, pp 170–9.

Robinson, N (2004) Bolts from the blue, *Supply Management*, 4 Nov, pp 32–3.

Robinson, PJ, CW Faris and Y Wind (1967) *Industrial buying and creative marketing*, Boston MA: Allyn and Bacon.

Rubinstein, A (1991) 'Comments on the interpretation of game theory', *Econometrica*, 59, 4, pp 909–24, in BR Munier and J-L Rulliere (1993) 'Are game theoretic concepts suitable negotiation support tools? From Nash Equilibrium refinements toward a cognitive concept of rationality', *Theory and Decision*, 34, pp 235–53.

Schramm, W (1955) *The process and effects of mass communication*. Chicago: University of Illinois Press, pp 3–26.

Schultz, RJ and KR Evans (2002) 'Strategic collaborative communication by key account representatives', *The Journal of Personal Selling and Sales Management*, 22, 1, pp 23–31.

Senge, P (1990) *The fifth discipline: the art and practice of the learning organization*. New York: Doubleday Currency.

Shapiro, RM, MA Jankowski with J Dale (2001) *The power of nice*. Chichester: John Wiley and Sons.

Sheth, JN (1973) 'A model of industrial buyer behavior', *Journal of Marketing*, 37, 4, pp 50–6.

Snow, C (2005) 'A trail of missteps in Epstein talks', *Boston Globe*, 3 Nov.

Starkey, MS and M Carberry (1996) 'The future of supply-chain relationships between small business and multiple retailers', Annual Conference of the Marketing Education Group, University of Strathclyde, July.

Steele, P, J Murphy and R Russill (1989) *It's a deal*. London: McGraw Hill.

Strauss, J, A El-Ansary and R Frost (2003) *e-Marketing*, 3rd edition. New Jersey: Prentice Hall.

Strong, EK (1925) *The Psychology of Selling*. New York: McGraw Hill.

Tarver, JL and RC Haring (1988) Improving professional selling: a social exchange approach, *Marketing Intelligence and Planning*, 6, 2, pp 15–20.

Thimm, C, U Rademacher and L Kruse (1995) 'Power-related talk: control in verbal interaction', *Journal of Language and Social Psychology*, 14, 4 (Dec), pp 382–407.

Thompson, L and J Nadler (2002) Negotiating via information technology: theory and application, *Journal of Social Issues*, 58, 1, pp 109–24.

Thompson, L, E Peterson and SE Brodt (1996) 'Team negotiation: an examination of integrative and distribute bargaining', *Journal of Personality and Social Psychology*, 70, 1, pp 66–78.

Tracy, L (1995) 'Negotiation: an emergent process of living systems', *Behavioral Science*, 40, pp 41–55.

Ury, W (1991) *Getting past no: negotiating with difficult people*. New York: Bantam Books.

Van Weele, A (2000) *Purchasing and supply chain management: analysis, planning and practice*. London: Thomson Learning.

Vitz, PC and WR Kite (1970) Factors affecting conflict and negotiation within an alliance, *Journal of Social Psychology*, 5, pp 233–47.

Von Neumann, J and O Morgenstern (1944) *Theory of Games and Economic Behavior*. Princeton, NJ: Princeton University Press.

Von Neumann, J (1928) 'Zur Theorie des Gesellschaftsspiele', *Mathematische Annalen*, 100, pp 295–320.

Walton, RE and RB McKersie (1965) *A Behavioral Theory of Labor Negotiations: An Analysis of a Social Interaction System.* London: McGraw-Hill Book Company.

Webster, FE and Y Wind (1972) 'A general model of organizational buying behavior', *Journal of Marketing*, 36, Apr, pp12–17.

Weingart, LR, LL Thompson, MH Bazerman and JS Carroll (1990) 'Tactical behavior and negotiation outcomes', *The International Journal of Conflict Management*, 1, 1 (Jan), pp 7–31.

Wilson, D (1999) 'Developing Key Account Relationships: The Integration of the Millman-Wilson Relational Development Model with the Problem Centred (PPF) Model of Buyer-Seller Interaction in Business-to-Business Markets', *The Journal of Selling and Major Account Management*, 1, 3, pp 11–32.

Wittgenstein, L (1953) *Philosophical investigations.* Oxford: Blackwell, p190, in Gabriel Y ed (2004) *Myths, stories and organizations: premodern narratives for our times.* Oxford: Oxford University Press.

Young, L and S Denize (1994) 'Super-glued relationships', *Industrial Marketing and Purchasing Group*, 10th Annual Conference, Groningen, The Netherlands, 29 Sept to 1 Oct.

Yuan, Y, M Head and M Du (2003) The effects of multimedia communication on web-based negotiation, *Group Decision and Negotiation*, 12, 2, pp 89–109.

Zagare, FC (1984) *Game Theory: Concepts and Applications.* California: Sage Publications Inc.

Index